ARBITER OF ELEGANCE

A Victorian Biography

ARBITER OF ELEGANCE

Mary Eliza HAWEIS

BEA HOWE

THE HARVILL PRESS
LONDON

Printed for the Publishers
The Harvill Press Limited
30a Pavilion Road
London, SW1
by Collins Clear-Type Press
London and Glasgow

CONTENTS

CONTENTS

ILLUSTRATIONS

INTRODUCTION

FOR CENTURIES complete male domination prevailed in the English home on all matters concerning domestic architecture and decor although, from time to time, a few outstanding women have left the mark of their personality and taste on their surroundings.

For instance, it was Eleanor of Castile, wife of Edward I, who first introduced carpets to England, and used tapestries and hangings to adorn the walls of her apartments which called forth the rather disparaging remark that 'they were hung like a church'; until then tapistry from Arras and Paris had been seen only in churches.

Another queen, the great Elizabeth I, delighted in the magnificence of her palaces, which became the gorgeous background of her splendid reign. It was for her that Sir John Harington invented his famous water-closet; for her that the ever active looms produced vast quantities of embroidered silver and gold hangings, and rich, cut-velvet materials, and for her that the finest Italian glass was imported from Murano to equip her banqueting table. In fact, Queen Elizabeth set the pattern for English taste in dress and interior decoration and demanded, according to their means, a more gracious and civilised way of life from her subjects.

Mary II was among the first collectors of rare antiques, china and curios. She had inherited much of her grandfather, Charles I's, artistic taste and knowledge, and collected in particular, fine Chinese porcelain, pottery figures from Delft and blue-and-white china, 'piling the china ware upon the tops of cabinets and scrutors', Dutch-fashion. This novel form of display was soon copied by others.

11

Queen Mary loved to visit City warehouses where the new East Indian calicoes and chintzes were on show. Her chintz bed at Kensington Palace was declared 'a great curiosity', inspiring many ladies to copy it. She also designed a marble bathing-room and water-gallery for herself.

The eighteenth-century, an age noted for its fine taste and subtle refinements, saw many domestic changes in the English home. New styles of furniture, new lacquered goods from the East, new kinds of furnishing materials, from English damask to Oriental chintz, hand-made wallpapers of English and Chinese design, all made their influence felt in the world of interior decoration.

It was the eighteenth-century, too, which saw at last the first entry by a woman into the hitherto masculine world of decoration. Moreover it was made at the invitation of a man, Robert Adam (1728-1792). The woman in question was Angelica Kauffmann (1741-1807), born of Swiss parents, and one of two women painters made founder members of the Royal Academy.

Four ceiling paintings in the vestibule of Burlington House, signed medallions in the back-parlour of Chandos House, and the ballroom ceiling at Stratford House are attributed to Angelica Kauffmann, as are the decorative paintings in 20, Portman Square designed by Adam for Lady Home in 1773, besides other work in country houses.

Angelica Kauffmann was content to carry out Adam's wishes as were the other interior decorators who worked for him, one of these was, Antonio Zucchi, whom she married. Although not an original artist, it is to her lasting credit that she participated in what till then had been regarded as a purely male province. In time other women followed her lead.

But it was given to another, a Mrs Delany (1700-1788) to help her contemporaries decorate their houses in a more practical and active sense than the professional artist Miss Kauffmann.

After an unfortunate marriage to an elderly and unpleasant

Cornish squire, Alexander Pendarves, who died in 1726, Mary Pendarves settled down in a small, elegant house in Little Brook Street, London, where she soon established herself with her exquisite taste and talents as an arbiter of fashion. A mania for collecting shells had struck eighteenth-century society, and well in the forefront of this fashionable craze was Mary Pendarves. She began to experiment in shell decoration for chimney-pieces, niches and ornamental vases; soon she devised a method by which she painted her shell garlands and wreathes so that, when finished, they resembled delicately carved wood in the style of Grinling Gibbons. A superb exponent of cutpaper work, she contrived ornamental panels in this craft which were said to be like the best Italian inlay work in marble.

After her marriage to Patrick Delany, Dean of Down, she lived at Delville where she became her own house-painter, paper-hanger and decorator, while at the same time advising her friends on all domestic questions including shell decor. She might well be called the originator of the 'Do it yourself school' for women.

But it was not till the youthful Victoria ascended the throne that the real change took place in the English home. Till then, the master of the house had had the entire ordering of it, employing the best architects, cabinet makers and decorators to help him, while his wife accepted his choice. But about the 1840's these roles were suddenly reversed, and with a pretty and determined young queen to lead them, women came more and more into the foreground of their homes, choosing what furniture, curtains and carpets they liked.

By 1850, it was generally considered to be unsuitable, even effeminate, for a husband to hold strong views—let alone express them—on how his home should be decorated or furnished. Given over to petticoat rule, English houses, both upper and middle class, began to reflect not only the highly moral spirit of the age but also feminine sensibility and taste. Everything that was vulgar or frankly immoral as the suggestively naked leg of a chair or table had to be discreetly hidden away. Window curtains now swept the ground and were made in heavy, rich materials, like velvet, or rep, dyed the new dark colours: bottle-green, indigo blue, or crimson. Chairs were low, broad-seated and armless, with sloping backs to accomodate a lady in a billowing crinoline dandling her child. Like sofas and sociables of the period, chairs were luxuriously padded, buttoned and fringed. Though chimney-pieces still showed a Regency feeling, their style coarsened. Short, stout columns supported a deep shelf which provided an ideal place for displaying an extraordinary assortment of unrelated objects dear to the female heart. These included French clocks, bronze statuettes, Bohemian glass, Parisian ware besides imposing bouquets of flowers in feather, wax and shells displayed under large glass shades.

Into this ornate and cluttered but comfortable world, typical of an upper-middle-class home, there was born on 21st February 1848, a little girl called Mary Eliza Joy, who was destined to lead her contemporaries not into the kitchen, like Mrs Beeton, but on a grand tour of inspection around the house. On this tour she pointed to new standards of taste in home decoration and established herself as an arbiter of taste and culture.

Mary Eliza Joy was the eldest daughter of Thomas Musgrove Joy, portrait painter. In her eighteenth year she married the Reverend Hugh Reginald Haweis, M.A., eminent preacher, music critic and writer of his day. They set up house at 16, Welbeck Street, Marylebone, close to St James's Church where the Reverend H. R. Haweis 'ministered in a fashion that was essentially his own' (*The Times*) and drew all London to hear him 'by means of somewhat sensational methods of preaching'. In the 1870s. Mrs Haweis came into prominence through her articles on decoration and dress. These were followed by books: *The Art of Beauty* in 1878; *The Art of Dress* in 1879; and *The Art of Decoration* in 1881. She illustrated her books with serious as well as amusing drawings and designs.

In 1884, Mrs Haweis went to live at Queen's House, Cheyne Walk, once the home of the Pre-Raphaelite painter and poet, Dante Gabriel Rossetti. Queen's House (known as Tudor House in Rossetti's day) was well known to me when it belonged to the late Mr L. F. Harrison. The house has historic associations with Henry VIII's great Manor of Chelsea, on part of whose grounds it was built, besides which it has long-established literary and artistic traditions. It is supposed to be the 'cheerful new house' named by Thackeray in *Esmond,* while George Meredith described it as 'a strange quaint place with an immense garden, magnificent panelled staircase and rooms—a palace.' The initials, C.R. on the wrought-iron gates are not those of Catherine Regina, wife of Charles II as Mrs Haweis thought, but belonged in fact to Richard Chapman, a City apothecary of means who built Queen's House in 1717.

On being taken by her elder sister Mrs Ned Burne-Jones, to a party given by Rossetti in 1866, Agnes Macdonald (later wife of Sir Edward Poynter) had this to say of Tudor House: 'It is beautiful till it makes one ache nearly, and I kept sorrowfully thinking of its lost mistress (Lizzie Siddal that was). Just fancy, large panelled rooms, narrow tall windows, a large garden at the back and at the front a paved court with tall iron gates to the road, and lastly the Thames in a flood of moonlight.'

How appreciative Mary Eliza Haweis would have been of this moving tribute to the house that she owned for a time and was in love with till the day of her premature death. To this house that she invited the titled, the rich and the great celebrities of her day. For many years, her At Homes in Chelsea to which men and women were invited to lecture on subjects on which they were authorities, were known throughout society. Among those who came to speak in the long panelled drawing-room with its seven tall windows were Holman Hunt, Herkomer, Justin Macarthy, Doctor Rae, the Arctic explorer, Sir Edwin Arnold, Professor Crookes, Miss

Sarah le Grand, Mrs Humphrey Ward and Lady Jephson. On her death a leading journal of the time wrote:

> Hundreds of letters and messages poured in from known and unknown people, witness to her surprising influence. These ranged from Her Majesty the Queen and the beautiful Queen Marguerite of Italy to poor creatures in obscure hovels to whom she had once been kind. She was never anxious to please everyone, troubled herself little enough with people's prejudices and was quite immovable in her opinions. . . . She was thought peculiar and so she was. But she was a unique woman, brilliant, fascinating, with the intellect of half a dozen men controlled by a bodily machinery that thundered away within and which at last tore her to pieces.

'She lived on her nerves,' said her doctor.

'There is no one at all like her left,' said her London editor.

'I could not to the last believe she was going to die. To me the world and life seemed impossible without her,' said her husband.

Today, like so many other vanished 'artists in living', Mary Eliza Haweis might never have been. But I, for one, would like to think that her small, elegant ghost has joined those others, famed in their day but equally forgotten, that are reputed to haunt the beautiful panelled rooms of Queen's House which still stands facing the broad sweep of the Thames below Battersea Bridge—the Thames which, dazzling in sunlight, or glimmering dark, mysterious under a full moon, first cast its spell on her as a child.

1. CHILDHOOD

1858-1864

It was a wintry afternoon, the day Monday, 18th January 1858, and the time about three o'clock. Two little girls, the one just seven, the other rising ten, sat alone in the top floor nursery of a tall house in Sloane Street, London. Dressed in pretty plaid-silk dresses with low necks, they were the daughters of the fashionable protrait painter Thomas Musgrove Joy and his wife, the beautiful Eliza.

Edith, the younger child, whose curls were tied with bows sat playing with a dolls-house which had once been a square box with a lid. But since Mr Green, the carpenter, had tinkered with it as well as her elder sister, Mary Eliza—or Sizzie as she called her—it looked more like a proper dolls-house with its four rooms, neatly tiled roof and pretty front door. Now and then, with a surreptitious glance upwards at Sizzie, Edith pulled out a chair or a little table from the house known as Rose Villa and laid it carefuly on the floor beside her. It was not often that she had the chance to arrange things in the dolls-house as she, and not Sizzie, liked. This afternoon, she was making the best of her sister's intense preoccupation in writing a letter.

Mary Eliza, her auburn hair held back by a circular comb from her wide, intelligent brow, sat at the baize-covered nursery table. Her small legs twisted round those of her chair, pencil in hand, and her eyes screwed up, for the light from the window had darkened, Mary Eliza was writing to her cousin Mary Horn.

Monday, January 18*th*

My dear cousin,

I hope you are quite well? Edith and I am except for a little cold which I do not mind in the least. Aunt Horn told mama in her letter, that you were beginning to draw, and papa says that I am improving in mine. I hope some day I shall be able to draw real pictures, like papa: very likely I shall, if I take pains: for people must draw, before they can paint. I must take great pains, too, for papa says that if I still keep improving perhaps it will be well enough to be sent to an exhibition—I forget what. Grandmama Spratt came last Sunday with Uncle Conrad and Uncle Eldridge, stayed the week, went home about half an hour ago. Last Monday we went to South Kensington Museum, and again on Saturday: I enjoyed myself very much and was excessively interested in the pictures. Also in the tapestry, which ladies used to make, before printing was invented; I believe it was one of their principle occupations. I saw also a great many models of machines, under glass cases. I saw plenty of models of shoes, but I should not like to be in any of them. I saw several globes, large and small. On one of them I found out, the Cape of Good Hope, New York, and New Zealand: besides a great many other places. Edith was seven years old, last Wednesday. I shall be ten, the 21st February. Will you write me an answer and tell me about your little nieces?

On New Years Day, we had a party, but we had so many disappointments that it was a very small one: however, we could not help it: I think there was quite enough. I had the twelf cake this time, for Edith had the last. They were very merry, and we danced the whole evening: we all had some jelly and some of us some blancmange at supper and Uncle George Tomkin came and helped us to cake and puffs while Mrs Franklin helped us to wine, tartlets, and blancmange at supper. Have omitted to tell you that 'Rose Villa' (did you know we had a dolls-house?) was in the dancing room, where everyone could see it. I will describe it. About a month ago it was an old square box with no lid; it was quite square every way, and I had been wishing to my eyelashes and was always curtseying to the moon, for years, and at last papa wrote to the carpenter desiring him to come to our house. Well he came, and mama told him what to do, and finally he took it home: it was made into partitions, so that there were four rooms in it, kitchen, the parlour, drawing-room, and a bedroom. We papered it ourselves, the parlour with light green, the bedroom a white ground with the outlines of ivy leaves in pink colour. The drawing-room is papered with a pale blush pink colour: imitating watered silk. The kitchen is not papered at all: for we have nothing now (nor had then) to paper it with. Nevertheless, the eldest doll Aglae, and her brothers and sisters (their names are Harry, May, Blondine and Annie; two other dolls, Mrs Williams and Miss Louisa Williams are staying at Miss Aglae's house) are quite satisfied with her house. Grandmama Spratt bought us a great boxful of furniture, besides the drawing-room chairs which I carved and covered myself, and the box of kitchen things I have had for years. She also brought us a little box of tea things for Aglae and I do not think I ever saw any so pretty. They are made of glass, and (I believe) painted white in the inside to imitate china. And on the outside are painted, bouquets of 'forget-me-nots' and a few green leaves. I am very fond of them, yet I am so exceedingly afraid of breaking them that I scarcely ever open the box even to look at myself. I keep them wrapped in wool; but I have forgotten to tell you that there are many little painted glass spoons (they have no bouquets on—they are plain white) and there are cups and saucers and such a lovely tea-tray! It is shiny on top, and of a beautiful rose-lake (if you know what that is or if you do not, it is a handsome kind of crimson colour). But to return to the dolls-house. Aglae has a dressing-table, in her bedroom; there is a little looking-glass for her. And Edith's clumsy red washand-stand quite spoils the whole room. But that does not matter. I must tell you that this house has been a great deal of contriving, to Edith and me, but I like all kinds of contriving. But I see my letter must now come to an end.

> Believe me, Mary
> Your affectionate cousin
> M. E. Joy

P.S. Please excuse the bad writing as it is getting dark! I have enclosed a drawing and some poetry.

As a child, little Mary Eliza always used to add drawings and a poem or two to her letters. Her drawings were of angels and cupids peeping out of clouds, funny people's heads, or dolls. Her father thought so much of her drawings that in 1856 when she was only eight, he sent some to an exhibition. There was nothing she liked better than to take her father's small narrow envelopes in which it was customary to send notes by hand to a house and, ungumming them, draw in the space inside exquisite tiny maps in sepia ink. Some maps, like those of the Brontë children, depicted imaginary countries, others, like the one she did of China, were real.

But it is in her 'dolls-house' letter that Mary Eliza Joy reveals for the first time her great interest in decoration: how she chose her colours and wallpapers and made her own little chairs. But above all, how she loved 'all kinds of contriving'. During the many ups-and-downs of her eventful life M.E.H., as she ended by calling herself, spent much time and trouble *in contriving*: contriving to find enough time to write her erudite books and articles while burdened by heavy domestic duties and family responsibilities; contriving to make both ends meet, financially. For as fast as money came into the

Haweis household, so did her husband spend it, not knowing —or professing not to know—how it went or to whom.

Her letter finished, Mary Eliza folded it, neatly, and put it in an envelope for Mama to address. By now it was quite dark. She scrambled off her chair—she was a small fragile child—and went over to her sister. 'Put those things back just where you found them, Edith. Put them back, carefully. It is time we went downstairs to see Papa.'

Downstairs in his large studio, Thomas Musgrove Joy sat plunged in melancholy thought. On the easel before him was the almost finished portrait of his wife which he was in the process of touching up. It showed her in a three-cornered draped shawl and a scuttle-bonnet, walking out of doors: a sedate matron, although a beautiful and dignified one, whereas some years earlier he had portrayed her as a delicious and lovely young wife. Joy wore a brown velvet coat with drab trousers. That poetic look, so characteristic of his youthful face had vanished, and his large hazel eyes were no longer luminous. They seemed much smaller and their expression dull, his thickening jaw emphasized by whiskers. Near Joy's easel was a round mahogany table covered by a heavily fringed plush table rug on which stood a big oil-lamp with a bulbous shade of ruby glass. Just lit, it shed a circle of warm light on what seemed more like a large, handsomely furnished sitting-room than a professional artist's studio. At one end, the long North window was masked by the drawn folds of a pair of heavy velvet curtains which had once belonged to Napoleon Bonaparte. They had been given to Joy by his life-long friend and patron, Lord Panmure, who had been dead now some six years. Another gift of his lordship's was the imposing Spanish leather screen placed before the door to exclude draughts. This screen was much coveted by Joy's sitters when they were told that the famous Lord Byron had owned it. Two great dark Stuart oak chairs upholstered in crimson, the usual litter of canvases propped up against walls, ponderous art journals and volumes of period steel engravings

that filled two book-cases and a wooden rostrum made up for
the rest of the furnishing of Thomas Musgrove Joy's fashionable Sloane Street studio. A studio which on that gloomy
cold February afternoon had become full of ghosts for him.
Ghosts, he thought moodily, which were soon to fade. For
only that morning Eliza and he had made up their minds to
exchange their present elegant address for the less salubrious
one of Number 32, St George's Square, Belgrave South,
Pimlico. Joy smiled wryly. How many of his titled sitters
would follow him out in their carriages to the wilds of Pimlico,
he wondered? For it would be a far cry, or rather, a long drive
from Georgian Mayfair or from more recently built Belgrave
Square, to his new studio. Especially when his lordship was
no longer alive to urge his friends to call on his favourite
painter and judge his work for themselves. Not that Thomas
Musgrove Joy cared if his commissions dwindled. He felt that
he had perpetuated in paint enough portraits of dukes and
belted earls to last his lifetime, for there were few noblemen's
galleries in which a Joy portrait did not hang. Since early
boyhood when, pencil in hand, and using the pages of his
school grammar for a sketch book, he had wandered about the
lanes and apple orchards of his native village, Boughton
Monchelsea, in Kent, drawing whatever took his fancy, from
little Billy Kemp munching an apple to old Silas Turvill, bent
double, hedging, Joy had shown a marked talent for 'catching
a likeness.'

Later, after his art training, first in London and then in
Paris, his romantic style and assured technique had attracted
many celebrities to sit to him. Critics, too, were won over
by his charm, and likened the rising young painter's work to
Thomas Lawrence under whose influence Joy had painted for
a time. But today, today, thought Joy moodily, he was
utterly bored by facile portraiture. If paint he must, in order
to provide Eliza and the children with the comforts to which
they were accustomed, he would return to his first love and
become again a subject painter.

Unheeded, his brush dropped from his fingers to the floor and he stared blankly not at the painted features of his middle-aged wife but at that dim company of ghosts peopling his studio. The present faded into the past and he was back in the year 1839. His *annus mirabilis*. For it was in this year that the handsome, convivial and generous William Maule Ramsay, (1771-1852) created first Baron Panmure and Navar of Brechin Castle, Forfarshire, by King William IV had commissioned him to paint the portrait of England's heroine of the day, Grace Darling. How excitedly he had said goodbye to his beloved Eliza, to whom he had been engaged for seven years, and raced North from London.

On reaching the Darlings' home, the much publicised lighthouse on the Farne Islands, Joy, at the peak of his good looks and charm, had been captivated at once by Grace Darling's dignity and modest beauty. His portrait of her was outstanding and he was equally successful in painting her rugged, honest father, William. Buoyed up with youthful ambition and enthusiasm, he began work on his third commission which was to be a great seascape depicting the dramatic rescue by William and Grace Darling in their tiny coble of the sole survivors of *The Forfarshire*, wrecked on Hawker's rocks. Delighted with his protegé's three pictures which when exhibited had been praised by all the leading art critics of the day, Panmure presented Joy with a handsome cheque. This enabled him in December of that never to be forgotten year, 1839, to marry his beautiful, faithful Eliza, daughter of Charles Spratt, Esq., of Drummond's Bank, London.

When the attractive young couple set up house in Frith Street, Soho, Joy's studio was besieged by prospective sitters. Scarcely a day passed without the jovial Lord Panmure turning up with a fresh visitor who, on being introduced to the painter, fell an immediate victim to Joy's charm and high spirits, to his gay wit and amusing conversation. The young Joys, admired and invited everywhere, decided to move from Soho to the more rural, but up-and-coming neighbourhood of Brompton. Here they took a house which backed on the lovely, leafy grounds of Henry Holland's villa, The Pavilion, with wide, sweeping lawns, ornamental lakes and a soaring elm grove with its old established rookery. The ceaseless 'cawing' of the glossy-winged, jet-black birds delighted Joy, reminding him of his Kentish childhood.

Here, in the 1840s, Thomas Musgrove Joy reached the zenith of his fame as a portrait painter. The fair and the famed flocked to his studio. An early and influential arrival was Prince George of Cambridge, first cousin to the Queen, who brought with him the beautiful young Drury Lane actress, Louisa Fairbrother, with whom he had fallen madly in love and was later to marry morganatically. Joy's portrait of Miss Fairbrother (who became Mrs Fitzgeorge) was executed in his most delightful and eye-appealing manner. He shows her seated in a stage box, dressed in a low-necked dress, her sleek hair demurely parted in the middle, her small hands clasping a lace handkerchief and a furled fan in the best sentimental tradition. On the edge of the box lies a rose. All his life Joy was a great lover of flowers. His 'The Moss Rose' was, according to the art critic of *The Times*, the 'perfect chrysolite of art' and the gem of the 1843 Royal Academy.

Under the anonymous title of 'Portrait of a Lady', Miss Fairbrother was hung in the Royal Academy and the *Morning Post* burst into a paean of praise declaring the picture 'to be one of those magnificent incarnations of womanhood which he [Joy] alone of all the portrait painters of the day can produce.' It was about this time that he heard His Royal Highness Prince Albert had bought his 'Gil Blas'. Not so long after, he was working, absorbed in his studio, when he heard the door open quietly. Glancing up, he saw the elderly figure of Lord Panmure standing a little to one side as if to allow another to pass into the room first. Suddenly to Joy's astonishment, a slender, tall, upright man came in, dressed in the height of sartorial fashion. The dark-blue eyes stared at him somewhat coldly, the handsome face was almost expressionless. Struck

Mary Eliza and Edith painted by their father Thomas
Musgrove Joy (1853)

'Self Portrait' (T. M. Joy, 1839)

'Wife of the Artist' (T. M. Joy)

Mary Eliza at 14 (pencil and crayon, T. M. Joy)

by the august young man's exceptional good looks—even as the youthful Victoria had been struck—Thomas Musgrove Joy rose hurriedly to his feet and bowed low.

Graciously, Lord Panmure presented the painter to Prince Albert. There was a slight pause, and then, his stiff manner relaxing a little, and a faint smile warming the immaculate features, His Royal Highness asked to see some of Mr Joy's portraits of which he had heard such good, such flattering report, from his lordship.

A tour was made of the studio, His Royal Highness pausing every now and then before some canvas which took his fancy to make a courteous, and always apt, remark. He admitted that he much liked to sketch and paint, himself, in his leisure time. In fact, one of the reasons of his visit, that afternoon, was to ask Mr Joy to give him some drawing lessons if a time convenient to them both could be arranged. Joy bowed again. His time was His Royal Highness's, he murmured. The Prince smiled, hesitated, and then turning to Lord Panmure to include him in the conversation, announced that he would like Mr Joy *very much*—the two words were stressed—to paint his dogs, dogs that were greatly loved. In particular, he wished the head of his greyhound Eos to be done in oils.

So Thomas Musgrove Joy found himself at Windsor painting the Royal dogs and giving drawing lessons to His Royal Highness. Soon after his first visit, Her Majesty The Queen received him privately. She made the suggestion that he should paint the Royal children, the young Princess Royal and Edward, Prince of Wales, in fancy dress. Later, in her so faithfully kept diary, the Queen recorded:

Windsor Castle   *January 23rd,* 1843
Mr Joy, a promising young artist, has made a delightful little picture of the children in their old costumes.

Some months of happy Royal favour followed for Joy who was, on one or two occasions, invited to stay to luncheon *en famille* with the Queen and Prince Albert. Unspoilt by success, and always himself, his natural charm, modesty and good looks appealed to the Queen. For when the question arose of how much he was to be paid for his work to date, and the sum of £50 was suggested in a letter from her secretary, Her Majesty wrote in pencil underneath: 'Certainly. He is a very modest man.'

When, on 5th August 1844, Joy's first and much adored son was born—his happiness and Eliza's knew no bounds; the child was christened John Edward Musgrove.

At the beginning of 1845, Joy was still basking in the sunshine of the Queen's graciousness. One February afternoon, wrapped warmly in her furs, her arm through her beloved husband's, Her Majesty appeared at the Royal Kennels to pat the head of dear Niger and Neptune and to enquire how Chico, a Cuba dog, and Gabbas, a Pyrenean, were standing up to an English winter. As usual, this visit was recorded in her diary:

Windsor Castle *February 1st*, 1845
We walked down to the Kennels and saw Mr Joy painting some of our dogs.

Ten months later, on the 13th of December, little John Edward Musgrove Joy died.

Remembering that fatal day now in his studio, Thomas Joy relived part of the intense pain and misery which followed his child's death. Two other sons died in infancy like John Edward. A curse seemed to have been laid, sometime, somewhere on the Joy family; for seven generations only one male child in each generation had reached maturity and Thomas Musgrove Joy was the last of his line. Bound up with his firstborn's death, malicious gossip had circulated in London that he must have displeased Her Majesty in some way; made an indiscreet remark, perhaps, or failed in courtesy, for he had not been recalled to Windsor. These rumours did not help either Eliza or him in their bereavement. They only consolidated Joy's belief that he had never really been accepted in the art world—a world plagued by petty jealousies and small, warring factions—in the way that he had been accepted from the first in London society.

As a clock struck in the studio, Joy started and looked round. He had the feeling that he was not alone. Beyond the circle of light shed by the big oil-lamp, were two small motionless figures, hand-in-hand. For how long had Mary Eliza and Edith been standing there, he wondered, during that strange voyage back to the past?

'Papa', came Mary Eliza's high clear voice. 'Papa' she repeated, firmly, 'You did not hear us come in, did you? 'She knew that they had caught Papa in one of his absent moods. 'No, Mary Eliza, I did not. Poor Papa was far away up in the clouds as usual.'

'Up in the clouds? Clouds! Where? ' Little Edith was always literal minded. She gazed about her, so many dark shadows in Papa's studio but no clouds; not the, high white clouds, she knew.

Her father put his arm round her small waist and drew her up to sit on his lap. Meanwhile, Mary Eliza had come forward and was gazing, intently, at his picture.

'Have you finished Mama's portrait, Papa? Is it exactly how you want it now? You have been a long time about it.' Her voice accused him.

Joy smiled. His daughter never minced matters when any kind of artistic work was under discussion.

'No,' he replied. 'It isn't yet how I would like it. It may never be—do you understand what I mean by that, child?' Mary Eliza nodded. 'Yes, papa. But it is very like dear Mama all the same. I like it, 'she added softly. Her father drew her by the hand to stand close beside him. 'I have something to tell you both, something of the greatest importance.'

In the familiar security of papa's studio with the faint sound of carriage wheels coming from the busy street outside, Mary Eliza and little Edith Joy heard how they were soon to leave Sloane Street, the only home they had ever known, and go to another in some place called Pimlico.

Thomas Musgrove Joy's house in Pimlico survives to this day. It stands exactly in front of the high iron railings of St Saviour's Church which rises, with its tall Gothic steeple, on the West side of St George's Square.

Number 32 is a tall gloomy house with a portico and a dark basement reached by a steep flight of stone steps. Close by is Lupus Street. Pimlico was, and still is, a very different district from Sloane Street, Knightsbridge. But the Joy children settled down happily enough in their new home as children do.

Between carefully ruled lines, Mary Eliza wrote in her neat round hand:

My dear Aunt,

We are very happy here; we like St George's Square very much; all the day, we hear the birds chirping in the Square. It is a very pleasant neighbourhood, I think, and we have, now something else to look at than Mrs Willis's bonnets and tiring yellow Opera cloak; and Doctor Whitfield (the chemist's shop) all smelling of pills, and rhubarb powders and physic! There is the Square; there are the children playing in it; not a grand lady in an open carriage or brougham, come for a new fly-away bonnet. In a few days Mr Naismith or Mr Hartry will take out, perhaps, four teeth, two single and two double; one day papa said, (as I was eating a pinch of sugar) 'I can tell you—I wouldn't eat that trash—spoil all your teeth—Mr What's his-name'll tug 'em out after it.' I hope you are all well, as we are. Our playroom is like a room of everything to us: now, aunt, as I am tired of writing,

Believe me
Your affectionate niece
M. E. Joy

Beneath her signature there is an ornamental scroll and in printed letters—

GIVE MY LOVE TO ALL.

EDITH SENDS HER LOVE.

Children soon forget the immediate past when it is followed by new joys and compensations. Ever since she could remember Mary Eliza had stood by the nursery window in Sloane Street waving her hand to the rooks crying 'Caw! Caw!' as they flew home to bed in the elm trees of Mr Holland's garden just like the little girl in *Good Night* and *Good Morning*, the book illustrated by Mr Walter Severn, a friend of papa's. Though the rooks were gone, she had the little brown sparrows in St George's Square garden to watch instead. Under the canopy of giant plane trees with curious trunks mottled like a snake's skin, they took their daily dust bath and this always amused her. There was the river too: the noble Thames which she had never seen properly until they moved to Number 32. How the water glittered and shone when the tide was high and they could see the river flowing past at the far end of the Square garden. She and Edith were always begging Mama to take them for a walk along the river to watch the innumerable boats sailing up and down: boats that were often accompanied by a flotilla of arrogant swans with narrow heads held high on their white slender necks.

The Embankment was not built until 1876, so Mary Eliza walked sedately beside an irregular brick wall broken at intervals by a crumbling flight of steep stone steps leading to small wooden landing-stages and rotting wherry posts set drunkenly in the glistening mud. Mud that smelt strong when the tide was out. It was a fascinating new world that Mary Eliza came to know, of old water-side taverns and leafy-green pleasure gardens, of horse-ferries and bumboat women calling out, coarse-mouthed, but friendly. This world stretched, she was told, from Chiswick village through Chelsea and Westminster to the distant Pool of London.

When papa was in a good mood, he would take them in a

rowing-boat as far as the picturesque old Swan Inn and Brewhouse. Here they would land and climb up some steps to the shady garden where, in season, they ordered a dish of delicious strawberries and cream. Beyond the Inn was a lane called Swan Walk and beyond again Cheyne Walk. Little did Mary Eliza Joy know how in the years to come she would make her most loved home of all in Cheyne Walk. Contrary to papa's gloomy predictions, their social life remained very much as it had been in Sloane Street. For a stream of titled visitors continued to visit Thomas Musgrove Joy's studio in Pimlico. So much so that one day his daughter, exasperated by the number of callers, put down in the childish diary she kept:—

Could not paint—Lord Strafford and Lord Exmouth called—Lord Andover and Lord Coventry came afternoon —Frith and Phillips—Some more lords called—Asked me to walk in the square—Angry—Wouldn't go—Duke of Cambridge came again—Pa too ill to see him.

Mary Eliza did not care a fig how many noble lords came to see papa so long as they left her unmolested in that secret hiding-place of hers which was under the studio table. To make a tent, she pulled down the plush cloth till its folds hid her from sight on three sides. On the fourth side, facing what light came from the window she crouched on her knees, drawing or writing on minute scraps of paper. To this retreat, she dragged heavy art journals or the illuminated gift books of the period to pour over their pictures, steel engravings and Gothic lettering, deaf to her sister's cries of 'Sizzie, come and play with me!' Play was all very well for babies, thought Mary Eliza loftily, but she was growing up and she wanted to become a serious painter like papa. She did not go to school and lessons given by Mama were very intermittent; so she taught herself, a mature precocious child, from the books found in 'Papa's studio'. In spite of her tiny size and her aptitude for catching colds or a cough, she possessed an iron will when it came to doing anything she wanted to. At this particular period, she wanted only to draw and write, no matter how much her head ached or her eyes.

Her eleventh year saw her next important letter dated Sunday, 24th April 1859. The carefully ruled sheets have disappeared and she writes in ink. Her hand is already formed and differs little from the one she used all her life.

My dear Mama,

I am sorry to say that I forgot to write to you last evening, so I write to you this evening. I hope papa is better; it is such a pity you cannot come with him! and (although I fear you will be very dull) Grandmama says she is determined we shall stay the week. Now, pray, have you taken one or two out of the book-case to amuse yourself during our absence? Will you, dear mama, write me an answer, to tell me what is going on in 'Belgrave South?' Grandmama has hired a horse and chaise, on purpose, for papa; and you really M U S T coax him to come down with you. It is so pleasant though today it has been very wet. Mrs Mattam is kind enough to curl my hair, when she comes to curl Fanny's. It is curled in rags—You must excuse my bad writing being rather late, and my having no lines. Grandmama, Edith, and Fanny join me in love to yourself and papa—therefore

> I remain, dear mama,
> Your ever affectionate
> Mary Eliza Joy

During their London childhood, the Joy children were often sent away to stay either with their paternal Joy and Tomkin relations at Boughton Monchelsea near Maidstone in Kent, or to Grandmama Spratt, their maternal grandmother who lived at Egham in Surrey. An animal lover all her life, Mary Eliza enjoyed best going to the old Kentish farmhouse known as Tilts Farm where the Tomkin family had lived since 1715. The old house had scarcely changed since the day when Grandmama Joy, then Susannah Tomkin, had left it to marry young Thomas Joy of Boughton Hall close by. The Joys like the Tomkins came from long-established yeoman stock. But Thomas Joy, the elder, had pretensions to genteel standing for he always signed himself Thomas Joy, Gent. He owned other property too (River Farm and Coombe Garden) in the neighbourhood and the family name survives today in a little wood called Joy Wood.

On Sundays, Mary Eliza was often taken by her Tomkin aunts to the ancient little church of St Peter's at Boughton Monchelsea. It stood on a steep hillside overlooking parkland where a herd of fallow deer roamed cropping the smooth fine turf and far away lay the enchanted landscape of the Weald of Kent. After church, Mary Eliza was shown the sunken, grey, eighteenth-century gravestones carved with the names of her Musgrove and Tomkin relations and the great table tomb where Grandpapa Joy lay buried and where her ashes, one day, were to be interred. But much nicer than walking sedately in her best clothes round a country churchyard with her elderly aunts was to wander, as her father had before her, through the hop yards and apple orchards, the latter foaming in spring with clouds of delicate pink-and-white blossom, the loveliness of which she never forgot. Another vivid memory was the large square stone inserted into a wall on a row of cottages. On this stone were engraved the words: 'With Industry. Economy. Honesty. Sobriety. Civility and Cleanliness. a Poor Man may live Happy and Respectable. 1827.' These words she had spelt out to her aunts, one day, never to forget them. Mary Eliza's letters from Kent are full of the cats, dogs, hens and chicks she knew and petted. Dried violets, a pansy or two, faded now and brown, still tumble out from the two-inch envelopes she used and sealed with a tiny blob of faded red sealing-wax (now broken) impressed with her initial M.

The last echoes of her childhood come from a cottage at Egham to which she and Edith had been invited to stay, on their own, by some friends of her parents called Gibbon. In their garden there were delicious ripe raspberries to pick besides currants and gooseberries. The lawn was 'beautifully kept and so elegantly laid out with white and red rose-bushes spotting it'. The lawn made a great impression on the Joy children because of the swing on it; a swing on which it seems they swung madly all day long. For when writing to 'My dear Mama', Mary Eliza asks to be excused her bad writing (as neat and clear as ever!) 'for I cannot write a bit today, I suppose swinging has made me tipsy with fun.'

She was not often tipsy with fun, for this word, a new one in her vocabulary, had a certain sad implication associated with her father. It was about this time, that Thomas Joy first began to indulge in periodical drinking bouts brought about by inherited melancholy or—as her mother once confessed to her daughter when she married—'because Lord Panmure, his great friend, had always been a confirmed hard-drinker and taught poor Papa to like good wine, cultivating a taste in him to drink.' When the day came for Mary Eliza and Edith Joy to return to London, to St George's Square, they both felt very low.

August 11th, 1860

My dear Mama,

We are both very sorry that the week is almost at an end, for we look forward with the greatest horror to the time when we shall begin lessons again. You can come whatever time you like to fetch us home. Yesterday we went to St Anne's Hill and the preceding day to Virginia Water, but we have not risen lately until half-past eight. Virginia Water is a lovely place. I don't want to go to Italy at all when there are such beautiful scenes in our own native land. The young rabbits ran out of their holes by the dozens. We got some ferns and purple heather from beside the lake.

I am quite contented with the waterfall there, especially when the men turned it on, to its full force; and I do not wish to drown myself in the Falls of Niagara like Francis somebody (The Hermit) did. I don't wish to go there in case I do—I hope it will not rain all day as it has this morning for we shall not go to Windsor or anywhere: on Tuesday we went to the River—the 'royal . . . . . . Thame' as Milton says. I dare say you will think this a very droll letter but it does not matter.

Now therefore, believe me

Your Affect. daughter

Mary E. Joy

P.S. We have eaten plenty of fruit without the least sympton of illness and we like eating it tremendously. Miss Gibbon says that you had better ask Mr David Gibbon about the trains: but don't bring Papa down, unless he is inclined to laugh and talk, because we are going to make him quite delightfully charming, et cetera.

Inside the flap of her narrow envelope is written: 'Love to all, tell Papa that he is to come down in a State of Joy not to be conceived.'

Below this command is drawn the round and jovial face of The Man in the Moon.

The winter of 1860 was to be a busy one for Mary Eliza and her father. Despite his recurring moods of melancholy, Thomas Joy had begun work on two mammoth canvases to be entitled Tattersall's 'The Yard' and 'The Ring'. Inspired by Frith's 'Derby Day' which had been the star exhibit of the 1858 Royal Academy, Joy was set on doing a painting that was to include two hundred, and more, of the leading noblemen, gentlemen, trainers, and others connected with the Turf. The fact that he was not yet a member of the Royal Academy rankled deeply: a wound that time never healed. Did he think—hope—pray—as he worked, alone, on these huge canvases that they might bring him this much desired mark of recognition by his colleagues?

As the winter closed in with its normal quota of dank mists and yellow fog swirling in from the river, Mary Eliza rarely stirred out of the attic playroom. Many years later, she wrote how 'after her sickly years of childhood' this teenage phase was the happiest period of her life. For it was spent in long, uninterrupted hours of drawing, painting and writing. It was now that she took up the study of book-illustration including typography and the composing of monograms. This latter skill of juggling, alone and concentrated, with the juxtaposition of one capital letter with another in relation to their different form and shape fascinated her.

Mary Eliza Joy was not alone, however, in this entrancing new hobby of hers. Illuminating had become a fashionable pastime for ladies and their daughters, superseding Berlin wool-work. It was considered a highly suitable occupation too for Sunday; much more so than crotcheting or sketching.

The introduction of the 'illuminated' gift book in 1860 was part and parcel of the Gothic Revival in which Mary Eliza Haweis was to play an important role. After her marriage in 1867, what had first begun as a juvenile hobby developed into a serious study. The fruit of this study led her to designing professionally not only the covers, letterpress, chapter headings, and tailpieces of her own books but those of her husband as well.

Meanwhile, escorted by her mother, she went regularly to the British Museum to pour over the medieval manuscript and illuminated missals and to make sketches from them. This occupation she kept up long after her marriage. Her first monograms, exquisitely done in paint or sepia, still survive. On small pieces of paper—or again on the backs of her father's envelopes—they are nearly all signed and dated between the years 1860 and 1862. Mary Eliza composed monograms for most members of her family, including several for her father, T.M.J., and for her godmother, Lady Murray.

At the Summer Exhibition of the Royal Academy in 1861, Joy exhibited as usual and received a splendid press for his portrait of the well-known veteran angler Henry Farnell. According to the Art Journal: 'It is an admirable work and a true likeness—perhaps the best production of this always careful and skilful artist who has few rivals in the art of combining the style of the master with accuracy of details and manipulative finish.'

But still those much coveted initials R.A. evaded him. 'A thing of beauty is a JOY forever,' the art critic of the *Civil Service Gazette* might exclaim and his confrère in the *Daily Telegraph*, 1861 wrote 'Mr Joy is an old friend and a welcome one. He can be most humourous and most original if he pleases', but Frith (the President of the R.A.) still avoided recommending him for the accolade of his profession. It was not surprising that his depression increased and he took to spending days in bed or else retiring in moody silence to his studio.

Time passed, and on 21st February 1864, Mary Eliza celebrated her sixteenth birthday. She was quite the young lady now with her auburn curls piled high over a frizette. Her hands and feet were tiny; the latter so much so that she suffered all her life when she had to walk any distance.

It was about this time, during the first months of 1864, that a dynamic young man barely five feet high with an olive skin, long narrow eyes of brilliant hazel, and a club foot began to draw large congregations to St James the Less, Westminster, where he was a curate. They came to hear him preach. Among his many admirers who attended regularly, was Mrs Joy accompanied by her daughters, Mary Eliza and little Edith. It was not long before Miss Joy, who went every Friday to the Vicar, Mr Dickson's, Confirmation classes, discovered to her girlish excitement that Mr Hugh Reginald Haweis, for that was the name of their favourite preacher, actually lodged in St George's Square with Mrs Chisholm, whom they knew. Mary Eliza called on her immediately and learned that the intriguing little Mr Haweis, with his dramatic gestures and vivid phrases that stressed the most original religious views, was the son of Doctor Haweis, D.D., a well-known clergyman who lived in Sussex and the grandson of the even more notable Reverend Dr Thomas Haweis, founder of the London Missionary Society. But alas, Mrs Chisholm told her Mr Haweis was soon leaving St James's for St Peter's Church, Bethnal Green. The news made her feel very downcast. She longed so much to meet him because 'of something very attractive in his face as of a man who commands respect and affection from all who see him'.

She wrote this on 1st of April in her Memoranda, a Memoranda which she had just begun to keep.

2. MARY ELIZA IN LOVE

(1864-1867)

ON 23RD APRIL 1864, Mary Eliza Joy records her first meeting with the dynamic young curate of St James's. Only twenty-four hours earlier, arriving as usual for her Friday Confirmation class with her mother, they were told that in the absence of the Vicar Mr Hugh Reginald Haweis would take his class.

I never expected to speak to him, Mary Eliza recorded naively.

My very fertile imagination often pictured scenes and speeches to me in which he and I were the principal actors, but I repeat, that I felt a chance of our introduction was vague and improbable and therefore never expected it. But goaded by the triumph of Mimi Boulger [a girl-friend] who had tried to prevent our going into the Vestry, crowing over me that I was on Mr Dickson's list and must be examined by him, I said to Mama, 'do ask Mr Haweis to examine me instead of Mr Dickson.' I was greatly excited. Here, I fancied, is a chance of bliss and eagerness making me bold, I followed Mama into the vestry. We began by saying, would he mind examining me instead of Mr Dickson. He hesitated at first replying 'I cannot undertake, I think, to take you off Mr Dickson's list.' My heart sank, then beat high when he agreed to see me the next day at half past one when several candidates, including Mimi and Emma Langhorne, were going to his lodgings. Then he bent to us and put out his little olive hand to us each: it trembled, perhaps with fatigue. **My**

heart was wildly beating—I could hear it: here was my
desire gratified. I had conversed with him (alone except
Mama), looked at his eyes, seen his smile at me, touched
his hand! Yet my joy was alloyed by fear that we had
been too bold—that he would consider our behaviour
queer. However, next morning, I went at the appointed
time. Once more he clasped my hand, with such a friendly,
gentle clasp. I instantly felt as easy with him as with a
beloved brother. His manners were courteous, princely.
He is a perfect gentleman in manner, and therefore I
sincerely believe he is so in heart.

The Confirmation class ended with a prayer; after it, Mr
Haweis distributed some religious tracts among his pupils.
Miss Joy received two papers which 'uninviting as they are to
read, I will treasure as a Keepsake from this dearest and best
of men'. It had been a memorable day for her, the happiest
yet in her life', she wrote the following day. But when, ah,
when, would they meet again? For immediately after that
Confirmation class, Mrs Chisholm informed her that her
clerical charmer had departed for Sussex. Life was truly a
blank. There was no possibllity—as she had hoped—for a
chance meeting under the plane trees in the square garden or
of running into him by the high iron railings of St Saviour's
Church which she rarely patronised these days. Then something happened which she could not have imagined, even in
her wildest dreams. Mr Haweis wrote to her.

Today, *May 1st.* I have received a letter from that dear
little man—Oh! what bliss! beginning 'My dear Miss
Joyce'. Sweet pet! To write to me from Colwood,
Crawley. He has fixed next Saturday at 2 pm for our
last meeting. But I trust not our last for life.

Punctually on Saturday afternoon, 7th May, Mrs Joy and her
elder daughter walked to Mr Haweis's lodgings and arrived a
little before the appointed time like the rest of his candidates.
In his sitting-room, a number of pretty girls had already
gathered. They spoke in low tones to one another, like a

flock of murmuring doves in their soft, linsey gowns of
pewter grey and leaf-brown, the latest spring colours; their
dresses featured the new, shortened bell-skirt which revealed
smart little cloth boots and white—not coloured—stockings.
Some misses, including the elegant Miss Joy, sported the
fashionable Zouave jacket. Like their chaperones, they were
all discreetly bonneted and held their prayer books carefully,
between their gloved hands. To stage an effective entrance,
Mr Haweis kept his class waiting for ten minutes; then he
emerged from his bedroom, beaming.

> He did not shake hands with us, for being about thirteen
> in number he could not walk round the crowded room, but
> bowed to us all courteously and said, 'I think you were
> quite right as you had to begin so many times last time.'
> Then he suddenly descried Mrs Boulger and Mimi and went
> and shook hands with them to my anger, but with nobody
> else!

On this annoying note, Mr Haweis started his Confirmation
class with the second part of the Catechism concerning the
Lord's Supper. Every now and then, in her Memoranda,
Mary Eliza breaks into her long recording of Mr Haweis's
learned discourse by describing exactly how he looked and
how he smiled and how he kept asking 'dear Mama' questions
to which she made quiet, dignified replies. Finally, Mr Haweis
suggested that questions might be put to him. There was
silence. Alone in that demure company Miss Joy, with a
pleading look and pretty smile, asked Mr Haweis if he could
explain the Parable of the unjust Steward to her.

> He instantly turned the light of his large dark-brown
> eyes on me (I think I may say with truth, the *light* of his
> eyes) for there is something in his glance which, though it
> neither thrills nor cowes you seems to beam upon you with
> such a calm brilliancy like a sunbeam if I may be allowed
> to make a true simile without being called a romantic
> stupid and here I intend to make a memoranda of his face
> for my own special pleasure. He has the long narrow eyes,

so rarely seen, so much admired which are capable of every possible expression fringed with long dark lashes, that give a soft expression to them. The irisis very dark brown, and the pupil large, quick, and mobile. Complexion dark and pale, telling of ill-health, stature five foot, left club foot. Hands very small and well-shaped. Brow high and smooth, eyebrows arched and nervous, whiskers thick and in good condition like his hair which is soft, long and black, lips rather thick, chin short and round. His smile is so bright, his eye so honest, and his expression quick and pleased as I asked my question. For I was his only pupil who did! 'The Parable of the unjust Steward? Oh, yes, I shall have much pleasure in reading it over with you. If there are any of you who would like to go now, please do,' he said but the stupids all lingered nobody knows what for . . .

Although Miss Joy realised that it was not going to be a thrilling tête-à-tête with her 'dear little man' as she had hoped, Mr Haweis did go over the parable with her and his other immobilised pupils.

In such a friendly and easy comprehensible way that I felt in paradise, and we took our leave of him for the last time. I had my glove off, so that his dear little warm hand should not be wasted on a kid glove and we parted after a hearty shake, or rather pressure. He opened the door for us, having rung the bell for the servant to shew us out, and Ma and I bent as we passed out which he gracefully returned. He is an accomplished and courteous man. I hope and trust that we have not parted for ever. I do hope to meet him again sometime and have the benefit of his counsels and advice from time to time.

But Mary Eliza was to wait eleven long dreary months without either seeing or hearing from little Mr Haweis.

In the meantime, her father completed his two enormous pictures of Tattersall's 'The Yard' and 'The Ring' which were exhibited in the old Subscription Room at Hyde Park Corner at a special exhibition of his work put on for the artist's benefit.

Society flocked to register approval of their favourite painter's work and the *Sporting Gazette* of March 18th, 1865, treated Joy to a long and magnificent notice of what they described as: 'An extraordinary picture. No work of modern times has equally these life-like portraits of well-known men, grouped in a most artistic manner, and in a well-known spot, every detail of which is given, so soon to be swept away, alas!'

To the regret of his family, for money was now in short supply, Thomas Joy refused the sum of one thousand guineas for what was to be his last work.

On the afternoon of 10th April 1865 as Mary Eliza sat writing in the drawing-room of Number 32 the front-door bell gave a shrill peal.

> I sprang up, went to the window and saw *him*! I crept back to my writing-table with a heart that throbbed to agony—I trembled so that I could not continue my writing. Edith came in—saw my trepidation—would not believe my wild guess—after a space that seemed an age, but during which I was utterly unable to move a single paper—Jane announced—'Mr Hoice'. He came slowly in —looked very delicate—greeted me with a manner I cannot describe—so cordial—so friendly—yet with a certain melancholy—'How do you do, Miss Joy?' I asked him to sit down . . .

On Mrs Joy's appearance with apologies that she could not introduce him to her husband who was ill in bed, the conversation turned on painting for a while and then changed to music; the music of Mendelssohn, Strauss and Beethoven.

> He went up to the piano, asked us if the piano was a good one—tried it, just like a professor, with confidence. Then made me play to him, Beethoven's *Pathetique*!!! He sat down close to me, turned over the leaves beautifully, and said it was too fast! I know I was scarlet, and my heart beat so dreadfully, I did it so badly. When I stopped and

said, 'I could not go on', he laughed merrily and said, 'Yes. Oh, yes, go on!' and beat with his hands and counted. I never saw such a saucy chap. At last, I threw up in despair.

At this critical juncture, Mr Haweis began fingering the music on the piano, picking up one piece here; asking about another one there. He was very glad to be back in Westminster, he declared, for he found the work in Stephney much too hard. Then looking straight into Mary Eliza's flushed face he said, 'I called here to say something about the Sunday school. Would you take a class? You have been down to our schools, I think?' 'Yes, yes, I have,' replied Miss Joy dizzily.

As Mrs Joy began to put her best Minton cups and saucers on a large black-and-gold papier mâché tray, Edith Selfe walked into the drawing-room. For no apparent reason, she blushed scarlet at the sight of Mrs Joy's visitor. To Mary Eliza's dismay, after Mr Haweis had politely shaken hands with her flustered girl-friend, he declined her mother's invitation to stay for tea and, abruptly, took his leave.

I followed him to the stairs, having rung for Jane, when he turned to me and said again, 'Well, Miss Joy, suppose you come next Sunday and take a class?' So I said, 'Yes, shall I come with Miss Cowell?' He assented. Then I ventured timidly 'I hope it won't require any great cleverness to teach for I am not at all clever.' 'Oh, no', he replied encouragingly, adding, with the greatest kindness, and quite affectionately—I can't describe the seraphic look he gave me as he said it—'it only wants a good will', and clasped my hand for a third time in silence and departed. I rushed back in a wild ecstasy of every imaginable emotion and dreadfully excited.

My wildest dreams realised, what more have I to desire? He has called! We are to have his Phot!! he is to lend me books! and instead of asking Mr Dickson about the Sunday school, Mr Haweis has come and asked me of his own accord, and quite pressingly, more than once! Desire is for a while lulled asleep; only the demon of jealousy awakes within me, and I hope sincerely, that he has not asked Mimi Boulger—as is more than probable, since she was prepared by him with me for Confirmation, and he does know something of them, I regret to say. I am now lying a second day in bed, ill of a rash, which Ma declares is brought out by Monday's excitement; what shall I do if I must miss Friday evening's sermon? Today is but Wednesday however. There is still hope, and Easter Eve late service with Mr Haweis's sermon—and Easter Day, when I suppose he will meet me at the Schools!

Thursday, April 15th. I have been allowed to get up today—Edith has excited me much by some news. She went to Church this morning and coming out met Mr Haweis in the porch who spoke to her and asked after me. Why had he not seen me in church? Edith told him that I had been in bed. He said he was very sorry to hear that and that he would be at the schools this Sunday—so polite! Mr Dickson also spoke to Edith, asked after me, and said if I was well enough, would I come and decorate the Church for Easter on Saturday.

Whether Mary Eliza decorated St James's Church at Easter as the vicar knew how well she could—floral arrangements were to be a great forte of hers during her life—or whether she was not well enough, she does not say. Her Memoranda remains a blank. But on 6th July there came the day so long awaited for by all the young ladies who lived in or around St George's Square, Pimlico. For on this day, the annual school treat arranged by Mr Dickson for his Sunday school children took place. And what a day it turned out to be, particularly as the morning was fine, sunny, and warm. In a white marcella frock with a pretty net shawl draped round her slender shoulders, her auburn hair frizzed up and wearing a straw hat trimmed with a single blush-pink rose, Mary Eliza—all her dimples showing—set out with Mama in decorous pale grey silk and plum, in a cab for Vauxhall Station near by.

Here they were joined by the entire Selfe family carrying fire balloons to entertain the school children. Mary Eliza's contribution was a basket of white currants which she dangled in her hand. They travelled by train to Richmond where, on arrival, they found two flies waiting to take them to the Park. The rendezvous was an enormous cedar in whose cool arc of shade stood Mr Dickson. He received them with open arms.

We enquired for Mr Haweis in great apprehension—he (Mr Dickson) said he was playing cricket with the boys,— 'Strip-shirt'. How jolly of him, thought I. Mr Dickson asked Mrs Selfe and Ma to superintend the dinner on the grass, and then Mr Haweis came and joined us. I didn't wish him to think I wanted to sit by him so dreadfully— so I went with Edith Selfe to the farthest side of the table cloth—but still, to my delight, he ensconced himself between her and me. He was very merry—did all the carving—and we did have such fun! Having no spoon for the currant tart, he was told to use a wine-glass instead so he served it out that way—he drank up his own sherry (after Ma was served) and then dug it into our laps—and gave us some sugar plums for the children to scramble for —so good natured! He took my fork to stir up the cucumber—and really proved himself the life and soul of the party as I expected. Then he blew out a bladder painted like a snake and sent it flying about.

After this gay little entertainment provided by the attentive Mr Haweis he vanished with the other clergy present. The ladies occupied themselves by tying the sweet bags on to the trees for the children to break off with sticks. When Mr Haweis reappeared he set the boys to run races for halfpence while Miss Joy coaxed those children too small to compete into jumping for the white currants which she had brought. All the time, though, her eyes kept turning to Mr Haweis's in the distance. After all the currants had been eaten, a game was played called 'Little Dog' and then 'Silly Old Woman' which absurd name sent Miss Joy off into peals of laughter,

laughter that brought Mr Haweis immediately hurrying to her side.

When the married ladies of the party disappeared to prepare tea in a Tea-Garden close by, Mary Eliza accepted Mr Haweis's invitation to stop playing with the children and to sit under the trees for a while. She and Edith Selfe removed their straw hats and sat down in the shade for a delightful twenty minutes' conversation with their attentive escort. Romantically, in the foreground, grazed a charming herd of fallow deer while the children, left to themselves for once, played what games they liked.

All too soon, however, came cheerful Mr Brown, the fat chorister, declaring tea was ready. So off they trooped to the Tea-Garden with the children. Here little Mr Haweis proved himself once more to be the life and soul of the party spreading jam on the rolls and getting some stuck on to his sleeve, which Miss Joy wiped off, of course, with her handkerchief.

After tea, he walked back to the Park with me and the Selfes quoting many verses from *In Memoriam* which I said I had not finished reading. Quoting them in so tender, so impassioned and solemn a tone that I was fascinated. We sat down and prepared the fire balloons for going up. Then I played with the little children at 'Little Dog' again while Mr Haweis sat talking to the elder ladies. After much bother we sent up some balloons. Then it began to rain and the last would not rise and got smashed among the children. It began to rain so fast that we had to rush under the cedar for shelter and the dear little man went (wilfully without an umbrella) in search of flies. Of course I formed vague hopes—never dreaming they would be fulfilled. We then entered a stables for shelter and Mr Haweis procured two flies and the children were packed into vans. Then in a pointed way Mr Haweis put the Selfes into one fly and us into the second fly—saying to me 'Mind your dress.' Edith got in with us—and so did he. He took his hat off, and threw his hair over his eyes in thick masses, and frowned and looked like a gnome —making us roar. Then he made fun of the dirt on my marcella dress—he said he had often admired the spotless whiteness of that dress—and when I pushed it down, he laughed and said, 'That's right,' and pulled my fan out of my pocket and commenced the fan-business indulged in by the ladies of his congregation. Now he pretended to go to sleep behind it, now woke up fanning himself violently—I was quite exhausted—yet he looked so handsome, so much younger, so affected, so disdainful, so vividly by turns that I could only marvel.

He handed me from the carriage when at his suggestion we put on our most solemn countenances—his little warm hand clasped mine so warmly—and to me *only* he addressed the sole remark—'Now, take care, Miss Joy, *do* be careful,' at which I laughed and so did he.

After vague and foolish hopes—after waiting in the station half an hour—he really did get into our carriage and sat by *me* (!), leaning back by me like a sofa. He did look so wicked! It seemed so strange for him to be reclining beside me in the train, talking in that low, tête-à-tête way of his. We all took our hats off, and he then began to talk more softly to me about Turner—and genius being a kind of madness—and I stared at the sunset, and sometimes glanced at him and found his eyes always on me, straight—Am I beginning to love him? I hope not! for I feel a thrill run through me whenever his fingers contact mine. He talked a long time to me—all the way home in fact, to nobody clsc. Now that must havc bccn his choice!

When we arrived at Vauxhall Station he handed me out with his firm little hand and placed us in a cab. Ma asked him if he would ride home with us and he said, 'Oh, yes, if there is room for two.' Then he and Mr Leonini entered. He talked to me about Tennyson's *Mariana*. He likes it. So we drove on to our house. The Signor got out first, and I was going to follow him—but Mr Haweis said 'Oh, I will get out next.' Taking the umbrella from Mr Leonini, he assisted me out, and walked not quickly but very slowly through the rain into the hall. There instead of hastening back to shelter Ma he stood talking to *me under the umbrella*, right in the hall, very coolly. Then after *mooning* rather, for some moments longer than there was any necessity for—he said an affectionate goodbye, and clasped my hand quite lovingly—paid the cab and he and Signor Leonini went away together.

So ended the annual School Treat where according to Mary Eliza 'I had awful fun and great bliss!' But heavy gloom followed. For she began to notice a certain detachment, a drawing back from her, on Mr Haweis's part. Their's had been such an instantaneous cosy and warm relationship, but all of a sudden, her new friend no longer teased or flirted with her, mooningly or wickedly, with gleaming eyes and mischievous smile. What was the matter? 'Will he never be tender with me again?' she wrote. 'Not that I mean any real tenderness, of course, he does not care a snap for me in that way, nor ever will, nor I for him, but I like the tender manner, it is awful fun, as long as we perfectly understand each other'.

There came horrid rumours to her ears, 'abominable reports that we are classed together in the Square.' In a panic, she sat down and wrote to her best friend Kate Elliot. She told her *dearest* Kate that Mr Haweis's manner to ladies was always flirtatious and that he had only gone so far as to make 'eye-signs to me across the table whenever anything is said that surprises and amuses him'. Unfortunately, this harmless little intimacy between them had been noted by Major Clutton who had had the cheek to tell her father. Whether Mr Haweis's aloof manner was caused by local gossip effectively putting him on his guard against her, she did not know, but, *but,*— 'I do so want your candid opinion, dear Kate.'

Here Mary Eliza must have been interrupted for she adds,

happily, to her letter next day (a letter which, though it survives, was never posted to Kate), 'Yesterday, Mr Haweis called and was quite his jolly old self. He put a bachelor's button in my mouth and then ate one himself and said, 'Now we are friends. Jolly dear little flirt.'

The next important entry in Mary Eliza's Memoranda is dated *October 3rd*, 1865.

On this longed-for day, we went to Knole with Mr Haweis and his sister Margaret. He sat by me in the train and we had a long conversation on domestic servants, and though neither could convince the other, I won, because he wandered from the point a good deal and I did not, and at last he gave up.

In the omnibus, going from Sevenoakes Station to the 'Crown' he sat opposite me. We had some lunch, ordered dinner, and went on to inspect Knole House. It is magnificent—the most beautiful and curious things.

With Mr Haweis by her side, Mary Eliza studied the historic furniture at Knole, and gazed at the pictures, little knowing how in the not so distant future she would be 'doing' not only other stately homes of England with the lively figure at her side but the famous palaces, art galleries and museums of Europe as well. 'In one of the rooms,' she records, 'I sketched a chair for Papa in Mr Haweis's pocket book which he got out so promptly—so jolly of him!' In their married life H. R. Haweis never failed to carry pencil and paper with him so that his wife could make her lightning drawings of the objects which interested her most while on a sight-seeing trip.

On leaving the House, we went round the park and I defied him to climb a gate which he said he could, if I would follow him. He ran up—not like another man climbing—but like a cat runs up a tree, marvellously fast, and descended by his arms alone—I was quite startled. Papa, in great anxiety for his dinner, ordered us all back to the Crown.

After dinner Margaret and I went out into the garden.

It was growing dark and cold, but we had good furs, and picked some flowers. All the rest of us, except him and me and Margaret went to the station in an omnibus. We went in a wagonette or dog cart thing. His sister made room for him but he squeezed in by me pointedly. We talked about the 'blue moon' and lilac flakes of sunlight on water, we mooned but cheerfully. It was very cold. He buttoned up his coat. And then . . . then . . . fut il jamais? . . . the dog cart jolted us very close together—and he put his arm on the back of the low seat, and then he had it round my waist all the way.

What the men are! and the clergy too! but it did feel so funny—and every time I felt the evidence of his hand's proximity more plainly—I could not laugh or smile, the feel of it banished my smiles in a queer way, and I was quite grave! but it thrilled me strangely—and it was dark, and cold, and he was very close.

Well! I could not have struggled or prevented it with his sister sitting opposite. In the rooms at Knole he put his hand on my back and held me by the gathers once or twice and called Mary Eliza. Once he said, 'May, ri, Eliza.' I wish he would always call me so. Once in my usual way I should have thought nothing could exceed this bliss. But now I know better. I have learnt that Imagination cannot anticipate the climax—that facts are stranger than fancies. I don't see how he can go much further with me, this tiny of tiny men, who looked so cold with his thin threadbare coat buttoned up like a policeman and the collar up to his ears as he sat so close in that cold wagonette, serious, not grinning, with his arm lightly round my waist. He had not got me squeezed up *tight* with his arm *far* round—only now and then a little press which felt queer and I was half tickled, half nervous, and I stopped laughing every time I felt his hand. He asked me if I remembered what Tennyson said of the night-orb, 'The Opal width of the Moon.' I could not hear and he repeated it close to my ear, 'width . . . width.' I can almost feel the warm puff in my ear now, as he said it. He looked so different then from what he does in a drawing-room when his eyes and teeth glitter with delight at anything. The flowers, the geraniums that Margaret and I picked in the 'Crown' garden fell out of my hair and he offered to hold them for me. I let him and as I gave him one sprig he took it from me in that ridiculous way he always does with both hands, so that his little warm palms passed over my hand. I consider it exceedingly impudent. I believe he knows the electric shock it causes, or else he is watching for some effect, for he has the queerest expression, a sort of complacent smug look, and has one eye fixed on me all the time.

In the train, he sat by me and showed me some photographs of St James the Less, said he would give me one and talked in my ear. . . . On our return home, Ma asked Margaret and Mr Haweis in to tea (she had prepared for them), he seemed willing but Margaret said she was too tired and preferred to go home. So he said he would go with her, adding 'if I can't get tea there I will come back to you by myself.' But he did not come.

November 10th. Is he such a flirt? I have just heard from Fanny S. that he was very sweet on Harriet Hunt once, only she despised such a mite. I don't believe it. It may be gossip. Besides many people might mistake his tender sort of manner. Mrs Boulger has spread the report that he and I are engaged. Brute!

Four months were to pass before Mary Eliza saw Mr Haweis. It was more than likely that at this particular time, with gossip rife, the Reverend Hugh Reginald Haweis, professionally ambitious and with small private means, had given no serious thought to marriage, except perhaps if an attractive heiress came his way. Miss Joy had no money and her father, however distinguished a painter he had once been, was now in poor health and straitened circumstances. That he was captivated by Mary Eliza's looks, her vitality, charm and marked talents was obvious to all. But she was young: He had no wish to break her heart. And so he kept away, fearful that he might be tempted, one day, to pop the fatal question. For in her presence—as in the presence of any pretty girl or woman throughout his life—the natural philanderer in him, the skilful executant of those 'tender and caressing ways' was immediately roused. This, in her shrewdness, Mary Eliza had already realised. He was a born flirt, but so was she. *Tant pis!* She wanted to cry but found that she could not.

So Mary Eliza Joy felt the first sharp sting of Cupid's dart. Emotionally stirred as she had never been before in her young life, she was at a complete loss. A terrible vacuum filled her days which long hours of serious reading, painting or designing her monograms could not fill as they had before. How she missed 'her dear little man'! That gnome-like figure with his endless tricks and jolly wiles. That alert intelligence which matched so well and struck sparks off her own. How dreary were the dank November days! When would they meet again to laugh and joke together, she kept asking herself? When, oh, when, would she feel the tender pressure of his warm little olive paw on hers? She wished there was someone to whom she could confide her fears and hopes. But there was only kind, beautiful and rather 'dumb' Mama; a sister who was still a child; and Papa, Papa who kept strange hours, alone in his studio or retired for curious and unmentionable reasons to bed. Still there did remain one outlet for Mary Eliza and that was to relieve herself of the complicated emotions and thoughts of adolescent love by writing them down. So she conceived the idea of keeping a 'Thought Book' which, in time, took the place of her Memoranda and which she kept up for the rest of her life. On the 15th November 1865, seated alone in her room at Number 32, St George's Square, Pimlico, Mary Eliza made her first entry. It was a miserable day with fog about. Fog that shrouded the dripping trees and empty paths of the square garden so that all was gloom to match the unmitigated gloom in her heart. She began seriously enough with a long quotation from Mr Emerson.

November 25th, 1865. 'A man should learn to detect that gleam of light which flashes across his mind from within, more than the lustre of the firmament and of bards and sages. Yet he dismisses his thought without notice, because it is his. In every work of genius we recognise our own rejected thoughts; they come back to us with a certain alienated majesty. . . . What I must do, is all that concerns me, and not what people think.'

Besides the turmoil in her heart there was ferment in her mind, for Mary Eliza's religious views were undergoing a kind of spiritual revolution. This was due to her having listened for so long and so seriously to Mr Haweis's unusual sermons. She thought so much of them that she transcribed many in longhand. She had read books, too, at his suggestion; books that were too advanced in theory and subject matter for an impressionable girl of her age. This rich intellectual diet had first disturbed then over-stimulated her mentally.

November 26th. I have been reading some of Bishop Colenso's writings. I see nothing so objectionable in them as to call down so much abuse as he receives, amongst such truths, cuts away many cords and breaks off many ends that one has leaned upon and trusted as infallible. Now, it appears that nothing is infallible. I wish I could find something that is—a book or a Person. I sometimes fear that reading so many eccentric books does me more harm than good, that, although to read and hear all doctrines and opinions is best to free one from narrow views and prejudices, and the mind will receive what it feels instinctively is true and good for its individual self, and reject what it feels to be wrong and untrue; yet I fancy at times I am losing some early good and growing worse not better, because I am growing less strict with myself and more lax—growing more liable to be blown about with every wind—because I want something that is infallible—mine is a heart without a rudder—nothing is infallible but God. And where is God?

She might have added 'Where is Mr Haweis?' For Christmas came and went without a glimpse of him. In the New Year of 1866, she continued probing into the why and wherefore of God's existence; of the evolution of man and the theory of the transmigration of souls; of whether the Sabbath Day should be kept or whether it should not be kept. For she no longer believed it was a crime to work, walk, or read other than religious books on a Sunday.

There is nothing in the New Testament, she wrote, to forbid us any particular pursuit on the first day of the week as there is in the Old to forbid the Jew doing anything on the seventh. Once upon a time I thought it a heinous sin to buy anything on a Sunday or even to carry a toy—now I see it is not. Beauty makes all things and all places and all seasons holy.

During Lent, that most dismal of Victorian religious seasons, a period set aside for petty self-denials, much esteemed by the sanctimonious church-goer, Mary Eliza led her solitary life, scribbling away in her Thought Book. She felt herself 'growing harder and more callous and more doubtful of God's individual Love and tender promises' because her prayers remained unanswered, in spite of their being so much more modified than before. 'Prayer is vain and God heareth not,' she wrote in her firm, clear hand.

In sad retrospect, she remembered the happy evening when after their excursion to Knole, she had dined *en famille* with the Haweises and noticed how teasing and affectionate they were with one another. It made Mary Eliza feel very much apart and lonely and 'the old longing for a brother which I thought smothered, came back!'

However fond the Joys might be of each other, they were not demonstrative as a family. In fact, Mary Eliza never remembered being kissed by her parents 'unless with a kind of bang before going to bed'. The early loss of their three beloved sons had acted, no doubt, as some kind of emotional brake when it came to showing their daughters spontaneous affection. If they became too fond of Mary Eliza or little Edith, they would be sure to lose them, they argued.

Suddenly though on March 16th, 1866, Mary Eliza's sky cleared. While she was out with the Selfes, little Mr Haweis appeared at Number 32, St George's Square and invited Mrs Joy and her daughter to go with him and his brother Willy to Deptford to see the *Northumberland* launched by Lady Percy. But the following morning it was pouring and—

sulks prevailed at breakfast because we never dreamt we could go. But suddenly it cleared a little and I despatched a note to Rennie [first use of his family nickname by Mary Eliza] and lo! the answer came he had gone to Stepney the night before and was not yet returned! I was in agonies. At last, when again all hope was dashed a ring comes, and Rennie tears up, in his old rough Inverness Cape all spattered with mud, a violet comforter on, and iron grey cloth gloves, such a guy but very larky! I received him with grim coldness, saying he was always so uncertain that we had not the least expected him to keep his appointment. He was pert: said he didn't bring the rain and ordered me to fly off and dress instanter. I cheered up and obeyed; he strummed on the piano meanwhile. We got into a cab and he made us yell by tying his comforter all awry, making grimaces, and twisting his hand like a wax dummy in the tailor's shop. We arrived at Charing X. Station where he bought us buns and would not let us see what was in them; said I was so curious. In the train we divided them amid many antics. He had been to a concert at the St Peter's Schools of Mr Sitwell [Incumbent of St Peter's, Bethnal Green] and slept at Green's. [John Richard Green the historian and H.R.H's best friend]. Did not return till it was time to fetch us. This evening he has promised to play at a quartette party at the Sullivans [Arthur Sullivan].

Madness! But he is so rash. At Deptford we arrived too early, Willy could not come till One. So we walked about the town, a beastly place with dead fish lying in the gutters that look up at you with decomposed eyes, with contempt, as much to say 'Here I have been for a week and may lie for another!'

We returned to the Station and ate our buns. Rennie sat by me and talked about Doctor Newman—a great man—and Doctor Pusey, his disciple who had refused 'to turn'. At last Willy came looking very jolly in his uniform. I could see he wanted to walk with me but Rennie would not let him. He was crumped and had to walk with Ma . . .

We rowed over the river but finding no room to land and the water too crowded to stay in the boat, we climbed with difficulty up a plank on to a barge and then from it up some steps on to a high scaffolding crowded with 'twopennies' [trippers]. My chinchilla tippet would blow up so Rennie kept his hand on it. He would stick so close to me; Ma was frightened but I could give her no more room. Suddenly Willy yelled: 'She's going to start.' I saw the Countess Percy's white strings and then the ribbons of the bottle were cut and the *Northumberland* crept out a little way and then got stuck irreparably on the mud. A great disappointment, but not to me! We left our high post and tried to find our boat but could not. Rennie gave me his arm and we walked along the river, a peculiar little couple, he such a guy, and I so beautifully dressed, but so snug.

Eventually Willy found the boat and his men and we rowed along to Greenwich where we had wine and sandwiches, visited the Hospital and saw the pictures and Nelson's relics. . . . We arrived home for a seven o'clock dinner. We had a horrible dinner; for we could not get Pa out of the room and he made it so unpleasant by being extremely queer.

Rennie left at eight but we got Willy up into the drawing-room where he made me play and then accompany his comic songs till it was too late for him to go to the Sullivans. He left about half-past eleven! I was so delighted he stayed.

Five days later, on Thursday, 22nd, March Willy Haweis squired Mrs Joy and her two daughters to the Zoological Gardens where they took the 'Coati' out for a walk and made frightening faces at the bears. Then gallant Willy suggested they should all go down to Woolwich to see some private theatricals taking place on his ship, the *Bee*, before an invited audience. But Mrs Joy, obviously not recovered from her last excursion on the river, would not go. Eventually she agreed to letting Mary Eliza and her little sister Edith go with Willy Haweis providing he brought them back early.

The delighted trio drove to Baker Street by cab, where they took the Underground Railway to Moorgate Street: then they went on by cab again to Woolwich. The performance was to be a 'free-mason' farce, enacted in Willy Haweis's cabin. Here little Edith was put on the wash-stand and Mary Eliza given a chair. She gives a detailed account of a most extraordinary performance that consisted of nothing less than the ganging up of all the junior officers in fancy freemason's dress against a poor man called Hancorn who, after suffering various schoolboyish pranks, was eventually tattooed with a large A.S.S. on his back with five needles lashed together and dipped in Indian Ink amid guffaws of laughter from the audience. After a supper of fowls, cold beef, and mince pies served in the Captain's cabin the Joy girls were given a 'cup of delicious negus'. Then,—

Willy gave us each an arm to go home. At London Bridge Edith got into the train as it was moving and we could not follow. So we took the next. We found her safely arrived at Charing Cross from where we walked home, it being a splendid night. Found Mama in agonies, having insanely expected us for hours before. Rennie was in the drawing-room, and had spent the evening with Ma, what he called soothing her. I call it the reverse. Saying his brother was honourable and all that—but hoped we would not mention it to the Selfes. Did not think it quite correct going alone with a young chap at night and all that bosh!

When they went away, Ma told me that Rennie's conversation had been all about me! He thinks me very clever and (!!!) quite equal in my drawing and painting to his in his writing, preaching and music! Fancy that! His mother wants him to be married; but he says 'No woman would be happy with an old worn-out bachelor like him and the more so if she was fond of parties and gaieties.' Ma did not know what to reply, so said: 'No. Certainly you could not be happy with a wife like that.' He mooned a good deal. Said he had been married over and over again by report. For some it was the eldest Miss Selfe. 'Now, perhaps, it is Miss Joy!' He thinks me 'so pure, so innocent, so charming—so seldom found in girls today—they know everything!' I cannot get over that! Thinks me not musical. My forte is more Art. He seems to have spoken of me very flatteringly.

So Mary Eliza's Memoranda comes to a full stop and her Thought Book takes up the story of her inner life; of her secret ambitions; her hopes and her fears. In this book, she gives many a frank analysis of her character; a character about which she had few illusions, neither did she admire it.

In the meantime, a portrait of Rennie moving in quite different circles than those of Pimlico comes from the pen of a girl who was a contemporary of Mary Eliza's and just as discerning. A Miss Colquhoun of Luss, she was 'doing the London season' from the Mayfair home of a cousin, and described her first meeting with the Reverend Mr Haweis in her *Memories of Victorian London* published in 1912 under her married name of Mrs L. B. Walford.

On a cold grey March morning, the morning of the Oxford

and Cambridge Boat Race, Miss Colquhoun was taken to the riverside home of George Macdonald the well-known writer whose *Annals of a Quiet Neighbourhood* had just appeared. There were more than eighty people present to witness the great race. So the wooden stand erected in the garden with seats only for fifty

spelt exclusion for us younger ones. Headed by a little Mr Haweis, a very imp of mischief and quite irresponsible, we ran about the garden hopping up into trees and all sorts of places—finally what did that gallant little lame man do but wriggle himself on to the roof of the house, and sit there at his ease, with his legs hanging down.

Years afterwards, when I met Mr Haweis at one of Mrs Vaughan-Temple's garden-parties (when I was married and he was married, and we were, or ought to have been old and sober) I reminded him of this feat. But though I had remembered him, he had, I must own, forgotten me; I had been one of a laughing pack of girls, while he was, even then, beginning to be known as a wit, a preacher, and a Court favourite.

Barely a few days after the Boat Race described by Miss Colquhoun, Mary Eliza and her father quarrelled violently. Rashly she had declared that she would not have put up with half that her mother had from him. Losing his temper, Thomas Joy threatened to brain his blunt daughter and picked up a bottle near him for the purpose. Calmly, Mary Eliza recorded in her Thought Book:

But I wasn't the least startled or affrayed because I knew the only way to conquer was to be fierce and let the passion of anger come out. 'There is nothing in the world I am afraid to do when my blood is up,' I cried. Pa was silenced directly and remained calmer all day—just snuffed out. I had lost my temper—very futile! I regret it now. It was truth and yet not truth. I trust I will never give way again to temper but I do anything when I am strung up. But to give way even in the smallest degree, seems to

weaken me somehow—I lose a little bit of myself in every
emotion good or bad. Therefore I always repress it in any
form. Is it wrong or best? Who can help me? To give
way before another is to give him a hold on you and a
power.

After this distressing scene which reveals poor Thomas Joy
to have become a very sick man, Mary Eliza was struck with
remorse. She could not paint. She could not write. She
longed to believe that the sun though hidden still shone
and would shine again on her. But, somehow, she was filled
with gloomy presentiments as if there was 'an abyss at my
feet and a sword hair-hung over my head.'

Very early on the morning of April 10th, Mary Eliza's psychic
sense of impending disaster—a sense she was to experience
several times in her life—materialised. The sword suspended
above her head fell. She woke up to find her mother standing,
pale and agitated, at the bottom of her bed. Following a
slight attack of bronchitis which had put him to bed the
preceding day, Thomas Musgrove Joy had had some kind of
stroke and lay in a stupor. Doctor Dudley was sent for but he
could do nothing. Thomas Joy never regained consciousness
and died a few hours later. In silence, after trying to comfort
the stricken widow, Doctor Dudley, who was an old friend,
signed the death certificate and left.

Confusion now reigned supreme in the Joy household and
Mary Eliza records how on that terrible morning:

I was really routed out of my apathy. I cried very much
until at last I was quite dried up, and grew hard and could
cry no more. I have slipped from the *terra firma* down the
dread, unavoidable abyss but as yet have not reached the
bottom. I have never seen death before, and on seeing
him just as he had died—and again after he was laid out—
I was greatly affected. But after the first shock was past a
little, came a feeling of mingled awe and surprise as I
looked at the still form that was once my father and that I
had never seen so straight and stiff before. . . . It was hard

to believe that that sheet did not move a little with faint breathing; that the quiet well-known face (looking so much quieter and younger than it had for so long) would no more be animated. It only looked like a peaceful stupor, even pleasant to see. But away from him, my thoughts went on so rapidly to the dread future; what we must do, what we could live on—how I can add to the income. If only I could have made a commission before this with Daziel! How much I have thought about it lately like a presentiment. I do not cry now. I feel no fear. Only a strangeness when Mama first tried on her widow's cap and cloak. But now, now all is just as it was when Papa was away or in bed. Yet his death was the happiest —almost painless—sudden! If we have to live in lodgings and work for our living, the test is at hand of friends and relations. I shall miss Papa more and more. He has been a kind father and was very fond of us all. He had many troubles and his family will have much to account for. They had, for at this very moment his mother, [Grandmama Joy to his daughters,] lay semi-conscious surrounded by her three children—Aunt Sarah, Aunt Ethelinda and Aunt Augusta Henderson, who had taken complete charge of her. She survived her only son, Thomas, by a few weeks and left his penniless widow the miserable sum of only £50 in her will.

April 11*th.* Today I went in to see Papa in his shell. The long leaden coffin, covered by a long white sheet, looked so solemn—the calm face amid the paper-lace looked so very pale—I could not help crying. Where is my stoicism? I could not kiss him when Ma wanted me to on Saturday and I could not today. I just touched him with my finger—so cold it was, but the flesh smooth and limp. There is no horror in death to me. I would not wish him back because I know that his life of disappointment, of worry, of trial is over and I trust he is happy in Heaven. But I cannot help thinking what will become of us—no will, and so little money. His family are heartless. From pure pride, so that a Joy may not be buried like a common person, they are paying for the funeral. But they have not sent to ask after us, nor taken any notice of the death of their only brother. Uncle Tomkin has been very kind and was much affected on seeing poor Papa. As I looked at him today I forgave him everything—he was always a kind father—if only I could be better in the future than I have been in the past.

Friends of the Joys gathered round the dignified figure of beautiful Eliza mourning in her widow's weeds. Mr Frith called to offer his sincere condolences. Did his conscience prick at having cold-shouldered society's pet painter of late years? Particularly when that painter had been bereft by Time of so many of his rich patrons. Mr Frith offered to do all he could to help Mary Eliza in her art career. He believed in her talent and suggested that she sent a picture for the Summer Academy. This she did. It was hung on the 'line' and sold for £15. For two more portraits, one commissioned by their old friends the Taylors, the other by Major Clutton, she received the sum of £30.

On April the 28th, her mother sent word by the undertaker, Holloway, to the Joy sisters at Fitzroy Place that if they wished to see their brother in his coffin she would be happy to receive them. According to Mary Eliza on getting this message they thought better of their first intention which was not to come to St George's Square and told Holloway that they would be present at the nailing down of the coffin.

They came with the undertakers and going into the parlour where poor Papa had been placed, shut themselves in with the men, where they commenced roaring so loudly that one would have thought their sorrow great if one did not know their real characters. Deep grief is *not* noisy. They refused to see Mama. 'They were too upset,' they said and departed as they came, with Holloway. Ann [a maid] came and told us they were gone and would we like to go down for the last time. I went down, the leaden lid was removed for me. I just looked at him—he was just the same. I did not weep. I could not before all the men with their shirt sleeves looking so horribly like business.

On a characteristic April day of flying cloud and intermittent sunshine, when that great expanse of the Kentish Weald looked its loveliest and the fallow deer stood grazing in the park of Boughton Monchelsea Place, the coffin of Thomas Musgrove Joy was brought solemnly through the ancient lych-gate of St Peter's into the remote little churchyard he had known and loved as a boy. He was interred in the Joy family vault that is covered by a massive table tombstone surrounded by a high iron rail. The Uncles Tomkin were in attendance and Uncle Fred and Uncle Eldridge Spratt, Eliza Joy's brothers. Inside the shadowy church, hung Joy's painting of *Christ at Emmaus,* designed to be part of a three-panel reredos; a scheme which came to nothing. Today his picture can still be seen at St Peter's but the name of Thomas Musgrove Joy is all but erased by creeping ivy, moss and lichen stain on the family tomb. In all standard works too on Victorian painters, Joy's name is rarely listed and his pictures scattered no one knows where.

In London, in St George's Square, Mrs Joy bravely set about selling most of her best furniture, silver, tapestry, books and precious ornaments to raise money for the bare necessities of life. She planned to move out to Kilburn, thus severing all connection with Pimlico and St James's Church, Westminster. It could not have been a very happy time for Mary Eliza but she seems to have undergone a marked change of heart and, in a detached mood, wrote, philosophically, in her Thought Book:

June 15th. It is strange how soon we become resigned to what is inevitable—nay, content with it. At least, I do. I know I have been proud in every possible way—now, each sort of pride and vanity is gradually being taken quietly from me, and I don't seem to regret it. Once, I was in the greatest state of mind when **Papa** thought of selling this house and taking one much smaller. I was proud of our beautiful furniture, of our position with no lack of comforts even luxuries. Now I contentedly look forward to living in lodgings; of leaving here altogether. Once I was conceited as a peacock and how I loved admiration! But now, I do not care to be admired. I don't consider myself to be pretty. I should like to be clever and successful and beloved. I don't want to be rich; nor yet a pauper, of course. I am glad that I don't care for parties or gaieties as I did—glad that I feel more free and comfortable than I did three months ago—glad I am so different from what I used to be. It takes so little to satisfy me but that little must be of the right sort, and it is hard to get. Much as we must retrench and alter our mode of life, lose much that once I thought indispensable and put up with reverses, there is a wonderful amount of anxiety, uneasiness and trial removed. It was not a peaceful life before Pa died. There were so many things to dread; now there is only one—subsistence! If only I could succeed in etching and painting and keep myself if necessary. Things look so well now. My picture in the Academy and **Mr Frith** offering to help me in my profession.

But not a single word—not a mention—of Rennie: [of her *dear little man*; of Mr Haweis]. To where had he vanished? When the Joys moved out to Kilburn, their break with him was made complete. For it was a long and tedious bus drive to St James's, Westminster. Not that Mr Haweis was preaching there except at intervals. He was still based at Stepney, where cholera had broken out and he was kept very busy attending on the sick.

The dull weeks passed, the dreary months, but Mary Eliza gave no sign of how her heart ached for the gnome-like figure whose flirtatious arm had encircled her slender waist so often; whose voice had whispered such outrageous things in her ear

Mary Eliza Haweis in 1878; inset is the monogram she
designed and always used

The Reverend H. Reginald Haweis during his American tour; these drawings were printed in a San Francisco newspaper with the text of his sermon

to make her shriek and giggle. In the torrid month of July, in their new suburban home Cherwell House, Mortimer Road, to which they had brought only a few souvenirs of their former glory such as Byron's leather screen and those long, heavy velvet curtains once the property of Napoleon, bitter memories came floating up on to the surface of Mary Eliza's mind. So bitter were they that, in painful distress, she cried out violently in her Thought Book 'Why, oh, why, have I built my house on sand? Engulfing, disastrous sand?' Then she laboriously copied out a long quotation from her favourite author (and Rennie's too), Emerson:

July 21*st*. 'The things that are really for thee gravitate to thee. You are running to seek your friend. Let your feet run, but your head not. If you do not find him, will you not acquiesce that it is best you should not find him? For there is a power, which, as it is in you, is in him also, and could therefore very well bring you together if it were for the best.'

But the stars were set against any meeting between Mary Eliza Joy and her Rennie. For the time being she had to remain content reading her 'eccentric' books and settling down to their new life. One day, August 16th, she took a solitary walk out into the fields beyond Kilburn village.

It was a breezy day—smelling of the country—the wind-gusts laden with that mingled faint-flowery, wood-firey, birds-nesty, wet-bushy, fresh-earthy odour that seems to say more plainly that the town is left far behind. The sky was a rich cobalt blue and soft as feathers. It seemed to stretch millions of miles away into space. Here and there hung solid rounded masses of white cloud like indolent birds—rocs—poised.

Mary Eliza recalled the day of her father's death when she had expressed to herself three wishes:

One was that his talent might be mine for all our sakes; one was to die; the third was to be fit to die—the most earnest wish I ever felt in my life. There is only one wish now I have which may never be fulfilled, God help me! I think when I am old, I shall look back at the heap of fallen leaves that are past years and hunt over them. Perhaps, they will not all be dead. I think the happiest and the greenest in my life will be 1859 and 1865. The blackest and saddest, 1866, for this year is the sepulchre of all the others, of disappointment, of suspense, of separation, of change, of dispersal, of crises.

She must have been glad to see the old year die and New Year's day arrive, unheralded though it was by any celebration.

Some weeks later, Mary Eliza heard that Rennie Haweis had been offered, and accepted, the curacy of St James's, Westmoreland Street, Marylebone. The living was in the gift of the Crown and there was no parish attached, nor could christenings, weddings or funerals take place in church except by special permission. Persuading her mother to attend service there, one Sunday, the Reverend Hugh Reginald Haweis not a whit changed comes suddenly back into her life.

April 9th 1867. Cherwell House, I really can't wonder at my being so full of doubt and scepticism when I have such endless worries and so much to think about. First and foremost of all things is Rennie. He certainly is a queer one and although he may be my ruin, I am afraid I am destined to be his slave all my life. I am convinced he is very fond of me, and I believe that I shall be able to forgive him much. He now appears to be coming on again. I do think he has tried stopping away all this time as an experiment and found it an unpleasing one, so is trying it on again. Let him! For he cares for me. If he is not a real villain wh. I don't think he is. Sometimes, Ma says he is undecided whether I like him enough and he won't be rebuffed again—and therefore is waiting until I make some sign. At others, she scolds me for permitting those caressing little ways which are such a part of his character.

It was an attention coming home with us, Sunday

night, because we were alone and did not know how to get back. It was impudent to put his arm round me in the cab and his other on my lap. It is always cheeky, his pretence of deafness so as to oblige me to drive my nose into his hair before he can hear my remarks and answers. Today, he did not seem disappointed to hear Mr Dawson [a lecturer] had disappointed us when he arrived punctually at five pm for dinner. I ran in for a pin already in white bodice and zouave and told him there would be no lecture that evening. He soon made himself quite at home and amused himself by ogling me!

At dinner he sat by me and soon began a new dodge. I had my feet on a stool and he calmly put his feet on my dress on the stool for divers motives; because he likes a stool; because he likes to squeeze my feet; because it is useful to impress his arguments by treading on my dress; because anything of this sort makes me ticklish. We spoke about the British Museum. I told him I was quite safe so far as eloping was concerned. For it is very dull drawing there alone.

He admired the drawing-room, thought it looked quite beautiful. I made him admire my arum and moss plant. Kate played, saying I ought to begin. Rennie stood by me and said, 'She won't play to me. I once said she played a wrong note and ever since she won't play a note.' After much pother, when Rennie was engaged talking I did play *La Première Pensée*. Tho' talking, Rennie heard every note and said it was very pretty. I was not nearly so shy now about playing. I got quite bold—played by ear comic songs—Villikins and his Dinah and Lord Lovell. After wh. Rennie departed. I tried no end of keys to let him know my ear was pretty good!

April 15. This morning we heard his beautiful exposition of today's Gospel. I noticed him climbing oddly into the reading pew and thought the steps unfinished. His voice sounded tired. I saw his dear little head poke out of the

Vestry as we went away but we were too far down the aisle even if he did want to follow us. In the evening, a note from him saying his leg had begun to pain him again. He fears his old complaint [hip disease] was returning. He hopes 'it may be staved off but who can tell how soon my short day may be over!' Dear good angel! This speaks volumes. How could he marry while he believes this disease can or will come again? Directly the letter came, Ma cried. I did not. I don't believe it was anything more than yesterday's cold—enough to kill a Goliath. His weakest part is his leg. The fracture in his early riding accident as a child stopped its growth and walking too soon on his leg, together with the straining of his hip through being dragged in his stirrup, brought on the hip disease. But he was entirely cured of this, he says. I am sure if he marries anyone it would be very good for him; it would relieve his dulness, cheer his spirits, without his having to recourse to artificial excitement which wears him out in the end. God knows I would be willing to give my life itself to benefit this dear kind best creature. How sorry I am for his sufferings.

But repeating the old pattern of behaviour, so familiar now, Rennie, the lamed sufferer, vanished once more into thin air. Spring came and went; then Summer. At last, though, on one warm autumnal evening he walked, unannounced, into Cherwell House, never again to leave his Mary Eliza. Some long-fought battle of resistance to her abiding charm was over in his heart. He had decided, once and for all, to make her his wife.

Sept. 6th, 1867. At five or half-past, in came our clerical friend as sweet as ever. Ma took him to task about not coming or writing to us for all these months and I set about his having 'no' collection before the sermon at St James's, such ugly lamps and why was he using such a hideous stick? The stick, he said, was one which Margaret had bought for him in Paris. At tea he revenged himself by abusing my black bows and coral necklace. 'I never saw anything so hideous as black bows; and as for coral, if you can't have real, don't have any!' When I went upstairs to dress for the Dunbars, he entreated Mama to give him the name of our florist as I had told him I was going out to buy a flower. He gave Ma a book of Mr Gibbs' [his organist] hymns and then went with Edith to the florist. He brought back two lovely roses: a crimson one and one pinky-yellow. Seraph! I was in my sprigged muslin, half high, silver and crystal ornaments and no colours but the roses. He abused my velvet cape, my 'pall', put on my croquet hat and looked angelic in it though pert. To the Dunbars in an omnibus; sat by me though he need not. Ma on his other side had lots of room. Talked about my poems and writings. Edith had told him I never paint now only write. Says he knows I have what will make a good writer but must let people see what I do. I yielded and promised to give him some if he could read them. Sweet all the way. After I had made myself killing—all my roses and silver were in vain, I had forgotten my white shoes and had to creek about and dance in my walking Oxfords! Awful! Could not be helped. All through the first dance Rennie and Ma were watching my feet—cruelly—I grinned and bore it like a Briton. He did not pay much attention first part of the evening, only to Ma. Later, he got much sweeter. He took Ma to Refreshments early and asked me if I would go but I don't like being number three so would not; sat with Mrs Dunbar's married sister. Presently, back he comes with a glass of claret for me, thinking I looked pale. I said I did not want it, and so he gave it to my neighbour. Dragged me off to choose for myself. Walked up and down the gallery with Rennie. All wanted him to join the Brazilian dance but he would not. I told him he looked as though he had consulted the oracle of Kophonius.—Very dunny and slow. He took Ma in for refreshments several times and sat with her a great deal . . .

Rennie took me into supper while the Major carried off Ma. Very sweet at Supper—evidently happier—getting even spoony. Then Major Dunbar proposed the ladies. All the gentlemen stood up. Rennie enlarged while he was drinking, half aside, on the mere toast—saying 'Health and happiness' and long life and every blessing to the ladies—and to you especially,' he added very softly looking down at me. Anyone who had heard would have set us down as engaged.

After supper, we had the game of 'Chairs'. I asked Rennie to play and he at once consented, on condition that I would keep with him and teach him; he glued himself on to me and never left my side till after a bit I was out. Then we had 'Hissing and Clapping'. I expected he would choose Mama—anyone but me—but when I went out the chair by him remained empty while I went the round. I knew he had chosen *me*. But I would not go to him and he looked very blue and doleful, never laughing like the rest and all by himself. At last, they told me that he had chosen me so I was obliged to go and sit on the vacant chair beside him with the assumption of the greatest indifference and disdain. He said dismally, 'You didn't come till you were driven to it.' I said; 'I thought you would be the last to choose me.' 'No! the very first,' he replied.

So Miss Joy tried to score off the suitably chastened Mr Haweis for his long neglect of her. But in the end, she succumbed; for when he asked her what time they intended leaving the Dunbars she knew, instinctively, that he would escort them home. Completely happy, she declared herself willing to depart at once, the hour being half-past two am.

Accompanied by Mr Haweis, Mrs Joy and her daughter left St George's Square, walking through the deserted streets to Victoria Station where they picked up a cab to take them to Kilburn Gate.

He sat by Ma, I on the other seat. I did not talk at first

but when I did, he got my hand and would do nothing but claw and maul like a goose. I have been trying hard for more than a year—and especially these last three months, to forget and not care for him, and have partly succeeded. I don't feel the delight at seeing him or hearing from him as once I did. But although my feelings are a little less quick they are as real as ever. He must know his power. It is all very wrong of him. When he dropped a sixpence, he tried to find it on the floor of the cab—but really he was pinching my feet. When I tried to stop him, he clawed and stroked my face until I bounced up in a pet and he asked me sweetly if I had found—his sixpence! As I held my white rose in my hand, he would smell it, diving his face down into my hand till my fist was very nearly down his throat. He has very soft lips.

We got out at Kilburn Gate and walked leisurely home watching the stars. He saw a meteor and showed me the Milky Way. I showed him the Pleiades. By the clock at home it was three-twenty. He first said he would just put down my cloak. Refused anything hot but ultimately had some sherry-and-water. There was no milk. Then we talked till five o/k!!! Then he began to think he could not find a cab or his way to the Ayre Arms. Lastly he yielded voluntarily to sleep here in my bed. Did so! So now we have got everything.

When Ma went up to arrange things in my room, I had him all to myself. As he tasted the noyau [sherry-and-water] we had made, he asked me to sip it to sweeten it for him. He suddenly caught me by the throat and tried to force it between my teeth, crying, 'drink or die.' I would not. He was so awfully spoony and stupid I became suspicious. I don't like him to go so far. For he would put his arms round me or his head on my chest and although I struggled, I could do nothing as he is so strong in the arms. When Ma came back, he pretended to be tipsy— Ma really believed him! Next time she left us he became sober again and clapping his hand on my back and chest as if he would squash me, and made me give him my writings. Said very spoony goodnight at foot of the stairs, —another even more cheeky one at door of room.

September 7th. He came down at ten. He came to me in the drawing-room. He did not seem so very bright and suddenly felt so ill he had to go upstairs. I was sure how it was. Bilious! He was sick and seedy. Went home about twelve with my mss.

September 8th. Today, Sunday, we waited for him after Church (St James's, Marylebone) with the Dunbars and he tore out. Made us go to his rooms—Dunbars would not. I think Mrs Dunbar sees there is 'something' up between Rennie and me; that indefinable something, that fruitless feeling between us, that I fear will be my ruin. I cannot help it. If it is true that he is ungenerous, so selfish, so careless of my feelings or future—but I cannot think so. He is such a dear good kind creature. Showed me my MSS in his desk in his rooms; said there was so much good in them and undeveloped power—but they lacked form. I said I knew nothing about the rules or laws of prose or poetry. 'But you have a very strong instinct,' he said. Seraph! Gave me a volume of poems by Emerson and lent me Ruskin's *Stones of Venice*.

In our omnibus, going home, Rennie scolded me for not letting people see what I do—it's no use doing things and working away in the dark uncorrected, he said. Yes, I am afraid I do love Rennie,—and not with a fit, or a warm sudden impulse, but with a long patient indefatigable love that if it can't be ever realised will take all the colour out of my life. I have tried and hoped—but I know I shall never be able to settle down peacefully and contentedly to any life or any occupation even, away from him. I wish with all the good he has done me, that I had never seen him.

But the die—if she had but known it jolting home to Kilburn—had already been cast by fate for them both. On Wednesday, 2nd October 1867, after three long years of weary waiting, Hugh Reginald Haweis proposed to and was accepted by Mary Eliza Joy in the drawing-room of Cherwell House. How he proposed, she never recorded, but when she went to tell her mother what had happened, such a feeling of relief from the strain of long months of weary waiting, of pretended indifference as she turned a deaf ear to wounding gossip, overcame her so that she could only blurt out: 'He's done it, Ma. Done it at last!'

Mrs Joy was so pleased that to give her dear Mary Eliza a really fine wedding planned to take place early in December, she went out and pawned more of her good silver. Of her wedding day, the most sentimentally remembered by any Victorian bride, Mary Eliza writes nothing in her Thought Book. Its pages remain blank from October 2nd 1867 to April 1st, 1868. From a bill, though, preserved by Mrs Joy, Mr F. Michels, High Class Confectioner of 19 Sloane Street was put in charge of all the wedding breakfast arrangements. Thirty guests were invited at 12/6 per head and a fine large Bride's Cake which cost three guineas. Eighteen Wedding Favours were distributed and in all, expenses amounted to £16 8s. 6d.

Mary Eliza had five bridesmaids, her sister Edith, Margaret Haweis, her dear friend Kate Elliot and Blanche Parnell and Miss Chave, daughter of Doctor Chave, clergyman, who probably took the service at Kilburn Church. John Richard Green, now incumbent of St Peter's, Bethnal Green, was best man.

Mrs Joy contributed a pretty touch to the wedding festivities by making five little white satin bags for the bridesmaids to carry. In one bag she put a gold ring to insure marriage for the lucky chooser; in another, a thimble symbolising a poor man for a husband; in the third, a piece of money for ultimate riches. The two remaining bags contained nothing! Amid peals of laughter, each bridesmaid chose her little bag before setting out to church. Edith Joy got the bag with the thimble and declared she wouldn't marry at all if it was only to be poor! And in the end, this was her fate.

Calmly on the arm of Uncle Eldridge Spratt, Mary Eliza walked up the aisle, demurely veiled, to take her place at the side of her diminutive husband. A little while later, equally calm but radiant, her veil thrown back, she came out of the vestry on the arm of her beloved. They were a well-matched though pocket-sized couple and great must have been Mrs Joy's relief, and pride too, as she watched her daughter go down the aisle with the 'dear little man' of her choice.

3. NUMBER 16 WELBECK STREET

1868-1871

IN THE SAME WAY that a prehistoric girl collected some brand-new animal skins and cooking pots to outshine her rival in the cave next door, or a haughty Georgian beauty relegated her mother-in-law's ornate Stuart furniture to the attic and substituted her own Chippendale or Sheraton pieces on becoming the mistress of her husband's stately home, Mary Eliza set out to make her first home as different as possible from any other.

Number 16 Welbeck Street still survives and is little changed since that momentuous March day when a bubbling and blissful Mrs Haweis, with husband in tow, drew up in a cab before its arched brick doorway.

Mary Eliza was out on to the pavement in a flash. First she gazed up at the windows then through the iron railings so reminiscent of those belonging to her father's house in Pimlico. But this was not Pimlico! This was Marylebone. A far better address. Peering excitedly through the railings while Rennie paid off the cabby, she saw the most delightful little iron staircase winding its way down, spiral-wise, to reach the basement entrance. It attracted her, immediately. How much would she have liked to trip down those steps to explore what lay hidden below. But there were more important things to do. She must meet the new maids and see if their bed had been properly aired. So she was up the front steps pulling at the bell, before her proud husband could catch hold of her and carry her over the threshold in the approved traditional manner as he had threatened to do, that morning.

'How long should a house flannel last?' wrote Mary Eliza to her mother some weeks later. Then she went on to confess that she did not think much of Kate as a cook or of Elizabeth as a maid—

But they are very civil and contented and Elizabeth is improving already I think. I have got a lot of things in from the Civil Service and we are going to belong to another Association, similar, nearer where we can buy our daily bread as well as groceries and I think it will be an immense saving. Rennie has promised me £5 for a silk dress which I am going to have made like the sixteenth-century, after an idea of my own. But I don't think I can really have it as we only have £100 for our half year and it is already gone. I don't know how we are to exist on nothing for six months. Rennie has lost his voice again which is very unfortunate as tonight [Sunday] he has to preach a political sermon for someone in the east, and he wants to be in full fig—otherwise he is very spry. The people are beginning to come back now—we let a whole pew last Sunday and eight sittings today all to 'nobs' which I think is very good for this time of year. We noticed today what a very nice set of people the congregation seem. . . .

Young Mrs Haweis, practical by nature and anxious to avoid getting into debt, a state which she had had some painful experience of when living with poor, dear, extravagant Papa, began what she described as a 'species of housekeeping', purely of her own invention. All through her married life, whether feeling like it or not, she kept a day-to-day account of her personal and household expenses and was never a farthing out. A feat which never failed to impress her husband who was vague and casual about his money affairs to the extreme.

Mary Eliza had hardly settled in when Mrs Morell Mackenzie, a doctor's wife, who was one of H.R.H.'s oldest friends, called and presented her with a Cookery Book with which 'she immediately worried Kate!'

This book contained modest bills of fare for a small family household for every day of the year with others for dinner parties, stating the costs. Mary Eliza found this book so useful that it led her to write her own beautifully produced *The Art of Housekeeping* in 1889.

Once her maids, Kate and Elizabeth, fully understood their duties, M.E.H., as she now began to call herself, turned her attention towards furnishing her home. All through her married life, she was to be, like eighteenth-century Mrs Delany, a great exponent of the 'Do-it-yourself school.' Besides having this strong talent, she always knew what kind of decorative effect she wished to achieve. In the case of Welbeck Street, it was an oriental one. For the recent opening of the Suez Canal had introduced by way of Turkey carpets, opulent draperies and cabinets decorated with sphinxes' heads, a fashion for all things from the East. By good fortune, Gifford Palgrave, whom her husband knew, was leaving England on a honeymoon trip to Trezibond. He was speedily commissioned to buy Mrs Haweis some geniune Turkish rugs and, if possible, an ottoman.

M.E.H. did not favour the use of pale colours in decoration; a fashion largely sponsored by Charles Lock Eastlake whose *Hints on Household Taste*, published in 1867, had become a best seller. A copy of it was a period 'must' for all artistic young marrieds when setting up house. However in the end Mrs Haweis, rather reluctantly, decided to have 'a white drawing-room'. A decision which she soon came to regret when she discovered how 'pale glossy or white papers so much in fashion for drawing-rooms and boudoirs today are ruination to any material or picture hung upon them and to any complexion, too. The same objection applies to white ceilings and still more to pale floors.' (*The Art of Beauty*.)

Still, like others, she had to learn by experience. With her bedroom she was more successful for she had aimed to make it

77

look like a sitting-room so that she could retire to 'Work there'. Mrs Joy was told how 'Rennie likes to sit and write in it much better than in the drawing-room!'

When the afternoons began to draw out and the light improved, she took herself off, a small resolute figure in a painter's overall, to the shabby small conservatory which abutted on to the mews at the back of the house. With a pail beside her, her rags and brushes, she painted the dingy walls 'a flatted pink' and then stencilled a leafy dark-blue pattern all over them. Cleverly she camouflaged hideous lengths of festooning hot-water pipes to look like pillars and adorned them, too, with dark-blue stencilling.

Thoroughly pleased with this operation, she began another. Telling no-one, she got to work outside on her front door, determined to change its colour. To her, Welbeck, Harley and Wimpole Street were 'featureless black ravines' which badly needed brightening, especially as so many of their tall narrow houses once painted delicate cream had by now discoloured and presented a very drab appearance.

As she splashed moss-green paint happily over her front door, relieved by thin lines of elegant black, a fascinated crowd gathered. With some trepidation, they watched her climb up and paint the first floor balcony railings scarlet. What would the pretty young lady decorating the front of her house do next, they wondered. Such a thing had never been seen before in Marylebone!

Delighted to be the centre of so much attention Mary Eliza Haweis recorded later that evening in her Thought Book 'The shock was so great to passers-by that they remained all day long till I finished as if a raree show might emerge at any moment from my door.'

A few days later, another Welbeck Street house turned scarlet with moss-green door while Sir Charles Lyell painted his door sky-blue in Harley Street close by. Mrs Haweis was delighted.

From her home, she turned her attention towards improving

the interior of St James's, a Crown Chapel which had been long neglected. She saw that more pews were taken up to insure her husband a better stipend and insisted that the collection was taken before, and not after, the sermon. For each service, Mr Haweis's 'bands' were freshly laundered and ironed. Lastly, she arranged for a series of pictures illustrating his Sunday sermon to be hung in the vestry and changed, weekly. This proved to be a most popular innovation, people thronging into the vestry after each service to see what pictures had been chosen and by whom engraved or painted. Then only with both her house and Rennie's church put into good order, did she sit down on April 1st, 1868, and open her Thought Book to inscribe this momentous entry:

Wonderful! There is no other name for it. I have not written a line in my Thought Book since 27 September. I was not happy then. Had not been happy for a long time. I am happy now—as happy as any mortal can be. I am glad I have written nothing so long. Tho' I have often wanted to—I think it often well to write, madly, strongly, when one feels strongly which is not always—but I am glad, because one remembers when one writes, and it may be sometimes good to forget.

Since 27 September I have been engaged and married, whereof I had no idea then. It is like a dream—that strange mystical two months of my engagement, the dropping off to sleep, when things are getting double. And then, four months of marriage, the slumber hardly yet thinning towards waking. In the first weeks there was much doubt and distress, disappointment almost discontent. I suppose there is much to forgive when a being bred in a bottle is first married. But it is forgiven now, it was real sorrow, but I will not write it down, because it may lose its sting unwritten, and recorded it might grow painful again. I am so happy now. I am glad there are no bitter thoughts here to record my first married life. My own love, and my own dearest husband's, and Green [John Richard Green, the historian] have helped me. Green may have had himself in mind when he talked, talked, in the first days, but he spoke very kindly and I owe some of my content to him. I have so much to be grateful for that I can never write down.

A being bred in a bottle! So the nineteen-year-old Mary Eliza described herself in regard to her complete ignorance of sex matters before marriage. For what Victorian mother moving in genteel circles had ever imparted the horrid Facts of Life to her daughters?

During the many months she had known her 'dear little Mr Haweis' she had welcomed—greatly enjoyed—the caressing touch of his dear little brown paw on hers. The endearing way he had snuggled up to her in a cab, breathing down her neck, had given her many a strange, exciting thrill. But when it came to the marital bed, to the ultimate act of physical love between a normal man and woman, she was deeply shocked by its crudity. Although she never denied her adored 'Dovey' his rights as her husband, she never got over her first repugnance to physical love-making. Equally was she to dislike bearing children.

The autumn of 1868 flew by in a round of social gaieties. The Bishop of London and Mrs Tait took up the young Haweis couple and they were invited everywhere. Assisted by his pretty, artistic wife, the up and coming young parson began to draw larger and larger congregations to his church. Every week, his name appeared in the Pall Mall Gazette announcing where he would preach, for by now he was recognised as a growing power in the church.

Early in the New Year, M.E.H. was expecting her first baby and went to stay with her in-laws at Colwood where she was made a great fuss of. Soon after her return to Welbeck Street, she wrote and told her mother of a horrid accident—

I was coming down the stairs in my usual light and airy manner when I slipped just at the turn where the banisters cease and alighted on my left eye at the feet of Rennie and the carpenter who happened to be having a solemn meeting in the hall. The latter I have reason to believe nearly lost his sight of one eye through the sudden application of my heel; my own eye being of stronger material simply turned black and the skin literally left my chin out of sympathy, perhaps to see after the Eye! Somehow or other they got me on to a sofa where I instantly went mad. Doctor Mackenzie was sent for and carried me upstairs to bed where I was physicked and remained four days. On the fifth day, I was allowed to get up but have not been out since except once to Church on Sunday. My bones have not been right since and I am not able to walk much. My bruises etc., and black eye are gone and the stiffness wearing off—I told Rennie not to let you know as you might have been dreadfully frightened and come bolting over. Rennie wrote to Colwood and they were all very frightened. The news is even now spreading and kind enquiries are pouring in. I go out of an evening but not in the day. We have dined with the Tollemaches as Mrs Tollemache wrote a very gratifying but lugubrious letter to me to thank Rennie for a sermon he preached. I wrote back one of my angel wife ones; you have never seen me do the angel wife. It is very striking and quite natural and suits Cabinet Ministers to a T. The Tollemaches are my prey; they idolise us like the Cowper Temples. I think I told you Mr T is Mrs C's brother . . .

You should hear Rennie talk about his anxieties and troubles! It would do you good. He is very blue about his congregation, though every sort of nob swarms and fills the empty pews which are at the back of the gallery, all the rest being let. The Archbishop of Canterbury and the Dean of Westminster are going to preach in the Spring which is a specimen of his ill-luck—especially as he did not have to press them one scrap and they don't go everywhere I can tell you! The Marquis of Salisbury says it is a pleasure to go to our church simply for the music—and the M.P.s and Q.C.s say Rennie is the only preacher fit for a man to listen to—men of Science like Sir Charles Lyell, Vice-Chancellors and Judges, of whatever creed, come and hear him, those who are not Unitarians or anything take pews regularly, and send him cheques directly he preaches for any object. It is very depressing, but I am afraid there is nothing to be done but grin and bear our griefs.

Slyly poking fun at her husband's little idiocyncrasies, M.E.H. was as light-hearted about his self-confessed depression and silly fears as she had been about her accident, not two months before the expected birth of her child.

One afternoon, she found a white hair in Rennie's black whisker and told him it was a godsend. Now he really could complain of increasing age and forgetfulness. For there was one thing she was very much troubled about and that was his appalling vagueness. She wrote to her mother saying it was getting past a joke.

He is always smashing things wholesale and forgetting saints' days, which are worth £30 a year to him; going to oratorios weeks before the right day; and sending wrong letters to the wrong people who return them to him with witty replies.

It is obvious that Rennie, relying more and more on his extremely methodical and capable wife, was cleverly manoeuvring her towards taking over his correspondence so that he could devote more time to free-lance journalism and lecturing. A selfish move on his part, but justified if he could augment his income thus.

In one letter to Mrs Joy, her daughter dwelt on her husband's extraordinary ways of book-keeping which often drove her to think that she must be married to a madman.

If I see an entry for one week £16 2 11 (which he will weep over as such a dreadful expense for one week with nothing to show) you may be pretty sure without adding up the total that the right total is £2 16 11, which is not

quite the same thing. I always remember that in his book,
1 penny for cabs, and 3 guineas worth of stamps for 3
letters are not to be relied on as correct entries, I enclose a
phot we have done recently which is, however, so awful as
to be valueless as a portrait of the popular West-end
preacher and his Angel Wife. Rennie looks like a ruffian
and I like a Sneak. But never mind—they looked worse
before I painted them.

To pass the tedious hours while carrying her child, she had
taken up her drawing and painting again. She had also borrowed a sewing machine and made curtains, at last, for her
bedroom. They were of chintz; sprigs of white may with dead-
brown leaves on a green ground. An enchanting pattern.

Mary Paynter (her husband's eldest sister) came to stay for
the last four weeks of her time to look after her and the house.
There were fears of a difficult confinement owing to her recent
accident. Four days before the birth of her child, Mary Eliza
Haweis understandably frightened of the coming ordeal, took
out her Thought Book as she rested, alone, in her room:

March 15th, 1869. It is curious to re-open this book after
leaving it untouched for nearly a year and read what my
feelings were then in general. It has been an important
year too. I have been married one year and four months
and now things will change—as there is no possibility for
a change for the better, it might be a change for the worst
with this new life coming to join ours. Only the Maker of
the Future can tell. Perhaps, I may like It when It comes
and our happiness increases. Today, I cannot pray either
for myself or for It. I don't want It. Tho' alive today,
there is fear in my heart that every time I see my dearest
it may be for the last time—and my life is so happy! Still
I do not fear death as I did a twelvemonth ago.

But all her fears even to the one of not really caring for her
baby came to nothing. On the night before she was 'took' as
she described it later, she went out to dinner, gay and laughing, and Mary Paynter consoled her by saying how when she

was dressed up, 'No one could possibly guess you are having a baby!' which was just what Mary Eliza Haweis wanted to hear.

On the morning of 19th March, Mrs Hugh Reginald Haweis gave birth to a son immediately nicknamed the 'Stickleback' by his proud, delighted father. Early next day, with the morning sun shining through the windows of her room in Welbeck Street, Mary Eliza Haweis sat up in bed and wrote to her mother.

Saturday morning
March 20*th*

My dear Mater,

I consider you a nice species of mother for not writing so long and you don't deserve me to take the trouble to you when the Stickleback is just a day old—but I am of a disposition that amiable that I am doing it as you see. I meant to have written when I was 'took' but it was over by twelve o'clock and so there was no time. I had chloroform the last hour and could have written perfectly in the afternoon, only the paper was not given me. I am wonderfully well. The Stickleback is not very small, with a very large nose, and very small eyes—it has an unfavourable likeness of me, and has black hair an inch long and dark whiskers. Its hands are a very good shape otherwise it is so hideous I can't bear to look at it. It roars so that it can be heard across the street. The cradle basket and my sitting up jacket which Mrs Mackenzie gave me are Pink —a colour quite spoilt in effect by the Stickleback's complexion. Rennie complains that it bubbles like a snail. It has the voice of a cat—as you hear them even in friendly conversation on the house-tops at night. Its name is to be Reginald Joy. If it had been a girl it would have been put in the waterbutt at once; and if it refused to depart this life would have been Cecilia.

Dr Mackenzie attended me—Mary Paynter has been

staying here a month and is a real seraph. She sends you her love. Mrs Palgrave has sent me a shawl. Only one or two people knew of the coming event as it threw no shadow before! We told nobody except when obliged—and up to yesterday the rest never suspected it. So I think that rather good. I expect Colwood [the Haweis home] will come up with a rush when they hear about me. You see this is the first Haweis. You can also appreciate the extreme frightful nature of my fall two months ago. But there was always something cat-like in my nature which accounts for my nine lives. Rennie has just left off calling the thing 'Stickleback' and speaks of it now as the Vegetable.

Your Affectionate Daughter,
M.E.H.

At the same time that Mary Eliza Haweis deeply shocked her sentimental and conventional-minded sister-in-law by declaring in pure fun that she might have her baby killed on account of its ugliness, Mary Paynter drew the picture of a normal and proud young mother in her letter to Mrs Joy, whom she thought quite rightly, would like to hear from her as well as from her too jocular daughter.

May's recovery seems a miracle. She has had a beautiful night, suffers no pain, can turn about easily in bed, is in high spirits and threatens to go to church tomorrow and all other sorts of nonsense! She is very happy with her baby. Baby is a fine little fellow, tall but thin with a good deal of hair and perfectly healthy. May is going to begin to try and nurse him when he wakes up. She kept up well to the end, walking out nearly every day. Indeed, she has not even the average amount of pain and inconvenience.

With kind regards,
Believe me dear Mrs Joy,
Yours truly,

M. Paynter

A month after the arrival of little Reginald Joy Haweis, his mother opened her Thought Book.

April 21*st.* I am still alive and nothing is changed. There is much to thank God for; in fact, there is not one of the least of His Mercies that I am either worthy of or properly thankful for. I am not sure whether I even try to be.

What can I teach my child—Rennie's child. I am not a Christian in so much as to believe that in Christ's divinity is Christianity. It is no use saying I believe in what I don't. As for the Virgin! But there is one thing I can teach my 'Stickleback' and that is to love its father.

But there was to be no time for that lesson. On May 16th, little Reginald Joy Haweis appeared to be ailing and it was decided that his aunt, Mary Paynter with her great experience of babies should take him out of London to Colwood where he would have plenty of fresh air, sun and quiet. He was carried down the steep stairs of Welbeck Street and out through the front door to a waiting cab by his mother. She had never done this before—had not been allowed to—but her child was fretting and she insisted on carrying him, herself. That same evening she shut herself into her room and analysed her feelings, so mixed to her still, in secret.

May 16*th.* What a curious thing is mother-love. Some mothers seem to love their children, even little stupids of a month old, as they should (but don't sometimes) love their husbands whom they have chosen out of their heart's impulse, chosen before God, and promised to obey and cherish. I cannot see what there is to love in a little lobster devoid of sympathy—of character—of features even. I do not call new-born babes, children. There is much which is loveable about children; they are interesting; they have soft hands and birdie voices. I have sent my Stickleback to Colwood for a fortnight. I like him much better than I did; he turns his eyes now and sometimes tries to coo. When he is good, he is pretty. When Mary

took him over, squalling, into the cab, I was a little bit
sorry to think I should not see him tomorrow. But to
say he was a grievous loss is simply untrue. Even—I
believe it—if the poor little squealer died, I do not think
I should grieve much after a day or two. But if my husband died, I should pine. God keep me from such bitter
sorrow and the horror of remembering.

And then, alone in her room, she shed tears for her poor
little Stickleback who had cried so and got on her nerves;
tears which no one saw nor believed she could have shed.
For tears were to be her own private concern and only once
in her life did Mary Eliza Haweis cry in public.

Some weeks later, at the beginning of June, little Reginald
Joy Haweis died and no one knew why exactly.

On returning home from the funeral (he had been buried at
Slaugham where there is a memorial window to him in the
Parish church) his mother made the following entry in her
Thought Book:

June 6th. The first shadow in our happy married life has
closed in. Our child, our little peacemaker, our Stickleback,
is dead. I was not with him. I had let him go to Colwood.
How little did I know when I carried him downstairs that
he would be gone so soon. I thought it was for the best.
Everyone said I knew too little about babies and I should
do him harm, yet in the week I had him without a nurse
I had grown to love my Stickleback so much; and I did
feel very sorry to let him go. When he was gone, I cried
in case I should never see him any more. It must have
been a presentiment. He was well when he went and
Mary is so kind and experienced and she said she would
give him back to me so much fatter and bigger. So I let
him go. He was growing so pretty, with large dark eyes
and beautiful hands, and we thought he had a clever face
and that he would grow to be like my Darling. But the
next time I saw his little face, it was so old and worn with
suffering. Such a little sad old face as if he had tired of

living. He suffered so. But what he died of no one seems to know.

So our first, our boy that we prayed for, is taken from us. Now, I am sorry to think I was ever impatient when he hurt me and dreaded to hear him when he came in. But it was him—I should have enjoyed him more and learnt how to handle him if I had not been worried by the nurse and everything made so unpleasant for me. I am not so sorry he went for if he had died with me here, I should never have ceased blaming myself and thought I had left undone things in my inexperience. I know nothing was omitted at Colwood.

It seems a hard trial but G O D might have sent a heavier sorrow. If He will spare me my husband all other afflictions will be light. I pray that day and night. I pray to die first.

Summer came and St James's was full every Sunday of notable people who came week after week to hear the dynamic young clergyman with the club foot preach less like a humourless divine using pompous language than a Shakespearean actor with flashing eyes and clarion voice. The result was sensational.

The newly-installed Archbishop of Canterbury, Archibald Campbell Tait, who had always considered Hugh Reginald Haweis to be his protégé suggested that he should preach at St James's one Sunday and afterwards lunch with his wife at Welbeck Street. Mary Eliza's first thought was to let her mother know of this coming event and to ask her help.

July 17th, 1869

My dear Ma,

We are coming to you for pickings this week. We want your china bowl for claret cup—the tazza-spoons and forks innumerable—all the rarities you possess we shall take home in a cab this week. And why? We are going to have the Archbishop and Mrs Tait to lunch—likewise the

Cowpers—on Sunday!!!!!!!! Green is amazed at his coming! He ranks before the Duke of Cambridge and is next to the Queen! Mrs Tait wrote to us the day before yesterday, enclosing three invitations—one was last night and we went after the Townsends' dinner—to 'meet the Members of Convocation!' The great rooms were full of bishops. The Archbishop was very sweet. Greeny took us about. I had on my white grenadine trimmed with lavender and Mrs Mackenzie lent me a gold chain and I looked elegant. We had a brougham and Rennie had new trousers with *straps* and we both were most distinguished in appearance. The dresses were splendid. I had white Stephanotis in my hair and carried white roses and ferns. There were lots of people we knew there. It is a most wonderful thing the Archbishop coming to lunch and the William Cowpers. We want some splendid things about. So look out! And fork out everything beautiful and you shall have 'em back on Monday. We are going to have flowers from Colwood.

Yours affectionately,

M.E.H.

In August, the Haweises set out for their holiday which was to be spent sight-seeing in Belgium and Germany. It was the first time that Mary Eliza Haweis had been abroad and she never stopped filling her notebooks or any scrap of paper to hand with endless little drawings of things that struck her eye from an old carved doorway glimpsed down a lime-shaded alley to the lightning sketch of a Flemish girl wearing a small silver dagger in her hair. When not escorting his indefatigable wife into every nook and cranny of the picturesque towns they visited, Rennie was climbing like a monkey up the steep steps of every church tower en route. An ardent campanologist, he loved to explore belfries, those strange and secret caverns, bat-hung, in which from time immemorial bells have hung. Scrambling over their great bronze domes or seated astride their dusty clappers, while he peered about to discover the name of their maker, he would ring a sudden, mad peal out of sheer devilment much to the astonishment of anyone who heard it. Among his vast output of writings, his articles on *Bells* rank high for their intensity of deep-felt, poetic language.

On reaching Cologne, M.E.H. made a study of the different kinds of head-gear worn by the women attending service in the Cathedral in her sketch-book. There was an infinite variety of them, from stiff white lace coifs to gorgeous coloured kerchiefs. Later her drawings appeared in her book *The Art of Beauty*.

But it was the ancient town of Mechlin with which she fell in love. The old eighteenth-century houses, richly decorated in plaster-work, and all dated, with their steep tiled roofs, rising one behind the other like a flight of steps, and built for the most part beside a canal, bordered by weeping willows, fascinated her. They stopped at one old hostelry. A romantic building whose outside walls were painted with a frieze of golden halberds. Inside, the deserted rooms were silent; their furniture very old, and dark, carved oak. Lines of Gothic-lettered scripture decorated the china tiles. This inn of ancient times was called *La Grande Cigogne*. But the resident stork—if stork there ever had been—had long since flown away.

'I never saw a house I should like more to possess and live in than *La Grande Cigogne*,' wrote M.E.H. enthusiastically in her Thought Book.

They arrived for the Kermess at Antwerp which, with its crowded streets, hustle and noise, was a great contrast to the haunted stillness and melancholy atmosphere of Mechlin. Mary Eliza Haweis spent hours in the art galleries, entranced by the works of the famous old masters known to her only by name or through reproductions till now. Eventually, her absurdly tiny feet gave out under the strain of all the sight-seeing miles they had first tripped so lightly and then tottered, swollen and painful, at much the same time fortunately that they came to the end of their money.

On their return to Welbeck Street, utterly exhausted by all they had seen and done, splendid news was awaiting them.

October 8th. Such fun! Rennie is to be Editor of Cassells Magazine!!! My old Dovey an editor! I daresay I shall illustrate some numbers. I do hope this increase in brain-work will not be worse for my Dovey. He is very well now. If he does not overtire himself, all will be jolly.

We go out investing small sums in things together. For all our poverty (the poor little stickleback ran away with a good deal of money, this summer, which has left us in debt) we do have the occasional odd shilling and sixpence to devote to extravagance. Today we went to Baker Street Bazaar and invested 3/- in some odd bits of Chinese porcelain. One saucer we smashed just as it was tied up for us. So the man gave me another for it besides the bits broken no good to him! I have mended them all the same and it is just as good as ever. Now I call that enjoyment! Rennie bought me a fan for one shilling. And a little white china dog with loose head. I wonder, when we are richer, as no doubt we shall be some day—shall we be as happy as we are now with no banker and very uncertain ready cash? However rich, I should not care to change our way of life. I should like to give Mama a £100 a year for she is the best creature in the world and a very good woman though she writes me, sometimes, unkind and disagreeable letters! What a bother letters are—always misunderstandings particularly when writing to relations!

My old man should have a brougham in which to go into town and we would have geniuses to stay with us—but not too often! I don't like having people to stay, much. While my Dear is with me I shall never cease to be happy. Yes, I *do* live to be happy and I don't care what people say. I hope I may not live to be old and I pray that I may not survive my Dovey.

A prayer which was ultimately answered.

In spite of all that practical Mrs Haweis could do, budgeting so carefully for they did much entertaining, money remained in short supply. Although Hugh Reginald Haweis proved to be a successful editor of 'Cassell's', he did not consider the pay, £200 a year, sufficient for the work he did, and demanded £400. A compromise was reached by his acceptance of £300.

All was well at St James's with packed congregations and nine new coloured glass windows installed, besides money collected for a big east window. On his wife's advice, knowing by now her unerring good taste, Hugh Reginald Haweis had his pews cut low and ordered a splendid new altar-cloth and kneeling cushions. M.E.H. made herself responsible for arranging the altar flowers, while everyone who attended the services regularly declared the music to be of the highest standard at St James's. In the midst of such successful reforms and with not a single voice raised in dissent, Rennie suddenly announced he wished to throw up the Church and devote himself solely to writing and lecturing. To his surprise, he found his wife disapproving strongly of such a step. As she recorded in her Thought Book:

Dovey cannot possibly judge as I can of the great good he is doing all those who come to hear him preach. The letters, the grateful thanks, the assurances that he is always receiving should make him jump for joy. They make me! We have saved up £170 in the Bank and I have made nearly £50 with my blocks.

She was working very hard now at book illustration and hoped to enter into the magazine world with some small articles and poems. There could not have been a better time for her to start a literary career as a decade of educational revolution and school reform had begun with the passing of the first Elementary Education Bill in 1870. Girton College 'for the higher education of women' (and Mary Eliza Haweis was to become an ardent feminist and pioneer in the Suffrage Movement) had been authorised in 1869 though not actually opened till July, 1873. Through the ever-broadening channels for years ahead of mass-education a vast new reading public was coming into being while the introduction of mechanical methods of type-setting made printing cheaper. Pictorial reproduction was also on the 'up-and-up' and steel engraving reached a standard of quality by the 1870s unsurpassed today.

M.E.H. concentrated hard on perfecting her own talent for book-production and illustration by studying different kinds of typography and illumination. The past two decades—the eighteen-fifties and sixties—had witnessed the publication of many splendid books dedicated to the art of illustration and design. One of these, *The Art of Illumination and Missal Painting: A Guide to Modern Illumination* by Noel Humphries she found most useful, vindicating those long hours she had spent in the British Museum as a girl, studying ancient manuscripts.

On the chief qualities of a good illuminator, Humphries wrote 'Most important of all must he thoroughly understand the laws of colours and their symbolism, and, above all, he must possess a thorough knowledge of decorative art through the ages.' Agreeing heartily to this and full of boundless energy, M.E.H. proceeded to follow Humphries' advice. It was not difficult, for at heart she was an ardent medievalist and her artistic roots, like those of Morris, were nourished by her enduring love for the beautiful stained glass, the precious metal work, the tapestries and dress fashions of the Middle Ages.

Very soon, her research on the little studied 'Aesthetics and Pedigree' as she called it of women's clothes through the ages bore fruit in a series of articles which began to appear regularly in *The Art Magazine, The Queen, The Contemporary Review* and *St Paul's Magazine*. A regular contributor to many leading journals, her husband was well placed to help his wife submit her work to the right editor and to give her his expert advice on all literary matters. A task he much enjoyed carrying out as it pleased his masculine vanity.

By the time spring had changed into summer, the summer of 1870, Mrs Haweis was 'expecting' again. But this time she was determined, whatever the outcome, not to have her sister-in-law, Mary Paynter, taking charge of her house and confinement. So she laid secret plans to have her baby as far removed as possible from London. She engaged, too, the services of a woman doctor, Miss Garrett, M.D., later to be famed as Doctor Garrett Anderson, to look after her. In taking this unusual step, she put herself, firmly, on the side of those women battling already for the right to enter what profession they liked.

On 9th June, the whole of England was shocked by the premature death from a stroke of their idolised writer, Charles Dickens, aged only fifty-eight, at his home, Gad's Hill Place in Kent. The steel engraving by the young Luke Fildes called 'The Empty Chair' showing the great author's study with ink-well, pen and manuscript of his last and unfinished novel, *Edwin Drood*, on the plain wooden table before which a chair was drawn up was destined to become a best-seller among pictures for the Victorian home.

In the meantime, M.E.H. worked hard at her own blocks and completed a set of illustrations for 'Summer Idylls', one of her husband's books soon to be published.

On 30th June, before her departure from London, she made a short entry in her Thought Book:

The change is coming again and I have tried to be patient during these long months of waiting with constant reminders that I am not getting my happiness *gratia*. What do I want? *I only know I don't want children.* But if my Gub wants them I can but give him them. Perhaps, I may want them sometime. I should like to be stronger and more active and more 'cute' and more everything! My old Dear has not been well. Overwork and the weather, I think. We are going away soon for a month or two and I hope he will get better. I wish I was stronger: it bores him to crawl about with me who can't walk, can't climb, can't do anything without rheumatics or bad feet or back-aches or headaches or something or other.

I do hope we shall manage better with the next. I trust it will live and if so it will be strong, so that my Darling may not have the anxiety of seeing his own delicacy repeated in his child. I do hope it will be like him. I *can't* like what is like me. How can I want myself repeated?

The strangers' collections now average £6 a Sunday instead of £3, so we are really getting quite rich and this year brought the Chapel salary up to £450 (which is the utmost he will get). What talents my Gub has! I suppose he will get a canonry or something some day.

On 24th August, at the Swan Hotel, Lichfield, with Miss Garrett in charge, Mary Eliza Haweis's second son was born as fair a child as the poor little 'stickleback' had been dark. The day after, completely recovered and in good spirits, she wrote as usual to her mother:

> Swan Hotel,
> Lichfield
> *August 25th*

My dear Ma,

I suppose Rennie has told you all the necessary generalities. The Ugly Duck is what I expected, hideous and scarlet as the Puddles would prefer. Bab II and I are all right. He is a very well formed Bab and will soon get fat. We have just got a nice wet nurse for him and he takes to his food kindly. Miss Garrett M.D. was my doctor. I sent for her and the nurse and Mary and they all got down in time except Mary, so I did not get enough chloroform. I was only ill twelve hours. Everybody was very kind and attentive, indeed—the landlady lent me everything I could want, baby's clothes and nightgowns for me, etc.—two other ladies in the town offered nurses and cooking and clothes.

The hotel is a nice quiet country inn, a big rambling

house. I have nice airy rooms, large and well furnished. I think I shall write to the Joys soon [her aunts]. We have decided on no godfathers yet but I shall renew the dodge of naming the Bab. Green has written a melting letter of joy and congratulations. On everybody the event has come like a thunderbolt which is as it should be. Not even a doctor knew it a month ago. My present nurse, got by Miss Garrett, is an extremely nice person quite different from the last. I see hardly anything of her. Rennie stops with me at night just as usual; in fact, we ignore the whole thing and go on just as usual. One thing is I can keep quieter here than I could at home. Besides, being 'took' here allows Rennie to go to the Birmingham Festival which he couldn't have done from London. We have enjoyed our holiday very much. Rennie is writing a musical article and I have drawn a good deal. Everything is more satisfactory than last time and the country air is good for us all. So you see on the whole we are extremely lucky. Watch the papers to see when the announcements come out—*The Times*, *Pall Mall* and *Echo*—perhaps they are out now. I want to see them. You don't say whether you are glad it's a boy. The Haweises are in the most excited state about it and have enquired for the exact features and fingers to be described. He has loads of hair. I fear he has the Spratt hands but they may change. His ears are very ugly. But his forehead and chin promise to be very good. We are consulting whether to ask for one sponsor Sir Loll Doll (Reverend Sir Lionel Darrell, which they did) as the servants pronounce it, he adores us so. Sometimes, he is called Sir Lummie Dummie. Rennie is very well. He did not leave me all yesterday and had a dreadful day of it.

Your affectionate daughter,

M.E.H.

Unlike the majority of Victorian mothers, M.E.H's attitude

to having a baby was detached and completely shorn of all maternal sentiment. An attitude far more in keeping with the one held by mothers of today. Young Mrs Haweis always wished her pregnancies to remain unnoticed and so they were. Both Edith Joy and her two sisters-in-law found it hard to understand how strongly her aesthetic sense was revolted by human ugliness at birth. When it came to the plain facts of child-bearing, Mary Eliza Haweis simply could not don the rose-coloured spectacles so eagerly worn by many mothers of her generation.

In a subsequent letter to her mother she thinks it better for her *not* to come to Lichfield on account of the long, tiring journey and unnecessary cost. Their own expenses were totting up daily as The Swan Hotel was not so cheap as they had first thought.

Miss Garrett's charges are rather a blow—£21 for the day. She is a charming person and eminent even among first-rate medical men but her fees are higher than we had thought. So it is a very good job I can draw as I shall have to now!

The Bab is improving, the wet nurse seems to suit him and it is a much better arrangement than attempting it myself which would be a cat-like nuisance and keep me seedy besides. I don't think there is any more to say. Rennie sends his love and says he is as well as can be expected!

Your affectionate Daughter,

M.E.H.

Once back in London, the usual round of dinner parties and Church services, coupled with literary work, began again for M.E.H. Her baby son, Lionel, throve and gave her immense delight by his vigour and beauty. He had engaging, affectionate ways and 'a thatch of yellow-wool' which grew into lovely Lord Fauntleroy-like curls that were the admiration of all who saw them. His mother gives a full report of him in her Thought Book.

December 3rd. The Change has come and past and thank God all is well with him and me and It. It is a wonderfully strong boy, never ill, always goodish, pretty forward and has already begun to feel his feet, although not quite four months. I wish he was more like Rennie. But he isn't in the least, being fair with blue eyes. The first Bab was darker and had better hands, ears and eyes. My dear Love is well and I think as happy as he can be. I am still weakly but if I can but keep free from a third [she was to have two more children] I shall get strong. I dread having children with an almost morbid aversion although this is a dear little thing.

I have just read Huxley's paper in the Contemporary Review on School-boards and Education. I do not understand how an Atheist, as they call Huxley, could write that paper. It seems to me just what a good, religious-minded man who is an advanced Liberal would write. What is an Atheist? Rennie says, one who believes in a First Cause but not in a Creator having any sympathy with us individually or *en masse*. A Maker who has made certain laws—possibly *One Law* and willed that it should work out its own variations and carry its own unchangeable results along with it: not a Father, loving his children; an artist enjoying his work and sending it on its way for certain ends; not a Friend who feels with us and means to help us. My belief is, that he is a little farther off than we might guess or suppose.

From this point, in an introspective mood, knowing that she is not really an orthodox churchwoman though she attends service at St James's every Sunday and does all in her power to further her husband's career, she covers pages of her Thought Book analysing to herself what she really believes in —is it a kind of pantheism? That there is a God she admits, but He is a distant though kindly Deity, existing behind 'unending veils', though His Remoteness does not imply that,—

He to whom distance and time are nothing, cannot bridge these spaces by some splendid sympathy and even some communion? It seems to me that the more science unfolds to us of his Endlessness, the surer I feel how much more He can, and does, do. Why should there not be in Him an Intelligence, a Sympathy, and a Communication as vast, as wide, as minute as the systems and lives He has created? This is what I think my own belief to be.

It is a very interesting, perplexing and important question to me, too, the connection which exists between men and the animal world. It is a far closer tie than what most people think. There is the sympathy of some people for certain kinds of beasts, birds and even reptiles which argue to me that we, ourselves, have passed through all— or some of—the forms around us of those animals we consider 'lower things' made only for us to eat or enslave. We are distinguished from 'lower things' as Herbert Spencer puts it by feelings only more powerful and varied than theirs. I suppose many have had, as I have, sensations of a deeper sympathy with them than admiration or compassion.

In looking up into a tree in full leaf, I have often felt a queer sensation for a moment—something between memory, a longing and a wild delight—which is not caused only by admiration of the greenness, the coolness, the exquisite crossings of its boughs. It is a pure animal sensation which shoots and is gone in the very first contraction of a muscle. Again, I know, my feelings of sudden objectless elation, my unreasoning antipathies for this or that thing are less those of a human than of some other creature. A sudden wild sympathy with certain plants or colours which are never enduring but experienced in a flash, a fleeting moment, have no connection in so far as I can see with my real, enduring tastes, preferences, habits or reasonings. What is there to prove that all forms of animal and vegetable life around us have nothing to do with us and only exist to feed or work for us? Flowers may legitimately give us great pleasure by their scent and colour and shape; herbs may cure our ills. But is that all to them? Why have I felt sometimes in looking at a buttercup field in flower, a longing to enjoy them in some closer way than through merely sight and smell? I pick them—those blazing little flowers with varnished petals— but I inevitably regret breaking off a single one from its stem. It does not give me what I want. For I cannot replace it wilting already in my destructive hand. Would eating do it? I should often like to eat up quantities of flowers and grasses but this sensation is so quickly followed by the knowledge I can't that it is gone before I am really fully aware it was there! Is this the feeling known to a grazing beast to whom flowers and grasses mean an intenser but lower and simpler delight than to us who can only stand and stare? If I believe I have been a grazing animal, then why not another form of life? Bloodthirsty people may have gone through the forms of ichneumon, shark, tiger, lion, hawk, crocodile? Therefore why not at some time a Sound or Colour and developing from that existence to being a Plant or Flower till finally a bird, beast, child and man? There may be still myriads of other forms for us to take in which there will be, as now, periods of forgetfulness till in some final stage we remember all and know we are One with every other being in every other world and One with Some God Above All? It makes me happy to believe this. But Rennie does not like the idea at all.

Almost immediately after this entry, the Haweises called on Mr Emmanuel Oscar Deutsch, the Semitic scholar who had lodgings near them at 47a, Welbeck Street. Well known as the translator of the *Talmud* and a British Museum official, he was a popular figure in literary and artistic circles

on account of his wit and brilliant conversation. But report
had it that he was a sick man and withdrawing himself more
and more from social gatherings. Though never attracted to
Jews, on hearing of Deutsch's ill health Mary Eliza Haweis
called on him with her husband. Both were so shocked by
his haggard looks that they invited him to stay and recuperate
at their house for a while.

May 29*th*, 1871. The time has passed rapidly these last
five months and somehow left their mark on me. On
13th January, Mr Deutsch came to stay with us for a
week or so as he was so ill and lonely and uncomfortable
in his lodgings. Today he is still with us. And no better
either. He is a queer creature, better than the average
man—I used to dislike him once and think him plebeian
and ugly and a bore—but now I am very fond of him and
respect him very much. If he died, I should go into
mourning for him as for a brother which would scandalize
some friends!

The Bab is now nine months, very strong, fair and with
a pretty delicate face. I like the dear child immensely but
hope I shall not have another. The game is not worth the
candle—not to me! Greeny has just come back from Italy
and is delighted with his god-child. So is Deutsch. It is
touching to see the real and passionate interest in babies
some bachelors feel. Ours is a nice little good-tempered
child with long feet and hands. It is great fun to see him
crawling about a room. It is a great comfort to have him
so strong and well. He is very popular at Colwood and
they have given him some new clothes and a big bath.
Everything is prospering wonderfully. Rennie's church
is now crammed with two rows of camp stools along the
aisle. His sermons are growing more and more perfect
and make a great impression. One sermon he had printed
and sold it for 6d. 270 copies went off in one Sunday. My
Boffin is a clever old thing. His book on music [*Music
and Morals*] is coming out in the autumn and will pro-

bably be a great success because it is so readable. How jolly it is for everything to be succeeding so well. I pray it may continue and that my dear one may live and be happy with his Dovey for all her life.

The summer passed with M.E.H. busy designing the cover and binding for her husband's book. It was bound in navy-blue cloth with a musical theme and Beethoven's autograph in gilt on the outside cover. A best-seller, it went through many editions. She also illustrated a poem of Victor Hugo's, translated by Swinburne, for Cassell's Magazine. The great master was so pleased that he sent his signed photograph to her enclosed with a card:— 'Hommage à Mrs Haweis'. She was delighted! Several of her book covers were exhibited with others at the South Kensington Museum [later the Victoria and Albert].

At home, Deutsch, who was still with them, was no better. In fact, he was a dying man, stricken by cancer.

July 9th. There is nothing so terrible or so heart-rending as the sight of a man in the midst of his life and work being gradually pushed into his grave as poor Dyke is being pushed. He *was* getting better. If he could have thrown up the British Museum he would probably have continued improving but the eternal bothers and anxieties keep him down. How he is to work when he returns there next week, goodness only knows! It is strange to me how relative everything is to the mind which observes it and how things strike different people. Rennie said to me about Deutsch:— 'How he proves to me the necessity of religion under trial. If Deutsch had had some religion which could comfort him in his pain how different would he bear it; he is always railing and complaining. He has no God to pray to; no inward comfort or communion.' I replied: 'How strange! It has struck me how in real trouble and in view of an early death how *needless* religion is. There have been days when he believed Death was near and there has been no 'need' for spiritual consolation so far as I saw; no fear, no regret and no agitation either. It has seemed to me how wonderful, how *little* he has complained under exceptional trials; how calm and brave he has been throughout. It has gone far to convince me that his creed is wiser and higher than ours. No creed but belief in oneself, no vain prayers beyond what is our conception; no recanting at the last to what his whole life and learning has taught him to eschew. In this way, he seems to me a very religious man.'

By this time, Deutsch's gratitude to the Haweises for having rescued him from the discomfort and loneliness of his lodgings had deepened, in the case of his pretty, lively and kind hostess, to love. A love which her woman's instinct soon divined but never thought of reciprocating. Like Deutsch, M.E.H. enjoyed the thrust and parry of intellectual conversation and her daily presence at his bedside stimulated and kept alive the mind of the sick man. Now that she had got over her first aversion a mutual sympathy, derived from the exchange of their most intimate views, had brought them very close to one another, mentally. In her Thought Book, she recorded how Deutsch's face always lit up on seeing her.

It grows ten years younger when I come only into the room. It seems an honour to me to be loved, the gift is so immense and I am not worth it. I am fond of him and I would do anything to save and comfort him. I could even weep. For it might have been my Boff!—I am glad he has no wife and child to add to his anxieties. He would be a loss to my life now—because he loves me very much. He is very kind, too, and patient with me. Now I pray that my Gaffin may never be ill like that. I should die.

There was one person, though, who strongly resented the presence of Emmanuel Deutsch at Number 16, Welbeck Street and that person was John Richard Green. Up till now, he had had the free run of the Haweis home, constantly staying in it. He was not a little in love, too, with its charming mistress. But as an old pampered friend, he felt that he had been superseded and could not help showing his resentment at this new menage à trois.

July 22nd. I find Greeny so quiet, so vague and not at all the life of the house as he used to be. Altogether another and older man. Perhaps, he is jealous of Deutsch who is fixed here and has made him a Number 2! He has complained to Rennie of his being reserved and mysterious with him. All because Deutsch has been so anxious to keep his illness a secret and Green, as we know, is such a feminine chatterbox.

Soon after this entry, the Haweises left London for Venice where they were to take their holiday and where Mary Eliza's note-books and odd scraps of paper became filled—as always— with every kind of sketch relating to the clothes, furniture, armour, etc., she saw, and studied, in the pictures of the old Venetian masters on view in the museums and art galleries. Always at her side, advising and selecting with her what was essential material, what not, for her literary work, was her darling Dovey, Gaffin or Gubbles, according to whatever fond, ridiculous name she was calling him at the moment.

4. SOCIETY'S MOST POPULAR PREACHER

1871-1876

SOON AFTER HER RETURN to London with her mind
stimulated by all that she had seen and studied in Venetian
art galleries and churches, M.E.H. drew out her Thought
Book from the drawer in which it was kept and made the
following entry:

14*th October*. How time slips by! The Bab now walks
alone and crawls upstairs easily. Aunt Ethelinda dies and
I and my Boff have been to Scotland and Venice and now
we are come back to our dear comfy home and to poor
Dyke. How happy we are but he is suffering still and more
so as the weeks go by. We have lost all hope. He is terribly altered. His beard seems now to form the greater part
of his face. And yet he laughs and jokes and talks as well
as ever. How I wish there had been some Boswell to
chronicle some of the things he has said to us!

16*th November*. God—or whatever Dyke's Great Influence is on whom he is so silent—is very good to me. My
Boff prospers and his health has been excellent all this
summer and autumn. His beautiful book *Music & Morals*
is out, dedicated 'To My Wife'. The dear thing! He is to
publish a volume of sermons in the Spring. Critical Mr
Loftie's [at Macmillan] approbation of my cover is a great
feather in my cap. The Bab is so well and getting so
amusing. I enjoy the budding intelligence getting stronger
and clearer every day. The Church evening congregation
is growing nearly as large as the morning. We have now,
in the dead season, £6 odd every Sunday from strangers.

Boff is valued and sought after by all clever and intelligent men—Roman Catholics, Dissenters, almost all creeds meet and settle down in our Church and consult and trust Rennie.

All is well with us. Only poor Deutsch is sinking and suffering more and more. Worse is to come and his temper through pain is often very irritable. He scolds and abuses everyone—sometimes even loses his temper with me. But I do not mind. It is a comfort to be able to bear something since one can do so little.

Soon after this entry, Deutsch became so ill that he returned to his lodgings where, in permanent pain, he would see no one nor go out anywhere except to the British Museum. At last though, in the New Year, he consented to see M.E.H., on February 17th and told her that he was in pain 'night and day—night and day' and the only thing that kept him going at all was his work. 'He has not missed an hour of his B.M. time. It is uncanny. It is a kind of galvanised life there for which he suffers most terribly afterwards,' said a deeply troubled M.E.H. to her husband after this sad interview. The following day she wrote a detailed account of her relationship with the scholar.

February 18th. I cannot realize how bad he is; often I can hardly remember when I used to be so much with him here! Why has such a good, so kind and noble a man been singled out for this prolonged torture? He is more reverent to his God than any Christian I ever knew. We met Sir Charles and the new Lady Dilke today. Sir Charles Dilke talked about Deutsch. 'Five years ago,' he said, 'he was met everywhere with his little yellow gloves, his smile, and all that running about London. He was the best talker I ever knew. The only fault was, that as he was the only man on his particular subjects, no one could ever contradict him.'

Deutsch has taught me many things and untaught me as well. It is difficult to estimate between the good and the harm. If he has taught me to put less faith in Creed and Church, he has also shown me that these things are not necessary to righteousness. If he has taken from Boff some of the hours I should have otherwise devoted to him, he has given me much good advice and never abused the privileges Boff gave him.

Yet with all the serious feelings between us of affection and sympathy, we seldom talk sense together. Our conversation, if it could be taken down in shorthand would be found not only for the most part frivolous, but even inane. It is the same with our disputes. We quarrel like children about nothing, feeling all the time that it is nothing—and make it up again without apology or explanation like a play that is finished. We are both proud; and we do not like to talk on the horrid subject nearest to our hearts when we are together. He is dying and every meeting may be our last now—they are very rare. There may be things he would like me to do when he is dead—things I ought to know but never shall. He hates to talk of his own work—perhaps he feels it all too deeply. When we are together he only cares to keep quiet and look at me, and my only aim is to make him smile which is best done by the most childish sayings. But we both know better. I know he is really good enough and kind enough and true as steel. He knows I am not merely a fool. It is only, as he calls it, 'talking in domino'.

March 3rd. Last week the Bab was photographed. He came out pretty well—picturesque with rumpled hair, long and curly. But the rosy cheeks are wanting like the yellow of his hair.

My Boffin is getting out his volume of sermons. The dear old lunatic is always very mournful about himself but I don't think it means much. He thinks before and after every sermon that he is going downhill fast and every time he preaches as finely as ever. I am very happy.

March 17th. Green has just come back unexpectedly

from San Remo. He is much more his old self than when he was last here and is a lively as a cricket and as merry as a bird. He wants to read my articles on the *Art of Beauty*.

Tuesday, April 30*th*. Went to B.M. to meet Deutsch. This is the first time we have been to meet him there for he has always begged us not to. He took us downstairs to see the Assyrian bas-reliefs from Nineveh. He looked well enough, walked quickly and was enthusiastic in shewing us the vigour and fire of the lions that were hunted by Ashurbanipal. The dogs—Landseer's are not better drawn—the birdlets singing on the trees and the prancing horses, and the arrows that have maimed the creatures as they walk—the citadel and rivers with no perspective. Oh, how happy he seemed for the moment shewing us his beloved antiquities. Once he wrote to me, 'How I should like to spend years and years with you in my well-loved realms of buried bigness and beauty because you care for and understand these things without the help of Cyclopedias and the aesthetic sense is great in you!' He seemed very fagged when he walked back with us to No. 45 but he walked even then with his usual 'whisk' that reminds me so much of a bird in good spirits.

During May and June of this year the Haweis family were worried because they had heard nothing for months from Willy Haweis in New Zealand. His father was convinced that he had been killed by Maories. As Spiritualist meetings were the rage in London, Mr Haweis, senior, came to stay at Welbeck Street and attended several seances given at a Mrs Gregory's house with his son and daughter-in-law.

May 21*st*. We have just returned from Mrs Gregory where Rennie, Mr Haweis and I lunched to meet the well-known trance medium, Clara Harris. She is a somewhat good-looking servant girl with nothing offensive about her. We asked of Willy. She said she could see him over and over again but refused to tell us where. She said, 'I can't

pronounce the name!' Then, 'he does not wish me to tell.'
This unreasonable attitude of Willy's spirit made me
incredulous of everything.

June 5th. If my Dutchman dies I shall go into mourning.
Not because I care for this outward sign of feeling but
because in this case I will give an outward sign of inward
regret. Once I wore my little black rep with the white
collar and went into his room. He asked me if I was in
mourning and for whom. I said, 'No one. I am wearing
an old dress and I look quite hideous in black.' 'On the
contrary, you look very pretty,' he said with those grave
accents which take all the frivolity out of his compliments.
But I know this is not the case. I hate Black. I hate myself in it. But I will wear it for Deutsch if he dies. In
memory of his sufferings and of his affection.

A few days later, M.E.H. met Professor Liebrich, the great
German occulist whose lecture on Turner's eyes and colour-
sense shown in his pictures she had written up for *The Echo.*
Delighted with her notice which he declared was the only one
that seemed to understand at what he was driving, Professor
Liebrich asked to meet Mrs Haweis. After this had been
arranged she told her mother what a charming man he was,—

He wouldn't believe I was a British Matron and said 'Vy,
I thought you were a young Mees only just out.' Then he
looked at me as if I was a fossil. I got an immense amount
of information out of him and we are going to the Hospital
where he promised to shew us some experiments . . .

I made another conquest some weeks ago. An Indian
officer who is in England for reason of his health and
with whom I went out sketching. He turns out to be a
great swell in conchology and geology. One of the few real
swells.

This real swell was destined to play quite an important part
in the life of Mary Eliza Haweis. His name was Colonel
Godwin Austen, the notable explorer after whom the second
highest mountain which he had climbed in the Himalayas had

been called. Captivated by M.E.H's charm and vitality, he proposed an elopment with her in the near future because, as he told her, she was the perfect soldier's wife to go adventuring with in the Far East. Laughing, she suggested instead a visit to the Crystal Palace with their sketch books. When her invitation was accepted she was careful to take her sister Edith with her as chaperone.

June passed with great activity in the Haweis household. For though the season was coming to an end, Society's most popular preacher was busy seeing two of his books through the press.

July 15th. My darling old Spoffkin's book of sermons is coming out quite soon. The cover is to be as I meant it, with a growing vine *au naturel* on it in gold and the ground a dark bluish-green, the colour of Rossetti's book. It will be a first rate volume, I know, and worth a dozen of old Bottle Stopper (Mr Stopford Brooke) which are like a piece of bread soaked in milk and water and then left a long time till the bread is warped into a crescent. Bogle's ain't.

M.E.H. had every reason to be proud of her Spoffkin's sermons however loudly he groaned and moaned on Saturday evenings while he sat in his study preparing them. By now, he was recognised to be in the first flight of London preachers and his name was on everyone's lips. Even the Prime Minister's attention revealed in Lady Frederick Cavendish's diary was fixed on him.

Uncle W. (W. E. Gladstone) is anxious to hear all about Mr Haweis, a clever preacher beginning to be famous. (*17th November 1872*).

Did the Prime Minister suggest that Mr Haweis might be invited to be a regular Evening Preacher at Westminster or was it kind Dean Stanley, noted for his liberal views? During this year and onwards, the Reverend Doctor Haweis could be heard in the Abbey holding the attention of a spell-bound congregation for one and a half hours without a single note.

THE REV. H. R. HAWEIS AS HE APPEARS WHEN ARRAYED IN HIS MASTER OF ARTS HOOD AND BLACK GOWN.

Other clergy were mad to learn the secret of his oratory declaring he exercised some uncanny, hypnotic power to which he only replied, laughing 'I disclaim all the black arts!'

In *Thoughts for the times,* dedicated to William Francis Cowper Temple, M.P. who had done so much to launch him in London society and again, in *Speech in Season* that followed after, Hugh Reginald Haweis gave his views on the pure mechanics of successful preaching. They were not dissimiliar to those of the great Baptist preacher, Charles Haddon Spurgeon, who possessed not only a lovely voice but the gift of moving his congregation from 'laughter to tears, joy to pathos, heaven to hell.'

Mr Haweis told his readers he had learnt to be a good preacher when working as a young curate at St Peter's, Bethnal Green, a slum parish. At first however carefully he thought out and wrote down his long sermons, he received little attention except yawns, coughs, much fidgeting and often the discreet shuffle of departing feet down the aisle. One Sunday, greatly daring, he clambered up into the pulpit and holding his Bible in one hand, preached his first extempore sermon. Punctuated by appalling moments of complete silence, he stammered on as he picked up the threads of his suddenly forgotten discourse till he reached what he felt to be the inglorious end of a truly ghastly sermon. To his surprise, he found his vicar waiting to shake his hand in the vestry. Was he aware that, for once, there had been no coughing, no yawning, no shuffle of bored feet leaving church as he preached? From that day, he never delivered a written out sermon again.

Although there was a strong feeling in the church that the clergy should preach doctrines and not too personal ones at that, the Reverend H. R. Haweis believed that to preach doctrines only was of little use if they did not impinge on the ordinary practises of secular life. He also believed in the continual re-instatement of truths which to have any impact on people's minds must be expressed in simple, everyday language. Otherwise, he argued, truth was always passing out of living doctrine into dead dogma.

'It won't do' he told his Marylebone congregation one day, to the delight of his wife seated in her customary pew just below him, scribbling down his sermon in a peculiar shorthand of her own, 'to go and read old books of theology if you want the living Truth. The Church of the Future must take present forms, Creeds, Articles and Ceremonies and sound them to their very depths and when something is found that will not hold water cast it aside in the cause of Truth. *Vice versa,* when something is found expressed in old theology, take it and change its form, expressing it in a way that will meet present wants and capacities.'

By such forward-thinking, he made his mark and would today have upheld the modernising of the Bible into current speech. One Sunday while stressing the evils of drink, Doctor Haweis had a sudden idea and leaning far out of the pulpit shouted, 'Beer! beer! Bible! bible!' At the same moment he waved his Bible in the direction of the *Westmoreland Street Arms* owned by his arch enemy, Mr Broggins, the publican. His cry was delivered with such gusto and good humour that it delighted the hearts of the poor who were listening. There were few families living in the slums of Marylebone who did not rate their little lame parson with the club foot as 'a rare sportin' un!' When he inaugurated his first 'Sunday Evenings for the People' designed to give the poor, old and lonely the opportunity to hear good music free, besides supplying them with a dry warm place in which to sit in opposition to the local 'pubs', they flocked to them. Less, perhaps, to hear 'the Doctor' spout to them all about a chap called Wagner than to hear him give a marvellous display of musical fireworks on his violin, which fascinated them.

August came with M.E.H. indulging herself in a mad fit of painting in what she described as 'a new way' after the style of Gustave Doré whom she admired and who came often to their parties in Welbeck Street, a rendezvous now for the brilliant and famed.

I hope more painting fits will come on, she wrote in her Thought Book. I may yet paint as I was meant to paint. If only no more babs come! While I have my health, I am so happy. My articles in *St Paul's Magazine* are most satisfactory and I have another in hand on 'Head dresses'. So I may be a writer too! One day, I mean to bring out a sensational novel.

Revelling in her painting mood, she visited the Academy several times, particularly noticing Laurence Alma Tadema's portrait of his wife and another of his home, Townshend

House, Regent's Park, where she was soon to be a frequent visitor. A vivid description of it is included in her *Beautiful Houses*, published in 1882.

Before their summer holiday abroad, she wrote to her mother:

16 Welbeck Street,
Cavendish Square, w.
August 6th

My dear Ma,

I am better now, but was very ill with bronchitis for a time—Dr Mackenzie got me round. The weather has been very bad and wet. Mr Haweis is staying here and he takes me out somewhere every day. We had a grand little dinner on Thursday—twelve people, all swells. Two earls: Earl of Mar and the countess, the Earl of Dunraven, the Lushingtons, Professor Blackie, the wittiest old man I ever knew, Mr and Mrs Stopford Brooke, Mrs Gregory and Mr Haweis.

Lady Mar was just a blaze of diamonds. She had magnificent sprays in her hair, a necklace of single stones as big as one's nail, and a great pendant, and ear-rings, bracelets and rings. She was in white satin and silver. I never saw such a mass of jewels. I wore my plain white silk with Charles II sleeves and my big amber which beats creation. In the evening Sir Charles Nicholson came in.

When we come to you—Rennie will fix a day—we had better bring the Bab with us.

Yours affectionately,

M.E.H.

In the autumn of 1872, Deutsch made plans to winter in Egypt. The British Museum had given him six months' leave on full pay as a last chance to help him cheat death. On December 17th, he paid a farewell visit to the Haweises.

December 17th. Deutsch has just left me, he is going to

Cairo and has given me his address. I found him very dead and worn out. Codlin [a pet name for her son] enlivened him a little. After he left us, Deutsch roused himself and told me how sorry he was to go and how he would like us with him and how he should miss me. He came about half-past two—'for five minutes only' and left at twenty-five to four, a cab waiting all the time. Sometimes I wish he did not love me so much as I cannot love him in the same way. Six months is a terribly long time to look forward to. When the medium, Clara Harris, said I should be connected with sickness and death within six months, I was miserable and frightened' But, thank God, nothing has happened. Deutsch has not died.

Boffin went to Colwood by himself yesterday till to-morrow on account of Margaret's serious illness. I have not minded his going as once I should. It used to be nearly a mania with me—my dread of his leaving me. I made up my mind to conquer that dread when he stayed at Brighton without telling me and frightened me so terribly. What a night I had! Now I have conquered it. Yesterday it was a black fog like midnight. I have never seen such a thing before. Boff went in it but telegraphed from Haywards Heath to say he was all right which was kind of him.

I wonder if I will ever see Deutsch again. I hope all will be well with him—with Boff, with me, with Codlin. I hope he will get on well in Cairo. I hope he will come back better if not cured. I cannot help caring for him very much. He cares so much for me.

After Christmas, M.E.H. received two letters from Deutsch, who seemed in excellent spirits. It was not till March that she made her first entry for 1873 in her Thought Book.

March 1, 1873. It seems almost impossible that Deutsch has been away now nearly three months. About three weeks ago, he wrote to tell me to write no more to Cairo as he was going somewhere or other—he did not say where! It seems so dreadful for him to go in his state to a place where there is no post and only rare chances of reaching or leaving it! On the 10th March, I am to write to him as he will be back in Cairo by the end of the month —'if not dead'.

My Boff is, thank God, well; and I suppose I must not complain because my Rent [another child] is needed from me again. If God needs a tithe of all I possess I ought not to be so enraged and melancholy. I wish I wasn't but constitutions are very different.

In spite of her angry resentment at having to bear another child, she was enjoying the company of her little Lionel very much. Forced to rest more at home, she amused herself by teaching him 'a host of Nursery Rhymes and a verse of Nash's *Spring, the sweet Spring.* Her son sang in perfect tune and had inherited his father's physical dexterity, turning head over heels quite beautifully. But all too soon came the long-dreaded news.

May 15th. Now the great blow has fallen that we have been waiting for two years and a half. God knows, while my Boff is spared to me nothing can hurt me much. But this is the saddest that can come beyond my own dear Boffin. Deutsch is dead.

The last letter I had from him came the Monday before Easter. I wrote twice since—but no answer came. Every day I watched for the post, very anxious. Only on Monday came a letter, dated May 5th, from some gentleman in Alexandria, containing the last words I could hear from my dearest and tenderest friend, dictated, evidently, and most carefully composed that we might not be alarmed. I knew how bad he must be before he would dictate a letter to me. For weeks I have been anxious and worried about him. I thought he might be in a wax with me because my last letter but one had a sentence in it that might have seemed ill-humoured.

Oh, my Dyke, no one will ever love me again as you did; often you said so. You were considerate in all ways for

me, full of tenderness and care. If I could have seen you,
again, only for one minute, only just to know you recognised me, only to have the comfort of remembering that
you did not die alone with strangers—I think I should not
have felt it so much. It is so useless weeping for you now,
my dear, kind, faithful friend. Only I can't help it. It is
like a limb gone. I would have given any life for yours
but one; made a bonfire of everybody for your one life.
Only I knew that you knew well I loved you; how I should
mourn for you and wish you back. So I will put on black
for you as I told you I would and my coming bab shall be
called after you.

M.E.H's grief was deeply felt. For sensitive and tender as
a woman, domesticated yet an artist—characteristics all of
the Semetic race—Emmanuel Deutsch had both understood
and appreciated Mary Eliza Haweis's complex personality.
Above all, he knew that with her high moral code and intellect-
ualism, she would have been shocked at the idea of any relation
ship between them other than one strictly platonic. The more
so as she still idolised her husband.

At the end of May, Doctor and Mrs Haweis were informed
by a Mr Lang that Deutsch had died of advanced cancer in
the kidneys. He had been nursed by German deaconesses in
some kind of hospital and so M.E.H. knew that his old wish
of meeting death in his beloved East with his native tongue
spoken round him had been fulfilled.

Some weeks later, she took out her Thought Book.

June 5th. Green came in tonight and spent the evening.
What spirits he has. I laughed for the first time since the
15th of May.

It was obvious that John Richard Green was glad to resume
his old role of sole pebble on the Haweis beach at Number 16
Welbeck Street.

After another letter had come from Mr Lang telling Mrs
Haweis that while Deutsch lay dying, he kept repeating, 'I
cannot express to you how kind and good she has been to

me,' she began to sculpt a bust of her 'beloved Dutchman.'
July 14*th*. Miss Smith and Dr Smith think my bust of
Deutsch extremely like. When Green saw it I could tell
by his expression as well as by his word how much he
was struck. He came up laughing and joking—thinking
probably it was some fancy head or a portrait of Rennie.
He quite changed countenance when I lifted the cloth.
He thinks it extremely able and a wonderful likeness. I
have been thus curing myself homoeopathetically of my
regret; first by writing out copious extracts from his
letters—then by writing an account of his illness and stay
here, for Rennie; then by copying a photograph of him;
and lastly by making his bust. God bless him—wherever
he is.

In July the season ended and London began to empty fast.
Forced by her pregnancy to take time off from literary work,
M.E.H. kept turning to her Thought Book as a means for self-
expression. She filled many pages in trying to discover why
she had always felt so inadequate when it came to showing
her real feelings to anyone beloved.

July 14*th*. I was never kissed either by Papa or Mama
except with a kind of bang when I went to bed. My sister
and I never embraced at all. It is only now when I observe
other families and other children that I see how 'dry' I
was brought up. I raised Boffin into an idol and I was, I
suppose, as much in love with him as it is possible to be.
It was Boffin who melted out my poor dry heart and
taught me to have some human feelings. Every scrap of
love I had locked up in me went to him and for the first
time I loved him in a sort of (still) 'cracky' way—terrified
to have him out of my sight even in another room—
bursting into tears at the slightest thought of his possible
demise at any date however distant. Jealous if he so much
as looked at my first bab—hating everything and everybody that took him from me while he was in the house.
And then in three years, comes Deutsch just when I had

begun to see that my adoration of Rennie was too painful
and I must have other interests or go insane. Though I
cannot love two at once in the same way and my Boffin
must always have first place in my heart, I could not but
soon feel that I owe much to Deutsch for his forbearance,
his gentleness and uniform goodness to me. I cannot
comprehend people caring for me knowing how little there
is lovable in me. I cannot understand people thinking me
beautiful as Deutsch did. I often try to see it and can't.
A candle has been blown out, it seems darker than it really
is,—but I shall get used to it if God is merciful and leaves
me my darling.

In the middle of July, Mary Eliza Haweis put away her
Thought Book with its pages of long self-analysis and went to
stay for the first time with the Cowper Temples at Broadlands,
their historic home near Romsey in Hampshire. A letter was
soon in the post for Mrs Joy now living in cheap lodgings at
Ostend with Edith, who was still unmarried.

Broadlands,
Romsey

My dear Ma,

I have only time to write a line—we have hardly time
for anything what with excursions and the business of life.
The house is full of visitors, some great swells. The place
is perfectly magnificent, huge—and the treasures knock-
ing about something wonderful. Folios of old masters'
original drawings all loose everywhere, china of the greatest value in the bedrooms, tablecloths of bullion and white
silk, white satin chairs, splendid old pictures and ceilings.

The Bab is very well. Rennie is not quite the thing
today being subjugated by omelettes. I think I am a little
stronger. I have had a bad cough. We go for excursions
every day as if the grounds were not big enough. We have
been to Salisbury and Romsey Abbey, Stonehenge and
Queen Elizabeth's hunting Lodge, also Florence Nightin-

gale's home. The country is very lovely and so is the
weather. The Cowpers are delightful. Rennie preached at
the Abbey on Sunday night and he created a great sensation. Everybody down here is a Spiritualist. The Bab is
not much seen but has an Indian shawl and beautiful
frock when he is. I wish I had some decent frocks and some
splendid jewels but I have made a great stroke with my
old lace and acorns which I have made into a necklace to
astonish the natives. There is a Countess here who is
rather fun but very very old! We get on famously and
they all think me very lovely, which may not interest you
but does me and pleases Rennie. I dress in the Watteau
style—cheap which pays. Lady Paulet admires my Watteau hat. There are about fifty servants. There is one
hideous old gentleman here whom we call 'the ghoule'.
He is so spoony that I have to snub him very much.

Yours affectionate,

M.E.H.

Of the approaching birth of her child in barely two months
not a word. Her Watteau style of dress was designed expressly
to disguise her figure at this time.

London was unbearably hot on their return, and cholera
rife. Mrs Joy was told how Rennie has not been very well
owing to the heat and working too hard.

I think the death of Mr Deutsch in Egypt upset him.
It was a great shock to us both. We are going to take
a short run over to Rouen next week to see the Museum
of Pottery, but shall come back for Sunday.

After this trip M.E.H. departed to Hampstead where she
had taken a small house, Netley Cottage, to escape the heat
and danger of cholera infection. She took the blocks of
Chaucer For Children to finish as she needed something to keep
her mind occupied from worrying over Rennie who had to
spend many hours visiting the sick and dying round St James.

Returning to Hampstead, one evening, pale and exhausted,

he told his wife who had sat up to give him supper, how he had been the shocked observer, that day, of what was now becoming a frequent practice at a funeral service. This was to shovel the earth lightly over the coffin committed to interment before the mourners, then, when they had departed, raise the coffin and remove it to that part of the churchyard where paupers were buried. Thus grave-room was kept open on a paying basis and one grave sold many times over. A most un-Christian practice produced, in his view, by the overcrowded and insanitary conditions prevailing in London's graveyards. He thought that cremation which was being advocated by Sir Henry Thompson, the great surgeon, would be the only means of decent burial for the future, though it was not yet recognised by the Church. Agreeing entirely, M.E.H. urged her husband to write a book on this subject which he did. Published under the title of *Ashes to Ashes: A Cremation Prelude*, it disclosed many evil customs of the day still in existence, such as body-snatching for laboratory purposes; human bones being sold for manure; and coffins being burnt at dead of night to make room for others. Besides, a wholesale racket in coffin furniture (i.e. the everyday sale of name-plates, nails, handles etc. to marine stores).

But *Ashes to Ashes* did little more than gain Hugh Reginald Haweis a directorship of the Woking Crematorium when it came to be established.

On 4th September a daughter was born to Mary Eliza Haweis at Netley Cottage. She was a large baby and plain. Her mother made no comment on her appearance into this world, being far more concerned at the time over her husband's health. Three weeks later the grand house-cleaning ordered by her at Welbeck Street during their absence was completed, and they returned home. In the quiet seclusion of her pretty clean bedroom, M.E.H. opened her Thought Book once more.

September 25th. It is three weeks since our girl was born. It has been rather curious how all that I wished hard for has come. I was very anxious to get the confinement over for many reasons,—and at last in impatience wished hard for it to be 'tonight or tomorrow morning' and lo! the first suspicion did come that very night. It was born next day at 7.10 pm. Later, I wished hard that on our return from Hampstead I might find my little baskets that Deutsch bought me. And lo!—there they were—five dear little baskets—and a parcel from Lady Strangeford containing a pair of silver bracelets, two pipes and my poor little cigar case I gave him—besides these last gifts, two unfinished letters to me. One like 'a shout', so happy from Rome; the other only wanting me. Little did I ever expect to get letters of his again. A good many of my own letters were in the parcel too; he always said he destroyed them but he evidently did not, latterly. Some were worn through from long wear in his pocket. Mine and Codlin's photographs returned too. Lady Strangeford has certainly been most kind. All these things she need not have sent.

I walked today into the next room and was looking at the street opposite [Bentinck Street] and the brown houses against a salmon sky and thinking of Deutsch. Suddenly, I saw the tiniest, prettiest, and most delicate new moon that ever was. It gave me such a heartleap, it was so lovely. I remembered how delicious these things were to him. The notices of him in the papers called him 'a poet'. I had never thought of him as that before but I saw at once it was true. His poetic feeling had often struck me, things struck him from beautiful points of view. He would have been worth so much if only he could have been kept alive to write ballads!

So much has happened wrong all the spring and summer since Deutsch died that I got quite frightened. I hoped when the bab was born the spell would be broken and the luck change. I hope it has changed. My dear Boffin had the severest spell of illness last month that ever he had since our marriage. His leg was so bad that we both thought the old hip disease was coming again. Even Dr

Clark was in doubt. But God was very merciful and spared us that. I think it was the rheumatism and some strain brought on by over-walking in the heat and then catching cold. It was terrible both being invalids together; neither able to help the other. I used to get up in the night when he was in great pain and mesmerise him for three-quarters of an hour or even an hour and a half at a stretch and very hard work, it was. But it seemed to have an effect. He said it took the pain away. He certainly went off to sleep each time and slept for an hour or two when without it he could not sleep anyhow. What profound misery I was in! But God heard. For ten days he could not walk across the room; many mornings he stayed in bed. For several weeks he never left the house. He got better just before my time came. Now he walks with one stick again and seems well.

We have not heard any answer about his lecturing tour in America, but the fact of his having been asked just as Tyndal, Deutsch and others have been, shows that he is widely known as a speaker and writer. The success of his sermons in Westminster Abbey is another feather in his cap. I often wish Deutsch was here to know all this. He would say in his way, "He's an angel and as clever as the day." Greeny says we are the only couple he can think of without trouble of any sort. He recommends us to smash the thing we value most in the house as a sacrifice to the gods. But what can I sacrifice? There is only my Boffin and my own health which I could value enough. Even the children—well, I hope they will thrive and live but even they would not be like those. Perhaps, the loss of Deutsch could be considered a holocaust. I have been sorry enough. I went into black as a kind of sacrifice. But I am sorry that Rennie does not like to have the baby called Emmanuela. I always thought Deutsch should be godfather to the next whenever it came. Lately, I remembered my promise to him that it should bear his name. But as Boff does not wish it, of course I gave in. But I am very disappointed. Emmanuela is such a pretty name. But I daresay there would be a scandal. It is such a dirty world. The only other wish I have about the child is that it should be named after Boffin. So we must invent a name soon.

At the end of September, the Haweises went abroad for a short holiday. This over, there began a gay 'Little Season' for them with the Archbishop of Canterbury preaching at St James's, one Sunday, and returning with Mrs Tait to lunch at Welbeck Street. Little Lionel sat on the Archiepiscopal knee and played with the Archiepiscopal watch and His Grace was most amiable.

Later, that same week, Mrs Haweis gave a dinner party for Mr and Mrs Alma Tadema. She told her mother,—

I had several new lights about dinner decoration. I decorated the tablecloth with embroidered stripes in colours and put red tassels round the napkins. Mr Tadema is the artist who paints those wonderful Pompeian interiors and Mrs Tadema is a great beauty—Pre-Raphaelite style and dresses most curiously. Mr Nixon [a fellow guest] does not admire her—but does me whom he considers so beautiful as to be independent of all colours, lights, or other disadvantages! I have just got a grass green dress made by Ann [the children's nurse] very curiously.

By December, preparations were afoot for the christening of little Hugolin as she was to be called. Her mother made her a pelisse of white serge with a white fur cape, while Lionel, who always paid for dressing, was presented with a long green coat down to his heels, trimmed with grey fur. In this garment, he attended his sister's christening.

Suddenly, there came news that John Richard Green might be going to be married and Mrs Joy planned to live permanently abroad for reasons of economy. Her daughter thought this a good idea as everywhere round them houses were being pulled down and rents going up. Prices for milk, meat and Australian meat were high and steadily rising. Most joints were to cost 1/- more, while coals (mere slate) were 3/3, an exhorbitant sum, M.E.H. told her mother, adding: 'I believe before long the system of living in 'flats' will be adopted here on a much wider plane (and how right she was) for nobody can live on a fixed income at this rate.'

On 22nd December, the immense plain baby, destined to be both petite and pretty, was christened Hugolin Olive after her father and grandfather. Mrs Cowper-Temple and Lady Nicholson were her godmothers; Mr Stopford Brooke, her godfather. 'So she will never be called Emmanuela now,' wrote M.E.H. sadly in the last entry of her Thought Book for 1873, the year which had seen the tragic death of Emmanuel Deutsch.

Early in 1874, ready always to learn a new craft, Mrs Haweis sent for a Mr Saunders to come to Welbeck Street to teach her how to gild, as she thought this would come in useful. Soon she became as skilled at gilding as at mending old lace. No expert could tell the difference between her lace repairs and the original.

March 24th, 1874. D's works, his 'Remains', are out. They consist chiefly of a reprint of a few of his celebrated articles and notes of lectures. The memoir at the beginning is delicately done. All Jews, I have been told, have their private Jewish name. I never knew his till now— 'Menahem'. But Lady Strangeford's description of him is incorrect. His hair was a darker brown than mine and mixed with grey. His beard light-brown and thin and poor as beards go. His eyes bright hazel. A red stone covers his grave on which is inscribed the year of his death in Hebrew and a text: 'Arise, shine; for thy light is come'. I have put these words round his picture.

In June, Mr Lang, who had been the writer of Deutsch's last letter to Mrs Haweis as he lay dying, came to England and called on her. Hers had been the only name constantly repeated by the brilliant scholar, he told her, and he (Deutsch) 'fully meant, and believed himself able, to return home to them.' Considerably consoled, M.E.H. wrote:

June 6th. Mr Lang dined with us tonight and spoke with great feeling of our dear Deutsch. I was so touched by his many little memories of him. Ah, could I have been there with him! We shall never see his like again.

My dear Bogle is well; but his leg continues rickety since his illness last August. I wish I had more muscular strength. I think my children have taken all that from me. Yet, in myself, I am very well.

At the end of the month, M.E.H. heard disturbing news from her mother, now living in Belgium. The house that she had taken was suddenly declared unsafe. Practical and kind always, her elder daughter hastened to give her good advice and monetary help.

16 Welbeck Street,
Cavendish Square, w.1
June 27th

My dear Ma,

It must have been a great nuisance the house being found unsafe. But I do not see how in any way you can lose the money you paid in advance as they must, in all honesty return the money they have given nothing for! Likewise the piano—you wd only lose the money of carriage from one house to another. It does not matter to the makers where it is played on. I send you £5 now and we will try and send another before long. About moving and living in England. You know what furnished apartments are here when nice. Our curate, Mr Fisher, pays £200 for three very ordinary rooms near us over a shop. In Bayswater, they would not be much less. At the same time, there is always the loss in dragging your furniture about both in money and damage. And if you thought of remaining abroad and moving about, you wd be freer without furniture. So if you think of selling it, R. says he will see to it and do as best he can. Some of the things we wd try and take ourselves. The rage for works of art and old furniture is so much on the increase that I shd fancy now is the moment to sell. You might get good prices. Only I think it wd be too late this summer. You wd have to make up your mind and give Christie and Mansons, or whoever wd do it, time to sell it. Preferably, in the middle of next season or early spring. Their sales are made up for so long before. One or two things I should be sorry to lose and wd make a sacrifice to keep. But it is for you to think over it, and if you thought of doing so it wd be best for us to look at it and have a proper inventory taken and let you know about it before anything was done.

We have just got a wonderful fluke in the way of two large pieces of tapestry for the drawing-room. One fills one wall and the other a niche. I have always wanted tapestry vainly. It can hardly be got for love or money now the taste for such things is spreading so rapidly. But we found it by chance in a photographer's attic. He wanted to get rid of it and we risked the price,—a very small one for its value. We seem to have got a bargain! The large piece represents a battle of Alexander and the smaller a Royal Marriage of some kind, very early and curious but much defaced. There are not many colours left and it is very dirty. But I shall clean it, myself. The colossal figure in the big piece seems to me to dwarf the drawing-room. But other people think the reverse. Anyhow, we are pleased with our finds. On a bright day, they give the room a very handsome appearance.

We went to dine with Julie Farmer the other night,—a great many artists. I sat next to Sant [the future R.A.]. He has a lovely picture in the Academy of a child with peaches. There have been a great many theatrical parties recently to which we have gone. It seems to be quite the fashion.

Mrs Stopford Brooke died last Saturday. It is a sad thing for the eight children left.

I do not think there is any more news. We have got
Lionel a real fiddle to begin to learn on. He is very
delighted with it.

Yr. affect. Daughter,

M.E.H.

In the years to come, Edith Joy was to accuse her sister
bitterly of behaving in a hard and mean way to their mother.
On the contrary, her letters to her 'dear Ma' reveal
genuine affection and concern over her financial worries. Mrs
Joy was not a practical woman like her elder daughter.
Moreover, she had been used to living on a grand scale during
much of her life. M.E.H. was always coming to her rescue
with sound advice on how best to economise. With little
money except what she earned by sheer hard work, she knew
the value of every penny in her purse, and when she could she
sent her mother little presents of an odd pound or two. If she
bought an old family treasure from her, she gave her a fair
price always, though her sister ill-naturedly thought she
should pay more than its market value.

In July, her husband's article on Deutsch was published,
which brought about an odd quarrel with John Green. She
told her mother that:

He [J.G.] is as spiteful as a woman and still jealous of our
relationship with D. Nothing he can say will turn my
heart from one who was so good to me and loved me so
dearly. I won't go to any more picture galleries with him
for the present!

The summer of 1874 was extremely hot and the Haweises
made preparations to go for a long holiday to Florence, as
M.E.H. knew that Rennie needed rest. Canon Haweis, his
father, had just been offered and accepted the rich living of
Slaugham in Sussex. His family was delighted, including his
daughter-in-law of whom he was extremely fond.

Before the season closed, the Haweises were invited to meet

the Prince and Princess of Wales at a garden party given by Lady Waldegrave. M.E.H. wore her grass green dress with pink gloves and told her mother in great jubilation: 'It was the grandest party we have ever had and our names were in the Morning Post among all the grand people.'

Contrary to her advice, Mrs Joy insisted on immediately selling more of the Joy family heirlooms to swell her diminishing funds. Both her daughter and son-in-law attended the sale in London which was a disappointing one.

> 16 Welbeck Street,
> Cavendish Square

My dear Ma,

I got R. to write to Lady Mar who will call on you, so prepare for her turning up. She is very nice and pretty. Lord Mar you met here once, didn't you? You will get some introductions through them. As to the decanters (Dutch) and other little things and the tazza I described in my last letter, I bought in the lot they were in. They were going so low. We shall try and sell them for you, i.e. 1 tazza, 17 wine-glasses, an imperfect Worcester tea service, a wooden ladle, hot water plate, 2 Dutch decanters, a plate, inkstand and bowl. See catalogue. They were all going for a pound only and it seemed a sin to let them go. The hawkshood, fringed gloves and the 2 Etruscan lamps [from her father's studio] we did not send to the sale as they were unsaleable. I send you some money for them which we think fair. I hope you will. They are according to valuation. I include, too, the Albert Dürer book. When Jos [their solicitor and cousin] sends you your cheque don't delay the investment because of the money for the things we are going to sell. They cannot be much and we may not be able to sell till next season as so many are away now. That will be better than the Tazza going for £2 and the glasses for a few shillings! The Dutch decanters are worth about 7/6 each. Do you remember the price of the claret glasses with the stars on them? If so, you can tell us sometime when you write.

Your affectionate Daughter,

M.E.H.

Before reaching Florence, that summer, the Haweises stayed at a little village near Modane just below the Mt Cenis tunnel. Set high up on the mountain-side, it was a picturesque place surrounded by huge marble boulders in between which fell long, thin, silvery cascades of water. M.E.H. was enchanted by the exquisite views and walks, hating only the fine marble dust that was ruining all her clothes. She wrote to her mother:

> The dust is as fine as flour and very difficult to brush off. The mornings and evenings can be very chilly—the sun goes away so soon—and yesterday afternoon, we got back from an excursion into the hills, icy-cold. All the mountains seem composed of sheets of marble which wd be worth any money in England. But here they use it for building huts and walls to their fields. In the hamlets I saw that the 'country man' of the French stage is no exaggeration! The men all wear dress coats with brass buttons and gorgeously coloured waistcoats and trousers. Being Sunday, we saw them in their best—I never saw greater objects.
>
> We are going on to Bologna tomorrow. The hotels have all been spoilt by Cook—the prices of the dirtiest are the same as the best now—thanks to him.

Yr affectionate Daughter,

M.E.H.

5. THE LITERARY YEARS

1875-1878

DURING THE YEAR 1875 M.E.H's Thought Book remained without a single entry which can be accounted for by the fact that she was working very hard on *Chaucer for Children,* a book largely inspired by her carefully chosen readings from *The Canterbury Tales* to amuse and instruct her son, Lionel. As he appeared to enjoy them so much, why not other children, she thought?

New Year's Day, 1876, is recorded by a long letter to Mrs Joy who was told that Christmas had been close and muggy, with no snow, to the children's disappointment. Lionel and Hugolin, now in her third year, had been invited to numerous parties, and on Christmas Eve so many parcels containing presents and sweetmeats had arrived at their door from members of R's congregation that she had to confiscate a good few and distribute them elsewhere. She had been out only 'moderately'. On one occasion, she had met Mr Frith and enjoyed a long talk with him. 'He held forth on your beauty in the old days and asked kindly after you. He does not look a day older and is particularly fresh and hale-looking. Louey [his daughter] was with him.'

She then stresses the point that she cannot have her sister Edith to stay because

Our evenings at home are engaged in work and silence and anyone staying here would be wretched. I have often told you we are living beyond our income and look a great deal richer than we are and so every pound is of consequence. We ought to be saving up for the children's education as their welfare is our first duty. People have no business to bring children into the world whom they cannot educate.

I had a nice Xmas box sent me—a painted glass window from Mr Cottier to fit over the front door. I made the design, myself, a year ago and he has worked on it and presented it to me. But do you suppose he sent it to me for love? No. I shall have to write an article somewhere to puff his manufactory. People don't do things for love in this world. I have to write and draw as hard as I can to add to our income. I have never saved a penny out of all I have earned and often knock up with a headache for a week under it. Everything is ground out of R's brain and every pound we spend represents so many hours' work from him or me. Even the presents to the children have to be paid for one way or the other.

In February, during a spell of spring-like weather, the Reverend Doctor and Mrs Haweis went to stay with the Cowper Temples, again taking Lionel and his nurse, Ann, with them while Hugolin was sent to her aunts and grandfather in Sussex.

Broadlands,
Romsey

My dear Ma,

I don't know whether you have written lately as we have not had any letters but I write to say we are staying with Mr and Mrs Cowper Temple.

It is like summer here and quite different from London. There are a great many visitors. They come and go—all celebrities or else noble. They make a great deal of us and sometimes R. is asked to address the servants at Prayers which he considers a great compliment. Lionel is much improved and creates a great sensation by his beauty and genius. He has an early Charles II dress and an early

English one. The first is made of crimson velvet slashed with white and trimmed with antique lace and sable and the other is white blanketing trimmed with gold embroidery. He looks wonderful in both and comes down to lunch and sets a good example to everyone in the house. The butler says he is the most perfect child in every way he ever saw. The ladies dress beautifully. Mrs Temple has a dress of crimson plush and rose-point lace which is the first lace of all and plain diamonds. But Lady Asburton wears an ancient Keltic necklace of pure gold which I wd rather have than diamonds! If I am presented this season have you anything scrumptious to lend me? My eccentric dresses make me quite celebrated, I find, and Lionel keeps up the reputation of the family. Miss Marsh who writes 'goody' books and Lord Shaftesbury the reformer of ragged boys, Captain Maxse, another, several editors, and Lady Ashley are all here also.

R. preached at Romsey Abbey on Sunday evening. The Abbey is most lovely. Norman architecture. The servants's hall appals poor Ann. There are countless servants belonging to the house and every visitor brings two or three besides.

This house is very splendid with old masters all over the walls of every room and on the staircase, too. Countless port-folios of original drawings and prints of Sir Joshua's pictures lie about everywhere and are taken little care of. The furniture of the drawing-room is the palest green satin and gold; antique statues, orange trees and camellias everywhere. I think the place nearly as pretty in winter as in summer, there are so many evergreen trees planted.

With love,

Yr Affectionate daughter,

M.E.H.

Their visit over, they returned home and were at the

grindstone again, writing; always writing to earn the precious much-needed pennies.

Early in March, young Mrs Haweis heard that she was to be presented by Lady Nicholson. After this great event she dashed off a letter to Mrs Joy in high spirits, describing the whole scene and what she had worn.

I had a very pretty dress. The petticoat was of salmon (or as they call it, deep coral) very rich silk and the train of cream coloured brocade, very elegant indeed. The pattern woven in it was hart's tongue fern leaves, life-size but indistinct enough not to look too conspicuous. All round the train were puffings of cream coloured tulle trimmed with wallflowers and coral roses. The petticoat was trimd with brocade to match and across the front a lot of antique lace that I had on my blue satin. My train was $3\frac{3}{4}$ yards long from the shoulders and I wore gloves up to the elbows. My feathers were salmon coral and a longish tulle veil. I wd not have changed my dress with any there except two which were hand-embroidered. I had splendid diamond earrings, pendant, and hair aigrettes and five rows of large pearls round my neck—borrowed from friends, of course, and Mrs Haweis.

The Queen was not gone when I went into the Presence so I kissed her hand like a man and a brother. I was glad she had not gone; she never stays more than an hour. Afterwards, we walked about and looked at the pictures and the people. It is a very pretty sight to see all the uniforms, the Garter stars and ribbons. Lady Nicholson wore a pink petticoat and a claret train with pink roses on it. I saw none of richer material than my own which I believe would have cost £80 if I had gone to a swell *modiste*. But it will not be much more than £30 because I went to my own small dressmaker who knows my figure and fits me, always, to a T.

R. went to the Levee on Monday instead of going with

me to Court yesterday. He wore a black silk cassock and gown with a three-corner hat.

In haste,

Yr Affectionate daughter,

M.E.H.

This was not Mrs Haweis's only appearance at a 'Drawing-Room'. She was often seen at Court and her romantic reverence of Queen Victoria and the Royal Family was sincere and endured all her life. But she went to Court and to many great political and social parties of the day less to meet celebrities than to study the clothes, the magnificent jewelry and the priceless antiques seen on these occasions. Her steadily growing reputation for being somewhat of an art and dress expert had created a unique position for her in society as well as in the world of commercial fashion. In Society, it was said that many a London hostess with a flair for fine dressing often fought shy of meeting Mrs Haweis face to face in case the grand creation she wore failed to reach the high standard she exacted always from those of reputed taste. In the commercial world, she was the first lady to be treated, not as a gifted amateur, but as a genuine professional. But well-known Court dressmakers angled in vain to produce Mrs Haweis's dress expertise and knowledge on period costume. However hard-pressed for money at home, she refused all her life to write or design for the fashion trade.

In June 1876 the education of young Lionel came to exercise the minds of both his parents. What form was it to take and how should they cope? Quite naturally, they sought advice from his godfather, John Richard Green, the historian, who suggested that his mother should give him his first lessons and decide what subject he should take up whether art, history or botany. M.E.H. was frankly worried and wrote in her Thought Book:

June 1st. 'Make yourself a companion to your boy,' Greeny says. 'Go about with him.' I suppose I ought to

135

keep up my looks for that as much as anything. Boys are proud of their mother's beauty, and a mother gets an influence over her boys that a father seldom does. I see it is mental qualities wh. keep a child's love like a man; sympathy of tact more than silly weak affection. Green recommended my undertaking at least the art education of L. Every parent ought to be more like elder brothers and sisters to their children than they are!

Such a modern sentiment was revolutionary in 1876 when expressed in conventional family circles. Since the arrival of her children, both her sisters-in-law had been shocked by May's complete lack of what they considered to be true maternal feeling. They could not understand how she was incapable of being emotionally involved with Lionel and Hugolin in the sentimental way that most Victorian mothers were. From the day of their birth, she regarded them as separate individuals and, a strict disciplinarian, brooked no interference from her husband even in the nursery. Careful attention was paid to their health, and a wholesome diet insisted on. So were manners. Hugolin always had to curtsey on coming into a room when visitors were present while Lionel always said a short Latin grace before any meal taken in the dining-room.

When Sir John Lubbock's article on *Elementary Education* appeared in the *Contemporary Review*, M.E.H. was deeply interested in reading this eminent Victorian's views on how harmful it was to force children to store up a long list of unmeaning crimes and dull dates, miscalled History, in their poor little minds and imbibe yet more arid facts of dry-as-dust Grammar which did nothing to train them, either morally or intellectually. Much impressed, and agreeing entirely with Sir John Lubbock that a child's education should not be sacrificed to meaningless parrot-like instruction, or book-learning confused with real knowledge, M.E.H. continued working on her *Chaucer for Children*.

In April, she made this last entry in the second volume of her Thought Book:

April 19*th*. I close this book, chronicle of perhaps the most eventful ten years of my life with a sense of utter thankfulness. May He keep us all from harm.

Unfortunately, the next volumes were destroyed after her death by her husband.

Early in the New Year of 1877, M.E.H. completed *Chaucer for Children: A Golden Key to Knowledge* and dedicated it: 'To My Little Lionel, for whom I felt the need of some book of this kind.'

Side by side with Chaucer's own text, rightly accented for reading out aloud, she gave her own rendering of it in simple English. She also supplied concise notes on the social customs, dress and furnishings of the period together with a glossary of ancient words and their meaning. Considering the tender age of her readers, M.E.H. aimed high at their intelligence and neither her husband or John Richard Green were very sanguine of her book's success. But from the first day of publication *Chaucer for Children* had a deservedly popular appeal and went through many editions. In fact, it made her name.

No sooner was it off her hands and selling well, than she was busy on another, *The Art of Beauty*, based on articles which had already appeared in *St Paul's Magazine*. Her illustrations for it are among her best, witty and serious. The frontispiece shows a slender girl picking apple blossom on whose fair hair is perched a tiny red skull-cap which began a vogue for them as being the latest headgear 'à la Mrs Haweis'.

M.E.H. used her book as a platform for stating her clear-cut views on beautifying the English home by way of interior decoration which involved the use of more artistic colour schemes besides appropriate patterns for all furnishing materials, carpets and curtains etc. Like all individualists, she had strong likes and dislikes. A bugbear of hers was the opulent, upholstered furniture of the eighteen-seventies, so padded, buttoned and fringed (like women's clothes) that it had no proper form or shape. Others were the popular 'three-piece' suite, any form of cheap gilding, glacé silks, pale satins ('so boring'), or grass-green Brussels carpets with red spots. Nothing could be done with such things but to get rid of them, she declared. As for a chair covered in needlework showing a pattern of birds or butterflies:

It induces a very unpleasant sensation in me. A vase of flowers on a curtain is equally absurd. Most 'Italian' patterns are usually debased. Stout boys stand on scarfs attached to boughs in an impossible manner—swans perch on twigs of plants that could never support their weight—butterflies bigger than storks that stand beside them are bad because ridiculous; they hurt our sense of propriety and worry the eye. Choose good patterns—commonsense will guide you—and let your hangings be equal in tone with that of your walls.

In conclusion, she paid a small tribute to Whistler for

Vulgarity plus Unhealthiness.

Strong-minded young lady.

Grace.

Un-grace.

occasionally devoting 'his great but eccentric' genius to interior decoration and a much longer one to her friend Walter Crane for having done so much in the world of commercial design by way of producing his textiles, tiles and wallpapers to raise the standard of popular taste, saying:

While our carpets, wall-hangings, tea-trays, chinaware, presentation plate, metal and jewelry work, are left to designers of a lower order we can never rank as an aesthetic nation or aspire to possess a national school of art.

In 1879, with a fourth child regretfully on the way, M.E.H. followed the success of *Chaucer for Children* and *The Art of Beauty* with one on *Dress*, a subject long dear to her heart.

Ever since she had been a girl living in Pimlico with little pocket money, she had taken much time and thought on dressing herself as attractively and cheaply as possible. As the young wife of a clergyman moving in London's highest social and artistic circles, she knew that she had to make her mark sartorially somehow with the limited dress allowance of a parson's wife. Hers was no hour-glass figure suited to carry off the ornate dresses, so richly beaded, buttoned and draped of the period; nor had she the height or willowy appearance to attempt the 'aesthetic' style of dressing so much favoured by her Pre-Raphaelite women friends like Mrs Walter Crane and Mrs Alma Tadema. She had to strike out on a line of her own and ignoring the hated bustle, dress only to please herself. So when she put flowers in her hair for a grand party at the Cowper Temples, they were not flowers ordered from the little florist round the corner. She would pin a spray of lauristinus among her piled-up, auburn curls and be amused when this starry cluster was mistaken for expensive stephanotis. If she trimmed a bonnet—and how she loathed over-decorated bonnets with their bows, ribbons and even perhaps, a dead humming-bird—she used a tuft of feathery-pink, dried seaweed which instantly made 'fashion' news! As for 'that useless mask of cheap net miscalled by shopmen a "lace-fall",' Mrs Haweis would as soon be dead as seen in one.

Not since Miss Elizabeth Rigby (later Lady Eastlake) had treated women's clothes from a literary and historic angle in an erudite article called *Dress* published in the March issue of

The Quarterly Review, 1847, had a woman journalist thought of following her example till Mrs Haweis.

M.E.H. was well equipped for this task by having studied like Miss Rigby period costume in the pictures of old masters seen in art galleries and museums at home or abroad. From these studies, she had learnt 'the importance of clothes which

1750.

1860.

141

are destined to be our friends or foes during our lives, control-
ling our healths to say nothing of our worldly credit.'

She knew only too well the poor reputation in which Englishwomen were held abroad for unfashionable dressing. She was
quite sure, and bluntly said so, that this reputation would
endure 'till they thought more for themselves and individua-
lised their daily dress as a part of their individual character.
For the true secret of all true art is freedom to think for
ourselves and to do as we like.'

The best course open to Englishwomen was simply not to
pander to their modistes and milliners by agreeing to buy a
particular dress or bonnet just because they were fashionable.
They should remember, pointed out Mrs Haweis, how inde-
pendant of current fads and fancies was beautiful Mrs
William Morris and her daughters; not to speak of the great
Miss Ellen Terry. When these ladies went out walking, they
wore a practical dress topped by a graceful, circular cloak in
winter; a loose scarf and shady hat in summer.

'In fact, the pre-Raphaelite lady defies fashion when it is
bad but goes along with it if it mends its ways and becomes
good.'

Her views were equally decided on how children should be
dressed and she devoted a whole section in her book to juvenile
wear under the title of 'Nursery Hygiene'. She did not believe
in copying adult fashions for them. They should have special
styles designed to meet their requirements. Nurses were far
too fond of wrapping their charges up at stated seasons of the
year, irrespective of weather conditions. They should consult
the barometer outside the nursery window; that instrument
alone regulating the throwing off, or putting on, of childish
wraps!

If a hot day comes in January, throw off the thick petticoat
or hood and directly the wind shifts put them on again.
On some bleak August day, allow the child its sealskin,
despite the month's name. Many years of experience
assures me that no other plan can be wise in such a

climate as ours. While rashness is blamable, pre-prudence may be quite as mischievous. Children are made delicate by coddling.

No sooner had *The Art of Dress* been handed over to her publishers in the early summer of 1878 than M.E.H. made arrangements to leave Number 16 Welbeck Street which they had long outgrown as a family. New houses were springing up everywhere on the Portland estate and Cavendish Square and the nearby streets were noisier than ever. Carriages, carts and vans clattered about, unceasingly, during the day while, at night, more and more hansom cabs and growlers piled their trade as linkmen called out, noisily, for them. As for the smell of cow dung in Welbeck Street, it was stronger than ever! Every morning, a long procession of slow moving cows went past their door on their way to graze in St James's Park; in the evening, they returned to their byres in Marylebone. M.E.H. longed for more peace and quiet, not only for R. and herself during their long writing hours but for her children as well. Besides, they should have a garden now in which to play. A garden, she must find, somehow.

So she drove out in the direction of St John's Wood where an artistic colony was established among whose members, were the Alma Tademas and Frank Dickses, and many other of her friends. Very soon, she found exactly what she wanted; a roomy, two-storied house standing in its own garden just opposite Mr Thomas Lord's Cricket Ground. Number 34 St John's Wood Road (now vanished) was just the kind of villa residence of early Victorian date which John Claudius Loudon. the great horticulturist and architect designer, had upheld as a home for the professional classes of his day. M.E.H. was delighted with her new house because it was so unlike Number 16 Welbeck Street. There was ample scope for her to pursue different colour schemes and decoration in this countrified house. To begin with, she painted the outside a warm yellow for 'yellow was one of the finest colours which for years had been most unjustly despised'. Then, remembering with some amusement her failure with a white drawing-room in Welbeck Street, she decided that yellow should be the colour for her drawing-room in St John's Wood Road. How thankful was she that her taste was now completely assured and her touch certain.

Below a ceiling paper of a small amber pattern on a creamy background, she ran a deep cream frieze with an Adams design of classic gold swans and antique gold vases. For her actual wall-paper she chose a gold and white one and covered her chairs and settees in a silky Liberty material of the two shades as seen in a daffodil. Persian rugs in soft blue shades covered the floor.

A white marble mantelpiece had long been 'a most disagreeable object' to M.E.H. So she laid a deep strip of blue velvet stretched flat with fringe to match along this and then set her best pieces of Chelsea china on it. Above she hung an eighteenth century mirror whose frame of classic design enclosed, not shining glass, but a painting of Phaeton and his horses in dark, subtle browns, the shades of old leather. As a finishing touch to her shimmering, golden room, she placed between the door leading out into the garden and a tall window, a resplendent stool covered with orange silk, gold-embroidered, from Mr Liberty.

In Victorian times, an entrance hall often indicated the taste and status of the owner. Usually to be seen were such traditional features as a table to accommodate a papier mâché tray for cards and a niche to hold the latest design in an umbrella-and-stick stand.

The entrance hall of Number 34 St John's Wood Road was an exceptionally fine one with a black and white tiled floor. But it had a hideous grate. To hide this, M.E.H. put a large stuffed peacock with iridescent neck and gorgeous tail, outspread in the fireplace. As for that fashionable hall adjunct, a blackamoor lampstand which she loathed, she replaced it by bronze bust of Watt's Clytie. Finally, she painted all round the walls of her hall a fresco of tall, heraldic sunflowers which she loved, and christened her home The Amber House.

But before the children could see it, they were sent off rather hurriedly to stay with 'Granpie Haweis' in Sussex while their mother retired to Netley Cottage, Hampstead, where on 23rd July her fourth and last child, Stephen Hugh Willyams Haweis was born.

6. THE AMBER HOUSE

1878-1883

'When we got home, it wasn't home at all,' complained
Hugolin Haweis many years later in her book *Four to Fourteen*
which describes her childhood. 'But Ann said we had really
only changed houses. We were glad, for now we had a lovely
garden to play in!'

Indeed, it was a lovely garden that lay to the back of The
Amber House in St John's Wood Road. It had an orchard full
of apple, pear and plum trees laden with luscious, ripening
fruit. Prim box-edged paths that evoked a delicious smell of
spice on warm days wound their way past flower-beds crammed
full of brilliantly coloured autumn flowers; flowers like blazing
golden rod, michaelmas daises over which Red Admiral butterflies hovered, tall flaunting dahlias and pink, white and purple
phlox. There was a tangled thicket near the stables of rasp-
berry canes bearing a late crop of glistening dark-red and pale
golden berries which not only birds ate but two children
whenever they could steal away unwatched.

A hammock swung between an old medlar and mulberry
tree and on fine afternoons, M.E.H. would lie in it, swinging
herself gently to and fro with her tiny feet in bronze slippers
resting on a cushion. Sometimes she wrote in her hammock or
made notes; sometimes, she read aloud to Lionel and Hugolin
squatting on the grass below her. But if her mood was to
write, the children knew that they must go and play quietly
some way off so as not to be a nuisance. Neither must their
father be disturbed when he disappeared into the library to

146

write. They were very fond of their father who played funny games with them making swans out of wax or pretending to be an ogre. He was a better ogre than anyone else, they thought. But after they had moved into The Amber House, he seemed to be much away, lecturing 'to clever people so as to earn money to keep you, children,' their mother told them when asked.

They decided to earn money also and so their mother prepared a list of little jobs that they could undertake to help her in their new home. Wouldn't this be an excellent way to teach them the value of money in connection with doing honest work, she thought? So every time Lionel and Hugolin filled a sack with old newspapers they got threepence. Cook sold these sacks to a refuse collector at the back door. Another domestic chore was to pick up fallen branches or brittle twigs for firewood; another to help William clean out the chicken house; a job which they disliked much. Their mother had bought some hens to lay eggs for them. They were very small with beautiful pale blue combs and silvery plumage called Chinese Silkies. 'Just the kind of exotic birds your mother would have,' said Aunt Margaret Haweis one day, scornfully, when she was shown them. The latest Haweis arrival, called Stephen, was known as 'Apple Cheeks' because his cheeks were so rosy. But he did not come much into the lives of Lionel and Hugolin. He spent most of his days lying in his perambulator with its cream-fringed canopy in the garden. His sister would creep up, curious, to study him. Why did his milky-blue eyes stare so blankly in front of him, looking at nothing, she wondered? Much to her surprise, she had been given a nice plain holland smock to wear in the garden and, when it blew, a red tam o'shanter. Her long, high-waisted Welbeck Street frock with its blue sash and hated bonnet which made people turn round and stare at her in the street, saying 'Quite a Kate Greenaway' had been put away till Christmas, said kind Anny Fry, smiling.

Hugolin loved Ann who was always to be found when

wanted in the nursery. No longer the 'plain, immense' baby, she was very small for her age which was five. Her hands were 'like postage stamps', said her father when he held them. Her curly hair was kept short and she wore a pair of little gold earrings from France because her eyes were weak. By piercing her ears, her eyesight would improve, declared her mother. But of this Ann was not at all certain.

A curious uneasy relationship existed between Hugolin and her mother, for neither of them could express their real feelings to one another. They were, in fact, too much alike in character. Hugolin had all her wits about her and was quick and intelligent but undemonstrative. When her mother told her grandmother, Mrs Joy, that she wanted *hardening* and taught self-control and self-reliance because 'she is a poor, weak, squashy character, Ma, with no energy or sense of emulation' she was quite wrong in her analysis. Hugolin Haweis was to grow up anything but 'weak and squashy'.

Once the Haweis children had settled down at The Amber House an early morning routine was established in the nursery called 'Gymnasium'. Following some exercises like deep breathing and bending down to touch the toes, came drill in the garden where a trapeze was hung. Lionel had to stand up on it and sit down, three times while swinging on it all the time. Waiting her turn, Hugolin stood on one leg to improve her balance. M.E.H. wanted her children to be strong physically and agile.

Both Lionel and Hugolin stood rather in awe of their mother, knowing from hearsay how clever she was, writing books and painting 'quite beautifully' their father declared. Lionel who with his golden hair that stood out like a cloud from his head, Hugolin admired very much, had often been painted by her mother in his velvet suit with the lace collar. But she had never sat for her. Not even in one of her queer dresses. It never entered her head though to mind or even think about this, for what she liked best was to sit in the nursery with Ann, learning to read—not from her mother's

Chaucer for Children which was Lionel's book but from her own *Fred and Dolly* books which she much preferred though she could not say so except to Ann who merely replied, calmly: 'We can't all be clever like your mother, ducky!'

With Ann she learnt to hem dusters neatly and sew on a button as well as to read.

Christmas that year was celebrated by one Fancy Dress party after another for they were extremely fashionable. Hugolin enjoyed the one given by Mrs Walter Crane best at her house near the Shepherds Bush. Mrs Crane wore a lovely cape made of peacock's feathers which made her look like a fairy-tale princess, thought Hugolin.

In the New Year, she was sent to a small school for very young children at Brighton because she was so pale and needed strong, sea air. Lionel went to another school and only little Stephen remained at home.

Early in the spring of 1879 *The Art of Dress* appeared with its amusing drawings by the author. It set the seal on Mrs Haweis's reputation as *the* expert on women's clothes, both period and contemporary.

On her next appearance at a 'Drawing-room' dressed in a clinging gown of ivory Italian brocade with a train of brown plush velvet trimmed by cascades of Venetian point lace and clusters of bronze wallflowers and buttercups, her sole orna-ment the necklace of antique, cloudy amber she loved, she was surrounded by a crowd of enthusiastic admirers, anxious to hear her views on the dresses to be seen, that evening. Brought to a standstill under the glittering crown of a vast crystal chandelier decorated with drooping lustres like icicles, and ablaze with hundreds of little wax tapers, after she had left the Throne Room, M.E.H. held court with her husband standing beside. Years later, when writing his memoir of her, he proudly recorded almost word for word the witty commen-tary she had given on Court fashions, that evening.

'That sleeve, did you say? Why, it's a revival of the four-teenth century mode, but the loop has not been understood. The *modiste* had no idea for what it was originally meant. Besides, it really belongs to another period.' 'Those slashes? Quite absurd! The whole meaning of the slash was to reveal a rich under-garment and here there is none.' 'Loops without buttons and buttons without loops. Elizabethan? Yes, meant to be, but all that went with a different kind of dress.' 'Ah, that kind of pleat did come in with the Restoration but it was killed by the Duchess of Marlborough. I dare say that great lady over there with the lappet and pouch-like thing is not aware that it is a survival of the serf costume of Henry II's time and is really a badge of servitude . . .'

Then suddenly, with a characteristic little laugh, rather wicked, she turned on her small, high heels and made for the Supper room, followed by her husband leaning on his stick and smiling on all round him. M.E.H. could not help co-relating any question that she was asked with the endless historical facts, the art principles and dress customs of vanished days that were stored up inside her pretty head. Nor was she ever at a loss for a witty repartee if anyone tried to score a point off her. Invariably, it was she who came out best in an argument as most people already knew to their cost.

The summer of 1879 was spent as usual abroad. But this time Mrs Joy was left at The Amber House in charge of the children and servants.

Sept. 20*th*, 1879

My dear Ma,

I am glad you are comfortable—we are in the midst of lovely weather quite hot enough to be bearable and hardly any rain at all. We look straight on to the Jungfrau mountain and so the air is very healthy.

We went to see the Glacier at Grindelwald yesterday. It was a curious sight. A mass of blue ice and a cave dug

in to show effects of colour. It is very odd to walk on ice
in the midst of grass and wild flowers and strong sunshine.
It is many acres in extent and looks like a rough sea
congealed. I suppose Hugolin has returned to school by
now. She has been looking very pale in the holidays. I
hope Ann is not spoiling Baby.

We shall return on the 29th, I think, so I suppose you
will be leaving shortly as the servants must have a
thorough clean-up. I don't know where you think of
lodging but near us prices are ruinous—and no choice in
everything—especially food.

Yr Affectionate Daughter,

M.E.H.

It was after this trip that Hugolin complained bitterly to
Ann about her mother's love of dressing her up in unusual
clothes which she loathed. 'Mother *will* buy things from
abroad and bring them back to us. I wish she wouldn't. I
know they are always queer and original and I can see, too,
they are nice except when I have to wear them. Oh, Ann,
what shall I do?'

This time she had been given a pair of bright yellow stockings and told to wear them the following day. But their
colour enraged her. She felt like a hen in them. So she
continued grumbling:

I do wish Mother was more like other mothers. I like
being original and all that, but not all the time and never
when I am at school. Sometimes I don't think I like
Mother very much but when she makes funny faces and
laughs, I do! She is so pretty, too!

To all this Ann made no comment and continued knitting
for baby Stephen. Still, she did wish with Miss Hugolin that
the mistress would dress her more like other children.

But worse was to follow for Hugolin than her canary-
coloured stockings from Switzerland. In the Christmas
holidays she found a dress hanging in the cupboard of

her room which she hated on sight and remembered all her life:

'I had a black and white striped dress, the stripes very wide. The top was black and the sleeves were black up to the elbow. It really was a striped cover that was on a sofa and no one else had anything like it.'

They probably hadn't thought Hugolin's zebra-striped dress would be highly fashionable for a little girl today. Anyhow, her photograph wearing this dress survives and was used as a frontispiece to her book.

In the New Year of 1880, after Lionel and Hugolin had returned to school, M.E.H. sat down at her writing-table in the sunny, square little room which did duty for her boudoir at The Amber House and began work on what was to be her most important book *The Art of Decoration*. The time was just ripe for it as the 1880s saw the full domination of women in matters of household taste and culture. From the first small seeds sown by Charles Eastlake in his *Hints on Household Taste* a great tree had sprung whose branches spread now over the entire field of domestic art for women. Not for nothing had Mr William Loftie, F.S.A., who was a friend of the Haweises and on Macmillan's staff, become the editor of a series of engaging little books which appeared in 1878 under the title of *Art at Home*. The first one published *A Plea for Art in the House* Mr Loftie had written himself. The next by the Misses Rhoda and Agnes Garrett was called *Suggestions for House Decoration in Painting, Woodwork and Furniture* which that great exponent of the 'Do-it-yourself' school, Mrs Delany, would have highly approved of. Other volumes to appear were *The Drawing-room* by Mrs Orrinsmith who lived in a Beckenham villa and was considered quite an authority on house decor and the arrangement of flowers: *The Bedroom and Boudoir* by Lady Barker: and *The Dining-room* by Mrs Loftie.

But none of these good ladies could compete with the erudition and flair of Mrs Haweis when it came to writing such

Drawing of a tapestry bought by Mr. Haweis which M. E. H.
used as a book illustration

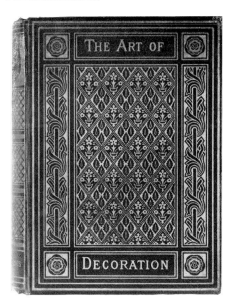

Cover and binding were
designed by the author

" *Yet Nature is made better by no mean,*
But Nature makes that mean; so o'er that art
Which, you say, adds to Nature, is an art
That Nature makes."—— SHAKESPEARE.

Frontispiece for *The Art of Decoration*

"In spite of all some shape of beauty moves away the pall from our dark spirits."
KEATS

Frontispiece for *The Art of Beauty* (1878)

A LADY CROSSING THE STREET IN THE OLDEN TIME.

Illustration from *Chaucer for Children* (1877)

an authoritative book as *The Art of Decoration*. Well over four hundred pages in length, it is full of fine illustrations that vary from a small-scale drawing of an *Iron bolt, French, 1550,* studied in M. Boucher des Perthes' private museum at Abbeville to a full page delineation of *A Pompean Room* seen in the *House of Germanicus, Palaces of the Caesars,* Rome.

The Art of Decoration is really composed of three books. The first deals with 'The Search After Beauty'; the second with 'A Retrospect of Rooms'; and the third with 'General Application' which embraces the treatment of walls, windows, lighting, ventilation and central heating in a house. In her opening chapter, M.E.H. stressed the need for the head of every English household: 'to care for beauty and to nurse our precious freedom to think for ourselves and to avoid the hated sheep-walk.'

In her last chapter she made an impassioned plea for all contemporary architects to be their own decorators as they had once been in the past. They should never be above designing a mantelpiece, wallpaper, carpet, furnishing fabric or piece of furniture like Mr William Morris, Edward Burne Jones, Walter Crane, Owen Jones or William Burges who have all had:

> more influence in raising public taste than others have had in half a century exhibiting at the Royal Academy or in Bond Street showrooms . . . Let us handcuff no one. Individual opinion is too precious to be sacrificed and in art matters it is better to bear with the blunders of those whose taste offends you, if their tastes result from thinking for themselves, than to reduce everybody to a dead level of propriety by Act of Parliament.

On finishing *The Art of Decoration*, M.E.H. gave a sigh of relief and resumed her social life with added zest. That autumn, she inaugurated the first of her 'Musical Evenings' at The Amber House. Her husband was a first-class violinist and as a boy so marked had been his talent for this instrument that he had thought of becoming a professional. But the call of the church had proved too strong. As music critic to *Truth* and *The Pall Mall Gazette* he helped to introduce and illuminate the music of Wagner to concert goers through his articles. Few musicians of note came to London without visiting his home.

For her 'Musical Evenings', M.E.H. designed herself a new dress from a piece of Japanese brocade bought at Liberty's which, lined in orange, was made after the fashion of a Court lady in Charles II's time. When she wore it her hair was arranged by her coiffeur in curls like a Lely lady, a hair style no one had thought of reviving.

Five days after Christmas of 1880 came the revolt of the Transvaal Boers against British rule which was to have such fatal repercussions in the years ahead. In the New Year, Kruger, soon to be known as *Ole Kroojer,* proclaimed the Boer Republic and inflicted a humiliating defeat at Majuba Hill on the British. But M.E.H. was curiously indifferent to the march of time, and like Jane Austen whose writings she admired, few contemporary events are mentioned in her correspondence or journals. In March 1881 Mrs Joy, still fighting a losing battle to keep up appearances on her dwindling income, is on the move once more. Her daughter writes:

The Amber House,
34 St John's Wood Road
March 2nd

My dear Ma,

So you are off again. You really ought to live in a gipsy's tent like Grandma! I think it must be dreadful changing so often unless you do it for occupation.

It is very difficult to send papers or articles of our own as we seldom have spare copies. I have not had anything small out lately except the description of a few notable houses in *The Queen* which is too fat to send and too expensive—besides not worth while.

I have a book coming out soon called *The Art of Decora-*

tion. It will be similar to *The Art of Beauty* but all about furniture and house decoration on which I am considered an authority.

We have been to some very grand parties lately, the Archbishop of Canterbury's and others. I met Lord Beaconsfield at one, among a number of distinguished persons and was astonished to see how young and handsome he looks, not over 50, and rather good-looking! Huxley and other scientific stars, Sir Stafford Northcote and various Ministers were all there and the Princess Christian. At one of the Aberdeen House Concerts on Wednesday where I went, there were some Royalties, and the Duke of Teck came and sat down by me and began talking about the concert which made me as nervous as a cat. I was very much astonished and when I got over it, pleased. I heard him whispering to Lady Mar something about the grey beads in my hair, asking if they were pearls— which they are sometimes taken for—but this was *sotto voce.*

I shall not go to the Drawing-Room this year, it is too expensive and, indeed, these parties are not cheap, but it is sometimes necessary to go, for the sake of being seen there.

Tonight we are going to a great party at the Countess Stanhope. I shall wear a cheap brown plush with petticoat of foreign stuff and Mrs James will lend me her fine diamonds. And everyone will think my dress worth £50.

I don't think there is any further news. The children are quite well. Lionel will be glad of any stamps.

With Love,

Yr Affectionate daughter,

M.E.H.

The grey beads in question were a species of Jamaican seeds known as Job's Tears which M.E.H. had pierced and strung into necklace form. She could admire but never envy the flashing diamonds, the rubies, the pearls worn by such friends as Lady Mar or Lady Waldgrave, knowing they were not for her.

About this time Lady Haberton pressed her to join the Rational Dress Society as Treasurer. But when M.E.H. saw how little real unity of aim and sisterly feeling existed among the members some of whom were advocating the wearing of the new 'divided' skirt, she resigned her post. Detesting clothes that aped masculine fashions—an odd streak in one who was such an impassioned supporter of the franchise movement—M.E.H. refused, steadily, to don 'bloomers' for the modish new pastime of cycling. But in spite of her position as a dress authority she could not fight a lone battle against the strong wind of change blowing through the world of Fashion. The eighties saw the firm establishment of 'artistic' clothes in London's leading Bohemian circles and the creation of proper sportswear, as young English girls took more and more to an out-of-door life, disdaining 'carriage exercise' like Elizabeth Bennett. Playing tennis on a country house or vicarage lawn, pretty young women displayed the latest 'tie-back' skirt topped by a Garibaldi shirt and mannish boater, or when 'botanising' wrapped themselves up in an Inverness cape or tweed ulster if the wind blew chill. On account though of her tiny weak feet, M.E.H. was never able to indulge in games of tennis or croquet or go on long tramps after wild flowers even if she wanted to. When she did ride a tricycle with her children or mounted a donkey in Morocco she wore an ordinary skirt and never one divided!

On April 5, 1881, England was forced to acknowledge the Boer Republic. Two weeks after, on Primrose Day to be, Lord Beaconsfield died, mourned by his Queen Empress and a nation grateful to him for long years of service.

That summer the *Art of Decoration*, destined to go into many editions, appeared and very soon after the Reverend Doctor and Mrs Haweis went North to stay with the Dowager Lady

Chesterfield, whom M.E.H. had first met at Broadlands and with whom she had got on so famously.

Bretby Park,
Burton-on-Trent
July 9th

My dear Ma,

We are staying with the Dowager Lady Chesterfield here and as it is too wet to go out I may as well write some letters! You asked where Cheadle is, it is near Manchester, a very big old Church quite a little Cathedral in its way. I don't think it is a good plan to write on postcards as the servants read them before giving them to us.

This is a splendid place full of every kind of precious object—much finer than Broadlands where the Cowper Temples [now Lord and Lady Mount Temple] live. There are all the State Rooms distinct from the living rooms, all stuffed with clocks worth £2,000 a-piece and that sort of thing! There is a niche or alcove in the dining-room for a silver fountain only put up on grand occasions. Lord Beaconsfield used to be here a great deal and Lady Dorothy Nevill told me he had made Lady Chesterfield an offer after Lady Beaconsfield's death. She is a very old Lady now but still very graceful and with beautiful features. The library is all carved like Gibbons' carvings and painted white with crimson and gold furniture, Louis Quinze time. Great galleries run along the house covered with old masters of every nationality like the National Gallery and the great staircase is very handsome with Turkey rugs. The park is full of deer and highly bred cattle. I daresay every other cow is worth £1,000! They have nearly all got foot-and-mouth disease so wealth is not without its thorns. There are a blue and a red drawing-room, a fine billiard room, etc., all very handsome and full of old pictures and marbles. It is politic staying at these houses when we are asked but not cheap. Lady Hester

Stanhope was a member of this family and Lord Stanhope whom we saw a little of last winter.

As to the Deanery of Westminster a simple Incumbent is never raised to that imminence at one step. I hear Doctor Butler, the Headmaster of Harrow, is to have it. It is said that the Bishop of Manchester was offered it but refused it. I do not think that preferment will come our way as R. rather aims at impressing the thought of his age and reforming the Church than looking after his own interests, and reformers are seldom rewarded in their lifetime whatever they may be afterwards. The Bishop of Durham has asked him to go up to Durham in October to address the Church Congress on the Subject of opening the Museums on Sunday: so that will be another expense.

I hear that Dr Bradley of Oxford is the new dean of Westminster.

Now with love,

Yr affectionate daughter,

M.E.H.

P.s. Our Church has been shut up for two or three Sundays —and while we are abroad it will be partly shut up for two months.

The days when the young Mary Eliza had dreamed, proudly, of her 'Dovey' becoming a canon like his father were over. By now she knew he was too unpredictable a person and too unconventional in his ways of preaching to be turned into a solid pillar of the Church wearing gaiters and a silk apron. Not that she had ever aspired to be a bishop's wife. Only a first-rate painter.

When autumn came, the Haweises went north to attend the Church Congress at Durham. They were put up by a rich Newcastle manufacturer and his wife who made much of them. On her return home, M.E.H. sent a letter to her mother now living at Malines.

158

The Amber House,
(Lord's) Regent's Park
October 9th

My dear Ma,

I sent you yesterday a Newcastle paper with 'the speech' of the Congress in it. R's paper is the only one which had a little paragraph in brackets after it, referring to the way it was received which stamps its importance and the impression it made.

We went to a big lunch in the Castle [Durham]. I sat next to Mrs Davidson, one of the Archbishop's daughters, and the Dean of Durham. The Cathedral is splendid and so is the Castle, all Norman architecture.

It is probable that you will see us next week as we are going to Rome and must pass through Belgium as R. has a fee to test some bells at Louvain. Hugolin wrote to say the Apron arrived safely. She liked it very much but I am afraid her letter was delayed.

With love,
Yr affectionate daughter,
M.E.H.

P.S. I send this cheque in case you want it but as R. is away staying with the Duke of Wellington he cannot put his signature to it till next week.

Just before Christmas, Mrs Joy asked her daughter to return several pictures of her Father's which up to now had been in her safe keeping. Ever since his death, M.E.H. had been most anxious that they should remain, intact, in the family. Once placed in her mother's improvident hands they might never be seen again.

The Amber House,
(Lord's) Regent's Park
Dec 21st

My dear Ma,

I will see about what you could have your things sent to

you for—but I think it is a great risk for the pictures and will probably be an expense to you which you would feel more than the pleasure of having them. They are all right now and I am much against varnishing as it is ultimately destructive of paint though it makes them look nice at first. You must remember you will have to pay their passage home one day as I ought to have them for Papa's sake. I am naturally solicitous that they should not be destroyed, lost or sold [which they were eventually].

I am just straight now having had rooms papered and two servants to find before Christmas, such a difficult time. The children are back. Lionel brought home a prize to our great surprise; his first report was not good but his Xmas one is, very. We had a nice time in Rome, lovely weather but I did not feel well, had bad headaches etc. There is no electricity in the air of Rome so I suppose it was that! I am all right in my native fogs. I never go out by day and that suits me. R. is very well, fearfully busy and so am I. I shall have to invent some new book after the holidays to bring in filthy lucre.

I think you are quite right not to winter in England. I wish you would cut out that bit about me in *Public Opinion* as I did not see it.

With best Xmas wishes,

Yr affectionate daughter,

M.E.H.

Never had there been such a Christmas holiday for fancy dress parties. Everyone seemed to be giving them. There had been even more than in the preceding year. But the palm for the most original one was awarded to Mrs Haweis for her medieval party. 'Everyone was so amused' wrote Hugolin. 'Mother had all the food laid out on a long table made of boards just as they would have done long ago. We sat all on one side of it only. I wore a dress down to my feet with long pointed shoes and fur edging my skirt and train and jacket. A long veil floated from the peak of my tall pointed hat. Lionel wore tights and parti-coloured hose, one white, one red, with a grand gold and red tunic. He carried a sword and there was a wreath on his head. Ann made our clothes.'

Her mother sent her own version of this party to Mrs Joy.

The Amber House,
(Lord's) Regent's Park
January 19*th,* 1882

My dear Ma,

I have not had a moment to see to your boxes and things but will do so directly the holidays are over. There have been a great many parties and I have to go to them as people won't have servants at them with big children. Our own fancy dress ball—a fourteenth-century one—was enormous trouble as I had to cut out half the dresses of the guests besides my own children's as the costumiers know *nothing* about such an early period! Several papers commented on it. For it was a great success. The rooms were decorated by Liberty at his own expense. I suppose he thought my name would advertise him and his loan would have cost anyone else eight to ten pounds. They were beautiful hangings. Lionel goes back to school on Friday. Hugolin a little later. They are quite well. We were at a fancy dress ball last night and go to another tomorrow. I drest up the tutor [John Brookes Penfold] as the Veiled Prophet of Khorasan in white calico and silver veil and he was the feature of the room. I went as Mme D'Aulnoy in white wig and one of my ordinary dresses. Hugolin had her nun's gown. It was a mixed party—not a period ball. Mine was much more interesting being just like the life of the time.

The 'evenings for the people' draw a great crowd. There is only one more. I have not been out for six weeks except at night. Does your *Public Opinion* arrive regularly? Let me know if not.

> With love,
> Yr affectionate daughter,
> M.E.H.

Ever since Arthur Lasenby Liberty had left the oriental department of Farmer & Roger's Great Cloak and Shawl Emporium and opened his own most fascinating shop named East India House in Regent Street, Mrs Haweis had been his patron. In love with the delicately coloured Indian silks and soft woollen fabrics he sold, with oriental china, Japanese fans, screens and bric-a-brac, she had helped him much by recommending her readers to visit East India House, the most fashionable shop for the diffusion of aestheticism in London.

In March, 1883, sad news came from Yorkshire while M.E.H. worked on her book to provide the much needed 'filthy lucre'. Walter Crane's charming sister, Lucy, had died from a heart attack during a lecturing tour. M.E.H. was much downcast. With her, Lucy Crane had been a pioneer in trying to educate women on art matters, though her medium had taken the form of the spoken, rather than the written word.

When M.E.H's *Beautiful Houses* came out, she sent a copy to her mother.

> The Amber House,
> (Lord's) Regent's Park
> *April* 12*th*

My dear Ma,

My little book is just out, so I send you a copy. It is got up in the style of the seventeenth-century books, you see.

I did all the illustrations, including the letters of the cover and the index and all the thinking! I have also been writing two Chaucer articles which will come out in *Belgravia* next month and the month after, I believe.

They cost me a great deal of labour and I had to draw two Seals of Chaucer which have never yet been engraved. It tried my eyes very much at the Records Office. I have parted with the copyright of *Chaucer for Children* which has been out six years and is still selling well. I have made £235 this spring and not before it was wanted! It sounds a large sum but it does not go very far.

I daresay you will notice that the red title and the lines of the book are not very exact. That was intentional—to be like the old rough hand-cut letters. I could have done them as exact as modern print if I had liked. I did not do the picture of the Villa Campagna. That is from an old plate lent to me and on copper. All the 'Initial' letters are portraits of portions of the houses I am describing; or something to do with them.

Mr Haweis is better, but has been very seriously ill. We thought a fortnight ago he would not get over it. Now he has been moved and is getting on.

Would you like to sell me your fan—not the thin wiry one that could not be used. I want a good fan badly. You could have it valued, or I would, at an antiquity shop. I may have a little cash coming in the month after next. I think as I never spend anything on myself I might invest in something I want after being so lucky. Some wives would go and buy some diamonds instead of sending their earnings to the Bank.

The children are very well. Baby goes to a day-school every morning. We have unsatisfactory accounts of Lionel. He seems very idle. But boys can do just as they like. He does not seems very clever either.

We are going out a great deal and I am looking forward to a month or six weeks by the sea. In Wales, probably.

Yr affectionate daughter,

M.E.H.

Beautiful Houses, which was published by Sampson Low,

is an attractive and well-produced book, every detail of whose designing was carried out by the author. It includes some of her best tiny-scale drawings enclosed in the 'Initial' letter which heads each chapter.

In all, M.E.H. described about a dozen 'artistic London houses' belonging to such celebrities as Sir Frederick Leighton's in Holland Lane and Mr Laurence Alma Tadema's in St John's Wood. In her Foreword she points out that the houses she chose reflected no well-defined period in art but were typical of certain minds and arranged with exquisite feeling and taste. One belonging to Mr Reuben Sassoon in Belgrave Square deserves special mention on account of an extraordinary fea-

ture described by Mrs Haweis. It possessed a lift, called the Stable Lift, which went from the ground floor up to the attic where a number of superb horses were stabled. Mr Sassoon was a noted collector of elegant carriages and it was his pride and joy to drive the lovely 'Jersey Lily' [Mrs Lillie Langtry] about London in a dashing curricle or four-in-hand.

The Sassoon horses were quite indifferent to going up and down in their leather-padded lift, M.E.H. was assured, and studying their immaculate loose-boxes lined with pale-coloured, artistic tiles, she thought this 'aerial stable' quite the latest thing in equine fashion.

During the summer of 1883 H.R.H. was much away involved with lecture tours that took him all over the north of England and M.E.H. found herself curiously restless. She had little work on hand except a dull text-book on *Chaucer for Schools* and she wondered if it was not time for them to move, again. There was little more she could do at the Amber House and even the garden did not need her attention. Like all interior decorators, she felt the urge to do up *another* house.

One evening while dining with friends in Chelsea she heard

quite by chance from a fellow guest that Dante Gabriel Rossetti's old home, Tudor House in Cheyne Walk, was in the market. In fact, it had been standing derelict and empty since his death the year before at Birchington-on-Sea.

Deep in thought, M.E.H. drove back to St John's Wood Road. She remembered the warm spring day when her father had taken her by boat from St George's Square pier to the landing-stage near the Old Swan Brewhouse. From here they had walked to Cheyne Walk where he showed her the home of the Pre-Raphaelite painter whom she admired so much. But with this early memory of a tall brick house with long, sash windows and a wrought iron entrance that faced the river, was another memory faint and vaguely disturbing.

Once in bed she felt so wide awake that she took out the second volume of her Thought Book from the drawer of her bedside table and began to turn the pages over, idly. Here and there she paused and read an entry. Suddenly, she came across one which arrested her attention. Dated the 5th of December, 1869, it described a curious dream in which her father had appeared to her most vividly. She had shown him over Number 16 Welbeck Street with its 'Orient things' that Gifford Palgrave had brought her from Trezibond. Then, suddenly, in the odd way things happen in dreams, there she was, standing hand-in-hand with Papa before a tall wrought-iron gateway looking into a paved courtyard while the sun shone down on a beautiful red-brick house: Tudor House, the home of Dante Gabriel Rossetti.

The following day, obeying a strong impulse, M.E.H. ordered the carriage round and told William to drive her to Chelsea. To Tudor House on the Embankment. Later that evening, she tackled R. on the question of moving house. Why not go to Chelsea and take Tudor House, Rossetti's old and very beautiful home? But he only replied that Tudor House was too far away from his church and it would be an expensive cab drive to Marylebone and back when the carriage was not available; that he knew the house was in a sad state of disrepair and the garden even worse neglected; above all, the rent would be too high and they should remain at The Amber House. To all this, M.E.H. turned a deaf ear and finally got her way.

> The Palace,
> Gloucester
> *September 5th*, 1883

My dear Ma,

I went to the fisheries to see about that picture ('The Wreck of the Forfarshire') and it *is* Papa's! It is hung over Grace Darling's own boat and the portraits of her and her father, also by Papa, hang at each side. They have been presented by the Duke of Northumberland to the Fraternity of Masters and Seamen of Dundee.

We are staying with the Bishop of Gloucester and Bristol. The Gloucester Festival is now going on. I suppose R. told you we are going to live at 16 Cheyne Walk, Rossetti's old home. The back of the house is very like Sloane Street. If you see the *Contemporary Review* this month, you will see a paper by me. But too technical to interest you, I think. It is on colours and clothes of the Middle Ages.

> With love,
> Yr affectionate daughter,
> M.E.H.

The die had been cast. She was going to live in the house of her dream.

7. QUEEN'S HOUSE

1884-1890

As soon as the lease for Tudor House was drawn up, signed and witnessed, M.E.H. set off by carriage again, to Chelsea. She went alone to see what most needed doing to the house before moving in.

It was a fine October afternoon with pale sunlight illuminating sharply the buildings she drove past. Such a light, a painter's light, always delighted her and her spirits rose rapidly as she sat gazing intently about her. It certainly was a long drive to Chelsea down Baker Street to the Marble Arch and beyond through Hyde Park. R. was right. But, in time, he would get used to it, she thought. When William drew up finally before the now familiar entrance in Cheyne Walk, M.E.H. jumped out on to the pavement with the same thrill of excitement she had known alighting, as a bride, before the door of her first home, Number 16 Welbeck Street. Once inside the paved forecourt which had jasmines growing up its two high brick walls, she paused to study the facade of the house now hers. One half of it was entirely covered by a fiery sheet of virginia creeper infested, at that moment, with drab little London sparrows sunning themselves. As their loud chatter met her ears, there came the hoot from a distant tug converging on old wooden Battersea Bridge. Her face lit up with pleasure. How lovely to be so near her beloved river.

With its blank, uncurtained windows very much in need of a good wash and polish, Tudor House had a withdrawn look. Had Rossetti so stood, she wondered, on the day of his first visit when a lonely unhappy and homeless man tormented by tragic memories of his dead wife, he had felt like her the all-powerful attraction of this house and taken it for twenty-two momentous years?

With the thought of Rossetti uppermost in her mind, M.E.H. opened the front door and entered the watchful, waiting house. Beyond an entrance lobby lay the large hall strikingly paved with black-and-white marble. The panelling was painted black and white to match. On either side of the lobby entrance was an alcove fitted with a seat for a servant to occupy when, in the eighteenth century, they accompanied their masters to make a call. Beside each alcove was a door.

Opening the right-hand door, M.E.H. entered a room once used by Rossetti as his eating-parlour which she immediately consigned to be the family's 'Little Dining-room'. It had a fine mantelpiece decorated by blue-and-white Dutch tiles put in by the painter who had also designed the mantelpiece made from a dozen handsome Japanese trays. In a corner her quick eye saw a curious object on the floor which was soon in her hand. It was a little whisk composed of a few mouldy peacock's feathers which she vaguely remembered reading somewhere Rossetti liked to make, calling them his 'Japanese brooms'. She laid it reverentially on the mantelpiece. It was as if she had come across the sign of some invisible presence, perhaps one of many haunting the house. What had its rooms not seen? What not experienced during the long period of their existence? She must tread delicately as if before a tribunal of unseen witnesses. Like on a sensitised camera plate, she felt past history had been recorded on the walls round her. Given time, she would try and piece together the fragments of a story heard from various Chelsea sources. She made up her mind also to re-create this dead house and make it a living entity once more which it would be her pride to inhabit and which would give aesthetic pleasure to all who came through its door.

Leaving the little room in which she had found Rossetti's 'Japanese broom', she went into the one opposite; an exact replica even to the same blue-and-white tiled grate and mantel-piece. Here, she thought, the Haweis collection of fine engravings and drawings could hang and it would be called the Print Room.

She crossed the spacious hall and entered Rossetti's studio, a large square room whose long north window overlooked the garden reached by an iron staircase from a verandah outside. From this window, M.E.H. stared out on to the garden so much loved and used by the Rossetti family, especially by Christine and her mother whenever they came to spend the day with Gabriel in Chelsea. It had a desolate air. Gone was the menagerie of fantastic animals once kept in it including that 'delightful creature', Rossetti's beloved wombat. Gone, too, were the peacocks whose raucous cries had made night hideous and who had been so detested by the inhabitants of Cheyne Walk. A little avenue of pollarded limes, leafless now, lined the weedy gravel path leading to the far end of the garden. What strenuous hours of work, of pruning and digging, of cutting back and clearing away that jungle of rank growth where flowers must have once made sweet the air lay here, thought M.E.H., peering out of the dirt-engrained window.

Very much depressed by the sight of a once lovely garden left to rack and ruin, she turned from nature run wild to admire the classic proportions of the studio with its four fluted columns painted black-and-white and a black ceiling encircled by a wide band of gold-leaf paint. In here, Dante Gabriel Rossetti had stood for hours, brush in hand, painting. Here had hung many of his finished masterpieces. Such works of genius as 'The Blessed Damozel' leaning from out her golden bar of Heaven; 'Pandora' clasping the box (now hers) from which her curiosity had loosed all manner of evils upon an unsuspecting world; 'Lady Lilith', that mysterious, beautiful woman whom Adam first loved before Eve. Had not Rossetti's favourite model, Fanny Cornforth, posed for that haunting face? For many years, M.E.H. had followed, step by step, the career of her favourite painter and attended any exhibition

where a picture of his might be seen. Now she stood, alone,
in his studio. It was a memorable moment fraught with
mixed feelings of which pity for his tragic end, prematurely
brought about by drugs and depression, was uppermost. She
gave a little sigh. Poor man! And then, she thought suddenly,
sadly, of her father. Dead, too, before his time. But the light
was darkening. She must attend to matters in hand, and
dwell no more on the nostalgic past.

After a careful appraisal of the whole room, she decided it
must become her 'old Darling's' library with bookcases lining
the walls where once there had stood a great army of canvases.

The bookcases she would design herself. On grand occasions, though, they would entertain here when it would become the 'Big Dining-room'. On the farthest wall there was ample space to hang her father's 'Supper at Emmaus' which he had designed to be part of an altar-piece for Boughton Monchelsea Church and which she had reclaimed as the present vicar wished to instal a modern reredos instead. Under the balda-chin of carved wood in black-and-gilt, could stand her hus-band's two Van Aerschodt bells, so dearly prized by him.

She knew that there were two stairs in Tudor House: the one of hammered iron that ascended, spiral-wise, to the left of the studio door she now took. It had a right-hand 'angled' turn followed by another that led to a half-way room with a double door. This very high and narrow room had two windows. A large one opening on to a small iron verandah: another, much smaller, set high up in the ceiling indicating that the upper half of this room had once been a 'concealed' priest's room whose floor had been removed at some time.

A few steps more and she reached the beautiful long draw-ing-room with its seven tall windows from which the broad river, busy with passing barges and tugs was visible and beyond it the misty outline of the distant Kentish hills. M.E.H's heart leapt at the sight of this elegant beautiful room whose fine panelling was lit by the warm rays of the westering sun. Here between the years 1862 and 1870, the poet-painter and leader of the pre-Raphaelite movement had entertained the art and literary stars of his day; here he had displayed his famous collection of Nakin china; his own pictures and antique furniture. Here, in April 1865, he had given a memo-rable party to his most intimate friends. The youthful Swinburne with his crest of flaming hair and green eyes, shrilly-tongued, had come; William Morris brought his beauti-ful wife, Janey; kindly Ford Madox Brown and his family struggled to arrive on time by devious routes from Kentish Town; Whistler with thick black hair and monocle stuck in one eye had tried to take the floor but failed; and gliding, quietly, from guest to guest, in plain silk gown, there was Christina, gentle hostess, low-spoken and kind to all.

But there were other ghosts besides those Pre-Raphaelites, who stood far off, as it might be said, in the wings of this long, historic room. Shadowy figures far more remote in time than those that had once peopled Rossetti's world and of whose presence the small motionless figure by the window was quite unaware. How fast the river flowed, thought M.E.H. It must be almost high tide. But where she could remember a low brick wall broken at intervals by a flight of slippery steps leading down to mouldering ferry-stages, there rose a stone embankment built by Bazalgette in 1874. This embankment now stretched from Chelsea to Blackfriars and might have reached the Tower if the 'City Fathers' had not put personal profit above public good. She was pleased to see that a line of fine elms, known as the Bishop's Walk, had survived. In the near future, she must walk by the river to see how many of the old familiar landmarks of her childhood remained or had been ruthlessly swept away. The old Swan Brewhouse, where they had once taken those delicious 'strawberry teas', did it still exist?

Reviving this happy memory, she stood by the long window till a sound from the court below interrupted her reverie. Poor William! Was he growing cold? For he had begun to stamp about on the paving. The carriage horse appeared to be restless, too. She really must continue her tour of inspection.

Turning from the window, she noted the exact colour of the walls. They were yellow, the colour she loved, and little faded. At the far end, the fire-place designed for burning great logs and complete with tall, iron dogs, was lined with beautiful old Persian tiles put in place by Rossetti. How fortunate they had not been removed at the time of the sale, she thought.

From the drawing-room she came to Rossetti's bedroom that appeared to lie over the studio below. Its long windows gave out on to a ten-foot verandah with lead flooring. She decided to make this room her own in spite of its air of gloom. An eerie gloom largely caused by the heavy shade of green paint used on the walls. What strange spells and visions this room must have known. Strange spells and visions emanating from the chloral drugged mind of a sick, haunted man, tossing to and fro, sleepless in bed. Not that she was in the least daunted by the sinister atmosphere of this room. On the contrary, she looked forward to sleeping here in her own carved bed, dated 1665, which she had picked up for a song.

As M.E.H. knew that the rooms the children and servants would occupy were reached by the second staircase ascending by the butler's pantry on the ground floor, she retraced her way to the hall where she decided to leave them for another day.

Gathering her skirt up in one hand, she decended bravely into the basement where she was appalled by the gloom and horrible smell of damp. The big kitchen was not so badly lit but the tunnel-like passages beyond were extremely dark. As for the sculleries and wine cellars she peered into, they were like dungeons! At the end of one passage, she caught the glimmer from a pool of stagnant water. How close did this subterranean part of the house lie in relation to the river, she wondered? Could it be flooded at times? She shivered. She must bring R. here to investigate.

Returning to the black-and-white paved hall, she sat down in one alcove and drew out her familiar little red note-book, while William continued to wait patiently for her outside.

The following week an army of painters, carpenters and cleaners moved into Tudor House. After a discreet interval, M.E.H. accompanied by her husband arrived to explore the cellars where the foreman said certain excavations undertaken for better drainage had revealed portions of a curious wooden gate at the end of one passage. To H.R.H.'s delight, this proved to be the remains of an old water-gate, obviously connected with King Henry VIII's vanished palace of Chelsea.

The extraordinary thickness of many of the cellar walls and the size and texture of their bricks bore out the local tradition, that Tudor House, reputed to be of Caroline date, must have been built on earlier foundations; quite possibly on those of some part of Henry VIII's palace which had once stretched east of Oakley Street to the Albert Bridge.

Early in the New Year of 1884, the Reverend H. R. Haweis and his wife moved into their new home swept clean of dust and cobwebs. The rooms no longer smelt of damp and decay but of scrubbing soap, beeswax and fresh paint. Very soon, M.E.H. was writing to her mother.

> Queen's House,
> 16, Cheyne Walk
> *March 3rd,* 1884

My Dear Ma,

The above turns out to be our address as the house is supposed to be one of the original row built by Queen Catherine, wife of Charles II, and the monogram CR is on the gate. I had not seen the notice you sent me, and should have liked to have the whole as Magazines are dear to buy. I am glad I am appreciated by somebody. I saw a notice in some paper stating 'Mrs Haweis is the queen of a very clever set'—I don't know what set or how a queen, but I am glad the public think I am one!

My books sell, which is necessary enough, for we have very heavy expenses. I find eatables, etc., cheap down here as I can get everything from the Stores, but it takes a long time getting them. House-rent is extremely high. Some of the red-brick houses in Cheyne Walk are £700 to £800 a year besides premium. I cannot imagine how people pay for it.

I was going to ask when you said you were not well if there was anything I could get for you at the Stores but remembering the abuse which my last offer of this kind provoked, I desisted. Still I will order anything you like.

Did I tell you I had Papa's bureau thoroughly done up? It turns out a very fine piece of furniture. All the inside drawers handsomely marked and two secret drawers revealed. But they are empty!

It had got very damaged in three moves. Now I keep it for house-keeping papers and my other for literary work. I have not had time for writing all this winter.

We are all quite well and the children at school.

Yr affectionate daughter,

M.E.H.

She was still very much occupied with Queen's House. For years now the rooms in which she lived had become of supreme importance. In other people's houses there were rooms that could make her feel 'physically ill' because of a bad cornice or ugly grate such as she had to contend with at The Amber House; a ceiling that was too low or a window set too high. The display of shoddy furniture or curtains of vulgar pattern and colour also got on her nerves, particularly when not expected, and she was quite frank enough to say so. But this was not affectation on her part as most people knew. 'I never knew anyone with so powerful a mind who was also so dependent on her personal surroundings and miserable without them' said her husband of her.

On account, though, of the classic proportions and innate elegance of the rooms at Queen's House, M.E.H. had few problems as to their decoration and furnishing. The first to be finished was the long drawing-room whose delicate yellow panelling was retained. In one corner where she could best see the river M.E.H. put the beautiful Moorish-Hispano bureau which had once belonged to a Spanish queen and at which she always wrote. On it stood a striking medieval drug-pot kept filled with fresh flowers and a handsome casket containing odds-and-ends such as string, sealing-wax etc., which Rossetti had once owned and 'painted' into his picture of Pandora.

A large settee made of dark Spanish oak, carved and dated

1605, stood against one wall; a china cabinet on another. Instead of the heavy Flemish brass chandeliers that had hung from the ceiling in Rossetti's day, M.E.H. suspended her own glittering Venetian glass ones on gilt chains which suited the room much better.

Treffry Dunn, Rossetti's companion who lived for so many years with him at Tudor House, has left on record that the poet's room was 'most unhealthy to sleep in' largely because the heavy dark-blue, crewelled hangings round his ponderous bed were rarely drawn. By the time that Mrs Haweis had done with Rossetti's bedroom, none of his friends would have recognised it; least of all Treffry Dunn.

Although she kept the forest green paint of its walls and Indian red dado, it seemed much lighter now. It was also more feminine. For it contained such charming personal things as her inlaid ivory toilet boxes, her silver brushes, her Etruscan table lamp and the little antique shelf that housed a falcon's hood and a pair of hawking gloves belonging to her father.

M.E.H. always affirmed that she slept neither worse nor better in the room where once the great painter had so feverishly tossed and turned. Like him, she suffered from insomnia but never took drugs or sleeping potions. To while away the long night hours she read, and, for years, had a candle always burning in a small glass dish beside her bed. She maintained a big reserve, too, of what she called her 'sleep' books ordered from Mudie's.

An odd sound which had always plagued Rossetti and others persisted in the house throughout the Haweises' tenancy. This sound resembled the heavy tramp of feet, and was heard at night on the front stairs. To try and deaden it, M.E.H. had the outside of the double door belonging to the half-way room covered with green baize. But this had no effect. The noise continued as it had always done, never to be explained.

At last as March was drawing to a close with high winds

but open skies and sharp, cold sunlight, M.E.H. set the final seal of her ownership of Queen's House by placing a statue of Mercury after 'Giovanni di Bologna' on the roof. For years, he stood there, against the sky. Mercury, messenger of the gods and of communications, the planet that governs writers, and by which she was greatly influenced.

Only then, with her home arranged more or less to her liking did she dismiss the old carpenter who had helped her with many a painting and decorating job. The Chelsea refuse cart appeared and took away the last bundles of torn newspaper, the scattered straw and discarded packing cases which mark the scene of a major move-in. M.E.H. breathed a sigh of relief. At last it was all over! They were 'in' and she could relax once more and enjoy in peace and she hoped, security, the lovely house of her dream.

One sunny afternoon early in April, she went into the drawing-room after hanging on the door-knob outside a neat placard inscribed: 'Please Don't Disturb': a long-established custom of hers. The seagulls, she saw, were wheeling and screaming high over the river, from whose surface came such a sparkle, it looked as if made of diamonds. All along the Bishop's Walk the elm buds were swelling crimson. Spring had come to Chelsea. She sat down at her bureau and, drawing two sheets of paper towards her, sheets that are so yellow now, thin and brittle, wrote the following lines in her firm, clear hand:

Queen's House, Cheyne Walk

This house is one of the most interesting in London and, perhaps, one of the oldest still standing in Chelsea. It is said to have been built for Catherine of Braganza, and the monograms containing CR introduced in the sixteenth-century ironwork of the gate are said to represent Catherine Regina. Anyhow it is a house probably built by Sir Christopher Wren, who did all the work in Chelsea for Charles II. The long drawing-room in which I habitually sit (as I am at this moment) with its seven tall windows

overlooking the Thames has various stories connected
with it. Queen Elizabeth—as a child—is supposed to have
paced up and down it and flirted with Admiral Seymour
with whom she had stolen interviews at the little postern
gate (now destroyed) in the garden area at the end of the
subterranean passage which is now blocked up. The ghost
of Queen Catherine Parr, her stepmother, is supposed to
haunt the stairs, and others, one a small girl in Tudor
dress following a little boy. But all this is impossible
legend because the whole fabric of the house is Caroline
and *not* Tudor except the foundations some of which we
uncovered and which are made of old narrow bricks of
Henry VIII's time. There is little doubt that his Palace
in Chelsea stretched along Cheyne Walk and part of the
old water-gate we found once belonged to it.

My interest in Rossetti who first showed me the way to
freedom though I cannot be called his pupil in any sense,
induced me to retain his colouring of the rooms which are
all panelled throughout. His studio, perhaps the finest
room in the house, is my husband's study; his old parlour
our breakfast parlour. Several of the rooms contain
mantelpieces actually built and coloured by his hand. I
have luckily inherited from my father's family much fine
old Caroline furniture which suits the house admirably.
It is difficult, and I think mistaken, to adhere strictly to
one period in furnishing, and while the main tone is
Caroline, we are sufficiently eclectic to admit pictures by
Sir Thomas Lawrence, Davis, Morland, Etty, T. M. Joy
and others, and such modern comforts as are indispensable. My well-known views on house decoration have been
fairly realised. The deep yellow of the drawing-room walls
with the old Spanish leather of Lord Byron's screen, and
curtains belonging to Napoleon Bonaparte form an entirely 'becoming' background. Of the deep green of
Rossetti's bedroom with its dado of Indian red, the same
thing can be said: even my hard-worked bureau of

Hispano-Moorish work is none the less picturesque because useful. You see, like Rossetti, I enjoy brilliant colouring and do not 'go in' for *the imitation Queen Anne!*

I do not go out as much as I used and the entirely satisfying character of lines and colours belonging to a fine period house, semi-human pugs and cats, and last but not least my up and growing family when I can get them are making me sympathise more and more with Cardinal Richelieu when he sighed '*Faut-il quitter tout cela?*'

On their return home for the holidays, Lionel, Hugolin and Stephen were entranced to find that they were living so close to the Thames. A far more exciting element than the high walled-in gardens and leafy groves of St John's Wood. Hugolin, in particular, was much intrigued by the view she had from her third floor bedroom window of old Battersea Bridge, gas-lit. Though it was now closed to horse-traffic, pedestrians could still cross it on a raised footpath for a half-penny each. As a treat, the Haweis children walked over it, learning from their mother how this old wooden bridgehead had been painted, many times, by famous painters like **De Wint**, Turner and Whistler.

One day they were taken to see **Mr** Carlyle's house in Cheyne Row; another time to see his bronze statue recently put up in Embankment Garden close by. But they failed to find the old Swan Brewhouse where their mother and Aunt Edith had once eaten strawberries and cream and listened to the old bumboat women shouting to one another from their bobbing craft in mid-stream. The corner where it had once stood had been demolished for the building of the Embankment. Though the enchanting river-village of Chelsea was changing rapidly like the rest of village London, it still retained much of its old character, especially along the muddy foreshore by Lindsey Row where Charles II used to bathe from the reeds 'in the Thames over against Chelsey'.

Hanging over the broken wall by Lindsey Row, the Haweis

children could still see men setting their eel-pots, or count the heavily laden coal barges swinging in to moor on the flood tide. Another fascination was the Chelsea lamplighter coming along Cheyne Walk at dusk with his ladder 'dropping stars in his track' as Hugolin put it watching him from her window.

At Queen's House, she soon realised that indoor as well as outside life was quite different from the one they had known in St John's Wood. To begin with, there was a new footman called Minnis who had to clean and prepare over twenty-seven oil lamps for daily use. Hugolin's sharp eyes missed nothing, like her mother's, and she was quite prepared to help Minnis at his irksome job if he told her enthralling tales of his double life. It seemed that he was really a female impersonator by profession and he only became a footman during the winter months. Come the spring, he would join a musical troupe booked to appear in June on a seaside pier. One evening, greatly daring and encouraged by Hugolin, Minnis dressed up as a woman and danced and sang before her and little Stephen with Cook and Ann Fry in attendance. This performance had to be given in great secrecy in the kitchen, as talking to the servants or hindering them in any way from doing their work was strictly forbidden. If Minnis' performance had been discovered severe punishment would have followed and all pocket money been stopped.

To Hugolin's sorrow, Minnis left at the end of the Easter holidays and a black servant called Selim was engaged, who created quite a stir in Chelsea circles. But when her mother was asked why she kept a negro page, she only said: 'It was very fashionable during the eighteenth-century. I am reviving the habit.' Still, in the end Selim left, like Minnis before him.

After the children had returned to school, the garden was tackled. Shrubberies were cleared, roses pruned back and new flower-beds dug. At the extreme end of the lime walk, several cages and tumbledown sheds were found hidden in the thick undergrowth. In them Rossetti's fantastic beasts had been housed. Save two they were demolished and in the couple repaired the elegant Chinese Silkies from The Amber House were put.

Absorbed in garden matters, M.E.H. decided that her next book should be about town gardens and its title *Rus in Urbe*: or *Flowers that thrive in London Gardens and Smoky Towns*. For ever since she had tended her arum lily and moss-plant in those days of dreary exile at Kilburn she had been interested in the cultivation of flowers and pot plants.

M.E.H. was lucky in her new publisher, Andrew Tuer of the Leadenhall Press, known to be a printer more aware of the past than the present. Although Tuer affected 'Ye Olde' styles in book production, it was said that he really did it more in fun than in seriousness. However, on signing up Mrs Haweis, he allowed her full scope as her own illustrator. The result was an attractive little book bound in yellow cloth decorated with a scatter of falling leaves in bronze, sage-green and crimson. The frontispiece—a drawing in sepia—showed two children picking flowers beside a stream. The small woodcuts of a picotee, a hollyhock, a primula, a perennial poppy and a foxglove were equally charming.

Although M.E.H. cannot be placed in the same category as those classic Victorian lady gardeners, Mrs Loudon, Miss Jekyll and Miss Ellen Willmott who all had great horticultural knowledge besides green fingers, *Rus in Urbe* provides many a fresh and unusual idea in garden matters and floral arrangements. 'Why not whitewash or redden like your front doorstep your leads on high, and then railing them round for security, create a *second room*?' asked Mrs Hawies.

This term 'second room' is constantly met with in women's journals of today when referring to the present fashion of making a penthouse garden or patio. M.E.H. who always used her eyes to great advantage when travelling abroad wanted the gloomy back-yards and roofs of London houses to be Italianised and made into little gardens by furnishing them with tall terra-cotta jars, urns and flower-boxes in which

attractive foliage plants and flowers could flourish. If a
London house did happen to have a garden—and in the
eighties there were many—why did it so often contain only
'One lilac bush that never blooms and an earwig?' she complained bitterly. She strongly recommended the cultivation
of plants with unusual foliage for:

Leaves never offend. Leaves can be velvet or furry; like a
hand; like a shield; like a feather or like a folded fan . . .
It is thought rather vulgar now to have much lavender on
view but in my opinion whole stacks of dove-blue blossom
are a grand ornament wherever they occur.

She anticipated Constance Spry's School of Floristry by
almost fifty years. Like her she 'positioned' her floral arrangements in her rooms at Queen's House allowing light, artificial
or not, to fall on them. Thus she emphasised the dramatic
outline of a single spike of hemlock placed in a tall jar on a
window ledge or high-lighted a massive bunch of curly-leaved
parsley. Original vases and containers, ignored in her day,
like a large Spode soup tureen, were utilised, beside a common
or garden saucer which she loved to fill to the brim with pink-
tipped lawn daisies for these pretty little flowers always
reminded her of Chaucer.

In conclusion, she made a list of 'Things That Please Me'.
Among them was a red-cheeked apple and a ripe scented
peach which she liked placed:

Not on the dining-room table but in a shell in my room
because of their smell and niceness to touch . . . a saucer
of purple beans on a Buhl table or a few brown beech nuts
on an old silver salver may point every lesson by a flower.
I like the Indian passion for stringing seeds into necklaces,
belts and bags: I like their soft rattling sound. I have a
weakness for cloves stuck in oranges and horse-chestnuts
are dear to me in and out of season in their bright-green
leather cases. In conclusion, I would say: 'Let spring,
summer, autumn and winter give definite tone to your
rooms'.

With *Rus in Urbe* finished in the spring of 1885, M.E.H. made plans to accompany her husband to America where he had been appointed Lowell Lecturer at Boston.

They left in July and their visit was an unqualified success. Wherever she went, Americans took Mrs Haweis to their hearts while she, in turn, fell in love with their go-ahead country; their racy speech with new words and phrases so descriptive to her ears; their independent way of life with few social taboos or class distinctions. America's climate seemed charged with electricity. She felt so well that she was her sparkling and most witty self.

The Haweises went to Boston, Philadelphia, New York, Detroit, Baltimore and Chicago. Everywhere they were feted and entertained, meeting many literary celebrities of the day like Olive Wendell Holmes and the Longfellows.

At Vasser and Ogontz (a high class school for girls) M.E.H. was introduced to the new Transatlantic Girl in whom she was intensely interested. She was enchanted by the best types of American girlhood and frankly said so. She found them more independent and intellectually advanced than English girls of their age and social standing. They moved quicker; thought quicker; and, in general, lived at a far quicker pace, both as spinsters and young 'marrieds'. Interviewed wherever she went (her books had been printed in the States and widely read) M.E.H. resisted all attempts to get her to speak in public. But later in England she lectured several times on American Womanhood.

On arriving home, she installed two bathrooms at Queen's House after the American style, one for herself, the other for the children. Of her own bathroom she wrote in *The Art of Housekeeping:*

The only real *bain de luxe* is one fixed in your bedroom or dressing-room in the American way, which saves trotting about the house. It is most agreeable when sunk in the floor instead of standing so as to require nearly as much clambering as a five-barred gate.

When visitors evinced an interest in the Cheyne Walk *bain de luxe* they were quickly taken to see it. A genuine American rocking-chair in bentwood was also on view, for M.E.H. had been much attracted by the American women who sat in their porch on 'rockers' knitting and passing the time of day with their next-door neighbours.

In autumn of 1885, it was decided to move Lionel Haweis from King's College School, London, where he was a backward and unsatisfactory pupil and send him to board with the Reverend Gammack and his wife who lived in Aberdeen. Here he was to receive special coaching at the same time as he attended the local Grammar School.

About this time, too, M.E.H's long correspondence with her mother to whom she had once wanted to give £100 a year because 'she was the best creature in the world though she sometimes writes me disagreeable letters' entirely ceased. In its place, there began a long and faithfully sustained correspondence with her eldest child, Lionel, which ended only at her death.

That autumn, Aunt Sarah Joy—the last surviving Joy aunt —died at Box, near Bath, and M.E.H. inherited more fine china and furniture. Assisted by Hugolin, the china was washed, labelled and arranged in the long drawing-room where a wall panel was opened to receive it.

In the spring of 1886, *Rus in Urbe* was published. Later the Haweises started on a round of visits in the West country. They ended up at Boskenna, the Cornish home of Mary Paynter (H.R.H's eldest sister). Writing to Lionel, M.E.H. tells him his Aunt:

Was a more agreeable hostess than she has been for years, as she had no incessant meetings and school feasts and could attend to her guests. I moved all the furniture and improved many of the rooms; hung up blue china etc. which if I can do nothing else, I can do well . . . Tell me how you are getting on at school and let's have a little news. All the people in Devon and Cornwall seem nearly teetotallers. Curious how the fashion is growing. Hardly any wine or beer offered. Like America. With love, Y. affect. Muz.

After the Christmas holidays, Lionel Haweis was sent to board with Sophie Kammerer, his father's old German governess who had nursed him as a child through his hip-disease. She lived in Brunswick where Lionel was to concentrate on learning German, perfect German, and nothing else.

Early in the New Year, M.E.H. fell ill and was ordered to take a rest, which she did, lodging at Madeira Hall, Ventnor, in the Isle of Wight.

> Queen's House,
> Cheyne Walk, s.w.
> *March 6th*, 1887

Dear Lionel,

I have heard nothing of you from Miss K. and so was not prepared for your shout of woe. I wish you'd say a little more—then I could judge better and would say to them what you wish. But I do think that operettas and Mark Twain ought to have been quite put aside for the present as every English word or even English thought discounts a German word in the first few months. I should grind if I were you at easy German books and poetry, not like a 'willing horse' as you call it, but a raging mad horse. . . . We have just come back from Ventnor where we have been nearly three weeks. But I don't feel much better, rather antiquated I fear. Hugolin has a cold and looks odious. Father is not very bright, working too hard, but bills must be paid and so must German lessons. . . . It is foully cold and raw here—the Thames a nice iron grey and the pavements white in comparison; which means frost. No buds out though in Ventnor violets and hearts-ease are already in bloom. I hope you will send me some sketches of Brunswick (some with pencil and some with pen). Let me know exactly the state of things. You must hold your breath and not say hasty things. I think they mean well—but I daresay you have trials. German life and ways are stricter than ours. Yr. loving Muz.

The cold persisted. Lionel heard that it was fiendish! 'You know the medieval hell was not a fire but ice regions, and I am very medieval'. To make the situation worse they were without a cook or manservant at Queen's House. Neither were to be had for love or money, it seemed.

A month later, M.E.H. was ill again, and they retired to Margate. A hateful but healthy hole. But weren't all healthy things hateful? And the cold! It was even worse at Margate. They returned to London where she caught a fresh and worse chill.

But summer came at last. The glorious summer of the Jubilee year when golden weather with not a cloud in the sky continued for weeks on end in England. London went mad celebrating fifty long years of peace and prosperity at home while an aging Queen-Empress, still mourning her beloved Albert, reluctantly consented to make a triumphal tour of her capital by carriage to attend service at St Paul's Cathedral. Bunting, flags and illuminations were the order of the day. Far away in Brunswick, Lionel was told that the decorations of Queen's House were considered the best in Chelsea as 'we all put our backs into it!' Bonfires were lighted in pails every evening in the forecourt. Chinese lanterns hung on strings above the portico and every window with curtains undrawn till midnight radiated light. As a final touch, the letters 'VRI' were picked out on the bow front in coloured lamps and a painted buffalo skin (picture side uppermost) labelled 'The Colonies' was hung by Hugolin from her bedroom window.

Before the Jubilee procession, there came the Naval Review in June.

Queen's House
(*Undated*)

Dearest Lionel,

We went last night to the Naval Review, staying on board a friend's yacht. The Review was pretty, so many hundreds of ships all 'drest' with flags which at Sundown were replaced by coloured lamps and electric flashings. I never saw the masts 'manned' before and it looks very handsome. All the men like caterpillars on end along the yards. The Queen was too far off to see except just the procession of yachts and men-of-war. But I don't like yacht life. It is so dreadfully monotonous and the difficulty we had in getting back was awful as everybody was off their heads if not drunk. We could not get a train for three hours after we reached the station and starting at twelve pm only reached London at five in the morning! I was as nearly dead as ever I was in my life. Father had strength to post off to morning service but I went to bed. It really was an awful business and not worth the agony, though the fireworks and illuminations a very pretty sight at night . . . Send me some sketches when you can of where you go. Grandpie is back from Switzerland—a little aged but otherwise wonderful. With bestest love, Your loving Muz.

By 15th July poor M.E.H. was feeling ill again and planned a seaside holiday for August.

We have three little new chickens, she wrote to Lionel. I should like queer beasts all over the place (like Rossetti) but your Father is made so miserable by any creature not human that we have to be merciful. I must say no more or Hugolin will say I have told you all the news. Are you rowing, cricketing, duelling? Thy loving Mutterlein. P.S. Are you reading Heine yet?

On 16th July an important ceremony took place just

opposite the iron gates of Queen's House, watched by M.E.H. Among a crowd of notable figures, Holman Hunt, R.A., unveiled a bronze medallion of Dante Gabriel Rossetti which had been designed by his friend Madox Brown, and placed above a drinking-fountain, the work of John Seddon which still stands today in the small public garden in front of Queen's House. After the ceremony, fully reported in *The Times,* the Reverend H. R. Haweis came out and asked any who cared to visit his house. 'A considerable number availed themselves of this opportunity to visit Rossetti's old home'. M.E.H. must have been delighted at such an invasion of celebrities.

In August, the Haweis family departed to Swanage in Dorset.

Toy Cottage
August 23rd

Dearest Lionel,

I weep to see how near the 24th is [his birthday] so that you won't get this on your birthday. It is not for want of thinking of you though. . . . I don't know how to send you anything as this is a Godforsaken place! I must tell you something of it at the risk of being thought dull. It is a mixture of Lee and Clovelly with pretty cottages in grey Purbeck stone; irregular roofs paved with stones; stone edges to the garden; stone floors which are decidedly cold to my poor feet. This cottage is temp. Chas. II. Built of stone and inside reeds and plaster take the place of laths. My bedroom is only seven feet high. The drawing-room is panelled like Queen's House. There is a pretty old garden full of old-fashioned flowers and a huge mulberry tree. The back of the house is covered by a huge passion flower in bloom. The drawback to these glories is, a dearth of food, harvest bugs and the absence of a cook. There is good bathing and Wuz bathes every day with his offspring. I sit and look at their unpicturesque gyrations. I never knew how hideous my relations were till I went thro' this trial. . . .

It has been lovely weather, very warm, and we have taken various expeditions accompanied by a very small and weak donkey which I ride with Pompey and Dolly [her pugs] on my lap. Wuz [Hugolin's name for her father] leading the donkey said, one day, he felt reminded of the old pictures of the Flight into Egypt by the Holy family. . . . Answer my question about German and don't spell light *lite* any more. With bestest love and enquiries after the waving beard. The loving Mutterer.

This is the last picture of the Haweis family relaxed and happy on holiday. From now on, a cloud at first no bigger than a child's hand appeared on the horizon which, in time, swelled to such dark and menacing proportions that it eventually destroyed the whole fabric and pattern of family life at Queen's House.

On their return to London, Hugolin became so troublesome that she was sent to Miss Buss's North London Collegiate School where, her mother declared, 'She will be in glory if she works and in Coventry if she does not.'

From Brunswick Lionel Haweis tiresomely gave out that he wished to be a musician. He was behaving in as idle and feckless a way as his sister, composing silly waltzes when he should have been consolidating his German. Very soon he received a sharp summons home from his mother.

Queen's House,
Cheyne Walk, s.w.
Nov. 27th, 1887

Dearest Lionel,

We have quite made up our minds that you must come back at Xmas. I hope you don't mind this dragon severity. . . . We shall probably send you to a brother of Mr Praetorius [Stephen Haweis's school-master] in Wiesbaden

as I don't expect you are firm in German yet. An extra
nail or two will be safer. . . . I wonder whether in a German curio shop you could find me a beautifully worked
antique key, cheap. I want an elegant artistic filigree key
to hang on my chatelaine and Germany used to be celebrated for its delicate iron work. Your affectionate
Mother. (P.S.) I want you to bring some Rhenish tum-
blers. They are very common greenish glass with a rib
round. I like them for flowers. How I wish you would
make me some sketches of Brunswick—you may never
be there again.

Nor was he, or at Wiesbaden either. For after a shocking
report from Miss Kammerer of his indolence, his old tutor,
Jack Penfold, offered to have him at King William's College,
Isle of Man, where he had got a mastership. Thus he would
be able to keep an eye on him.

As his grandfather offered £50 and his Aunt Paynter £20
towards his college expenses, Lionel was sent down to Boskenna to stay a few days and express his thanks. But once
there he took French leave.

Queen's House
31/1/88

Dear Lionel,
When you went to Boskenna you were told to return
on the 30th. When I found that Mr Walters would not
give you another day I wrote to you. When I say a day
I do not mean a fortnight. If you wish to be treated as
grown up it is sufficient to remind you what an important
time the present is to you. I am sorry you have forgotten
it. If you must be treated as a child, your aunts must be
telegraphed to, to send you, which we have now done.
You are due at Man on Wednesday night or Thursday
morning. School began last Thursday and only by favour
you have had a week's grace. We are very anxious not to

offend the Headmaster who only takes you as a pupil at
all by favour. I shall be glad if you will remember that!
Your affectionate Mother.

In March, the first shadow of that small cloud looming up
on the family horizon made itself felt. Lionel was warned by
his mother that 'there are awful rocks ahead in the money
way.' For some years she had been aware of these rocks,
partly submerged, and tried to steer her own financial course
between them as best she could by saving every possible
penny from her hard-won press earnings. The ever-growing
lack of ready cash in the pockets of the head of the household
alarmed her.

And not only did it alarm, it mystified. For scarcely a
week went by with R. not lecturing somewhere at a fee of £10.
Besides this source for money, there were his royalties for
innumerable books already published, and cheques for commissioned articles flowed in. The Sunday collections at St
James's plus the pew rents maintained a high level, yet R.
rarely had any cash on him. He also seemed to be a worried
man. Why, M.E.H. kept asking herself? Why?

To disturb her still further vague rumours reached her ears
that her husband was paying rather marked attention to two
or three lady members of his congregation. In particular, to a
rich spinster called Miss Souter. Could there be smoke without
fire, she wondered? Only too well did she know from past
experience of R.'s 'funny little caressive ways' which had
caused her such pain as a vulnerable girl. But it was one thing
for a young curate to indulge in agreeable philandering. Quite
another for a notable divine of the Church to attract gossip.
However she decided to say nothing for what was there to
say when nothing of a definite scandalous nature was attached
to the Incumbent of St James's silly flirtations? At least, his
wife hoped there might be safety in numbers.

That summer, with a view to launching Hugolin, rising
seventeen, on Society, M.E.H. began to take her to one or an-

other function. Together, they attended the Private View of the Royal Academy and went to an afternoon party at Lambeth Palace.

Queen's House,
Cheyne Walk, s.w.
July 12*th*

My dearest Lionel,

Pen says a report of you was sent a month ago. I wish the reports were sent to *me*. For Father has mislaid it. I am looking forward to the holidays as I want some triking. H. is very well, very bobbish. I took her to the Archbishop's in the old waisted high dress of my great-Grandmother. She was *much admired*—but don't tell her. She is considered *very pretty*. She is also getting quite sensible. I hope you don't get any headaches now. I do. Got one now. So can't write more. Your loving Muz.

It must be recorded that M.E.H. was sincerely anxious to make her teenage daughter as attractive as possible. As if she was composing a picture of her own, she decided what were the right colours that Hugolin should wear besides the right style to suit her petite, graceful figure so like hers. In any age, few adolescent daughters will take this kind of dress-direction from their mothers. The more so if, like Hugolin Haweis, they possessed strong wills of their own and were not in sympathy with maternal authority.

For years, Hugolin had detested the 'arty' type of Kate Greenaway clothes she had been forced to wear. Now she realised that contrary to any wish she might express, this 'aesthetic' style of dressing was to continue in her adult life. It was really more than she could bear. Still for the time being she said nothing. For she planned a temporary campaign of passive co-operation till she was older. There were days, though, when she moodily hunched her shoulders and wore an offending garment in the most unbecoming way possible hoping to show people how badly her mother dressed her and so gain their sympathy and pity for the future. There were others when she completely abandoned this attitude and did not 'look like a rag-bag' as her mother put it!

What with trying to stage-manage a successful debut for Hugolin in preparation for presenting her, early, at Court, and impressing on Lionel not to be so extravagant, M.E.H. was fully occupied. Her eldest son had taken to smoking, a habit she deplored, and having an excessively sweet tooth led him to pay constant visits to the school tuck-shop. 'Father' she kept telling him' is very much worried about money. I suppose he will never quite clear himself. I shall have to stop Hugolin's finishing classes if your expenses increase. But it can't be helped. You must be pushed! However, I think you are a canny old bird at bottom.' It was sad but they could not afford to go away to the sea that summer. Still, M.E.H. promised her children that 'We shall try by tricycles and other things to make the holidays bearable in London.'

Tricycling was very much *á la mode* and much enjoyed by the elegant Mrs Haweis who wore a suitable tweed skirt for the exercise. She had managed to obtain an old but adequate tandem for Lionel and herself to ride, or for him and Hugolin, while Stephen had a small 'trike' of his own given to him by Grandpie. Needless to say, the head of the household rode a brand-new Velociman. Thus the Haweis family were seen exercising themselves about London.

So the August and September holidays passed quietly in Chelsea and, later, for a brief spell H.R.H. took his wife to stay at the New Ship Hotel, Brighton, where he was engaged to give one or two lectures. M.E.H. was not at all well and remained in poor health caused by continual domestic and marital worry.

On their return to London, Lionel was notified that his mother was trying to organise some form of home entertainment for Christmas because 'There won't be much tricycling at Xmas and no money, so I feel rather up a tree unless we can fix some cheap dances. But you need not publish the cheapness!' She needed his help to get hold of some 'steady boys with respectable fathers' as dancing partners for Hugolin and her friends.

In March of 1889, M.E.H. and her husband went to stay with friends in Tangier. Her doctor hoped the change might do her good. It was a new experience for her to meet 'the Moors, who are so picturesque, and our garden a mass of arums and palms, and the housemaid, tho' black, a vision of loveliness.' She rode about on a donkey with R. at her side on a mule and enjoyed herself enormously. Just as she was beginning to feel better, they had to return home.

In May the financial position was no better at Queen's House, and the Matron at King William's College was asked to see if Lionel's vests were really past mending. There was no chance either of a summer holiday. 'You must begin to earn soon now for we can't keep up the expense' Lionel was told, and then 'Stephen has gone back to school. But Hugolin can't go yet. I want to save half a term—a great loss to her. However, she is very useful at home.'

By return of post, Lionel Haweis wrote a letter which so touched his mother that she immediately replied expressing feelings that go far to refute the many accusations levelled against her by her sisters-in-law that she was completely unmaternal at heart.

Queen's House
May 11*th*

My dearest boy,
I have read your kind thoughtful letter very carefully. I am most glad and thankful for what you say. Perhaps it would oftener be better to confide in me and avoid lots of little misunderstandings. You must not think we have such a low opinion of you or anything but the most heart-felt wish for your welfare. You must not think commerce discreditable or in any way beneath your father's position.

In these days, dukes' sons are glad to go into tea and barons' into beer. There is not the slightest slur. It is only that commerce is what you *make* it. It *confers* no honour like the learned professions but it *derives* honour from the honourable men connected with it. . . . I have never had any doubt of your future myself if you were willing to grind though I have sometimes had doubts about the grinding. We look to our eldest son—not to our youngest—to be Head of the family and to be the happiness he was when a small child and the only one. I cannot bear the idea of your not being all I would have you and it is really, dear Lionel, because I am sometimes worried and disappointed and I fear impatient, mixed up with all the squalid little details of housekeeping, that I seem irritated and cross, when I am only worried and longing for you to be better than every other boy in the world. I know it is a horrid grind working on in the dark as it were, with no prospect visible, but the light will come all in a minute as the Bridegroom came to the Virgins, and must find you watching and working. . . . I often wish I was stronger. I could do so much more for all of you but when I have a headache here and a backache there and something else every other minute, it is difficult to be patient and equable. I used to be so much stronger. Never mind about me and my holidays. I shall scriggle on somehow. The first consequence is to plant you out and give you *every* opportunity of 'growing'. I am sure you will not miss the chances. . . . I don't suppose you realise what a comfort and pride a grown-up son can be to his parents. Don't be afraid to ask me for anything you want. I shall always try and let you have it. You have never been extravagant. I wish we had more to give you. As soon as ever we can get you into something where you can earn, you won't feel that you are a drain. Never forget that I am your most earnest and anxious friend and will do everything I can think of. I have had a small weep. But I am all right now and hopeful of the future, colonial or otherwise.

Now about 'squalids'. Ask Pen about boots . . . Hugolin is learning something about housekeeping at home—that is one thing. She is very good-natured. I must not scribble any more. Grind on madly till we can hear of something however small where you can feel a free man. Your loving Mother.

With Hugolin at a loose end at home to save her school fees, her mother tried to interest her in the running of a house. Besides wishing her to be an ornament in society, she wanted her to be a competent housewife. So she wrote *The Art of Housekeeping: A Bridal Garland* which she dedicated to her daughter in the hope that it might please her vanity.

Mrs Beeton's formidable book on *Household Management* numbers over a thousand pages and has fifty glossy plates of delectable dishes in gorgeous technicolour. It sold over 60,000 copies during the first year of publication and is still going strong. Mrs Haweis's *The Art of Housekeeping* is a quarter of its size and quite forgotten. As usual, she supplied her own illustrations and her text reads like a series of polished essays on such subjects as: Houses For the Happy; Domestic Servants; Hints For The Storeroom; Costs and Quantities. No culinary recipes are given, for M.E.H. advised the young bride to go to Mrs Beeton 'with whom I generally agree, though I join issue on certain important points!'

One reviewer wrote that 'no mistress of a household would or could carry out economies which are almost Quixotic' to which M.E.H. replied, tartly, in print 'That is because no-one would take the trouble!' Certainly one person never did, and that was her daughter Hugolin. For instead of inspiring her to take an interest in the way her mother ran Queen's House and kept her faultless accounts, Hugolin was heard to declare that 'All domestic matters bore me!' She was intent on learning the banjo and saw a good deal of her mother's friends the

'Ionides who were so rich that you must not make comparisons between their scale of living and ours' warned her mother.

Money, or rather the lack of it however hard she worked, was still uppermost in her mind. In July, Queen's House was closed and the Haweis family moved to Novello Cottage near Worthing. Before their departure M.E.H. wrote to Lionel and in her letter there is a special reference to Miss Souter.

Queen's House,
Cheyne Walk, s.w.
July 7th

My dear Lionel,

I have seen Mr Carberry about your learning commercial German which you could easily get up on the top of the language in a general way. I don't know whether Father has told you we have a new East window and reredos promised by Miss Souter. It will be such an improvement. Miss Souter gives nearly every Sunday the most lovely flowers. She is very rich and liberal. We have been going out a good deal and I am very seedy and overdone and going away soon to recover at Worthing with the family. The house will be shut up. I am also advised for you to learn Spanish in case you go out to Buenos Aires, the coming place. Your last report is a much better one than usual. Mind you ask everyone you meet about commerce. Write to Granpie and Aunt Paynter too. They have not 'struck' yet about money. Very glad to hear of your cricket successes.

Your affectionate mother,
M.E.H.

At Worthing, H.R.H. fell off an enormous hired 'trike' and dislocated his shoulder. This accident considerably frightened his wife, and added to their expenses, as a surgeon was called in and had to see him every day. They were all glad to return home at the end of September.

Before Christmas was on her, M.E.H. started to plan some holiday amusements for her children.

Queen's House,
Cheyne Walk, s.w.
November 6th

My dear Lionel,

Will it be a pleasure to you if we give some 'afternoon carpet dances' at Xmas? It is a great trouble and an expense so if you don't care about it, you may as well say so. But I don't mind taking trouble if you all enjoy it. I am however this year very denuded of men and it will be no use giving the series unless you bag some presentable fellows and good dancers (six or more) from K.W.C. I thought of the parties being informal and merry; not stiff. Of course, good music and grub. It is really very difficult to know what to do with you all in winter, especially you, for you don't seem to enjoy the holidays in the least or be able to fall in with anyone's ways. So think over the idea. Hugolin is very pleased and written down lots of names. Your affectionate Mother (very seedy indeed for a week).

At this moment came a letter at long last from her mother to which her daughter replied.

Queen's House,
Cheyne Walk, s.w.
December 2nd, 1889

My dear Ma,

I was in Droitwich when your letter came. I am sorry to hear you are not well. I don't think any of us grow any younger. I suffer dreadfully from rheumatism and neuralgia, but I do not think it is the house. I think it is connected with Papa's gouty constitution which often becomes neuralgia in the next generation. I am much better this autumn but till then may I say I have been really ill one way or the other for one and a quarter years. Weak digestion is the worst pain though. So don't get that! I suppose you know Alcock's plasters. They are capital for chronic rheumatism.

You never told me if you began the all-wool style of clothing for which I sent you some cash as I could not send the clothes without duty. I wanted you to try the experiment.

I do not write because you never write, so I do not know what to say but I often think of you. We are thinking of putting Lionel in a bank if we can find a place. Boys seems to be a dreadful expense and anxiety. But he has had a stroke of good luck. This summer a friend took him travelling *en prince*—Vienna, Berlin, Dresden and everywhere else. Some friends took us too this autumn, all expenses paid, to Paris where we enjoyed the Exhibition. No holidays now except business ones. The other children are quite well. But expenses have to be met with increasing hard and strenuous work which one does not grow stronger to perform, unfortunately.

I will send you a copy of my new book *The Art of House-keeping* which has come out. I hear you consider I don't know anything about keeping house. This book will shew you. I shall not get any money for it till 1,000 copies have sold. . . .

Old Canon Haweis is going to have his birthday dinner here on Wednesday. He will be 85. Active as ever but rather deaf. I have a very bad head today and cannot write more now.

With love,
Yr aff. Daughter,
M.E.H.

It was sad that M.E.H. and her mother were no longer on intimate terms as before. This was mainly due to the fact that Mrs Joy lived abroad with her still unmarried daughter Edith, who had always been acutely jealous of M.E.H. 'queening' it so unfairly, as she thought, in London, while she was forced to live in dreary exile.

Conscientiously, M.E.H. made fresh enquiries about sending her mother another supply of Dr Jaeger's wonderful all-wool clothes. She rightly guessed that the money for their purchase had been spent on other things. Since 1883 when a Mr L.R.S. Tomalin had obtained the sole agency in London for selling Dr Jaeger's Sanitary Woollen Clothing, Mrs Haweis, Oscar Wilde (whom she cordially detested), Bernard Shaw and others had been ardent 'Wolleners'. She insisted on her husband wearing a Jaeger woolly vest next to his skin while travelling.

For the moment, he was hectically lecturing in the north of England. Manchester, Blackpool, Sunderland, Liverpool and other cities saw his small, ungainly figure stumbling up, hampered by his club foot, on to the platform of one dreary hall after another. But once enthroned above the crowd gathered to hear him, he was transformed from a puny maniken to a king-lion raging in action. With flashing eyes, dramatic, gesticulating hands that he used like an actor, he kept his audience spellbound. There was no doubt that the Reverend Hugh Reginald Haweis was a great orator. But it was a hard, wearing life for a man of his frail physique and medical history. For his travelling was mostly done at night and every weekend saw him forced to return to duty at St James's, Marylebone. But as he had come to be billed everywhere in large letters and drew enormous audiences, he rarely grumbled. For he adored to take the centre of any stage and be its focal point of attraction. It was the applause and adulation of people who came to hear him for the first time, people that he must constantly woo and conquer afresh that had become the very breath of life to him', so much that like a powerful drug it had become of paramount importance to him. In spite however of his lecturing fees collected weekly, there was never enough money to meet either the expenses of his children's education or those of Queen's House.

There remained only one thing to do, thought M.E.H., and that was to end Lionel's schooling, from which he had benefitted so little, in spite of all Jack Penfold's efforts and extra coaching. At Christmas, Lionel Haweis left King William's College, Isle of Man, to become a humble bank-clerk living at home in London.

8. THE BREAK-UP OF FAMILY LIFE

1890-1895

FROM 1890 ONWARDS, the pattern of family life at Queen's House underwent a dramatic change even as the face of London had begun to change rapidly. Historic landmarks were being swept away to make room for new City streets while many slum areas disappeared completely. As for the Aesthetic Movement which had seen its peak years in the eighties, this movement now received its final quietus at the hands of those who brought Oscar Wilde, its leader, to public trial and ignominy.

Long-established social customs and habits, fashions in clothes and interior decoration, were in a state of flux and the first seeds for the coming of Art Nouveau being sown in the Paris studio of Alphonse Mucha. But in this movement M.E.H. was to remain entirely disinterested. For her mind was set on other things. Good works were in the air and gay though the Nineties have been called such an adjective only applied to a small cross-section of Society. There was a sombre, reverse side to the garish glitter and ostentatious display of newly-acquired wealth in high circles particularly those bent on gate-crashing into the much envied 'Marlborough House' set.

Through London streets marched General Booth leading his 'Hallelujah Band' of ragged men and women while in Hyde Park, by the Marble Arch, men in rags with white, bitter faces and hoarse voices screamed out for social justice and the long-denied rights of the worker and underdog.

In her Chelsea drawing-room M.E.H. who had become an ardent Suffragette made her own stand to uphold the cause of philanthropic works. She wrote early in 1890:

At the present time I am helping popular movements rather by my pen than by my presence though I hold many lectures and drawing-room meetings—among them for the rights of women. I have no special work on hand except that I am involved in the preparation of the Chaucer Concordance projected by Doctor F. J. Furnivall.

It was just as well that she had no serious work on hand for hers was an uneasy and troublesome household. Installed at his bank and hating business life, Lionel Haweis was proving difficult to manage. A self-opinionated boy at this time and intensely reserved because of his innate shyness, he carried a permanent chip on his shoulder largely due to the failure of his scholastic career. To assert his grown-up independence he took a day off from work when he liked and without permission, thought far more of his writing activities than of being a good bank clerk and declined to follow the advice, however tactfully given, of his parents.

Hugolin, who had been presented at Court by now, and 'come out' was little easier to control than Lionel. With extremely decided views of her own, she could never be relied on for long. One day she would be most amenable; the next all prickles and thorns and glumly silent. She had developed a strong, secretive vein in her character like her father. But that was not all. Very stupidly she treated the boys of her own age that Lionel brought to the house with a superior kind of contempt which did not endear her to them and openly declared that 'she preferred married men.' She rarely invited her own girl-friends to Queen's House and, when she did, never allowed them to become friendly with anybody but herself. In fact, she regarded her friends as personal, private property and was hostile to any form of supervision by her mother. Believing strongly that girls should remain under parental authority until they married there was constant friction now between M.E.H. and her daughter.

Alone at Queen's House young Stephen, working hard at St Paul's Preparatory School with Westminster ahead of him, gave no trouble. At the end of January 1890, for economy reasons and because old Doctor Bird said she needed sea air and rest, M.E.H. engaged a cook-housekeeper to look after Lionel and Stephen at Queen's House and departed with her daughter to Novello Cottage, Worthing. Here she went for short walks with Hugolin and, sipping hot milk every evening, struggled to overcome the many ailments now afflicting her exhausted mind and body.

While she was away, H.R.H. remained in perpetual transit. His lecture tours took him here there and everywhere but with little ready money to show for his labours. He wrote almost daily to his 'Darling' begging her to whip up an egg and add it with claret, sherry or rum to her glass of hot milk at night. He wrote from grand addresses such as The Palace at Gloucester, or Manchester, or from dreary waiting-rooms in provincial stations, sometimes even in jolting trains, for it seemed he had his wife's health very much in his mind. And he always signed himself 'her loving but lonely Gumble or Giffin or P. B. (Poor Boffin).'

In February M.E.H. returned for a brief stay at Queen's House with Hugolin and gave one or two of her famous 'Lecturettes', a new kind of social entertainment which she had inaugurated. They took place on different days of the week depending on which month they were given, beginning at 4 pm and ending at 7 pm. Some lecturettes featured literary stars who spoke on subjects specially connected with their work; others presented stage celebrities who gave dramatic recitals. Famous singers and instrumentalists were invited to perform, too, whenever Mrs Haweis was 'At Home', musically.

In April, bent on further retrenchment, she rented a small

Surrey villa called Franklyn's Green for the Easter holidays. Here she decided to stay the whole summer, describing her rustic retreat to her eldest son as 'a funny little place' which he wouldn't enjoy much because of 'constant menial labours'.

Lionel Haweis was still being troublesome. Alone at Queen's House with Stephen and Alice, the cook-housekeeper, he kept complaining to his 'Aunts' and friends that the food was poor and he felt lonely and ill-treated. Naturally his stories came back to his parents and his mother wrote him a sharp letter.

Franklyn's Green
August 22nd, 1891

Dear Lionel,

I hear you have been complaining to Father that I wished you to eat a diseased fowl. This is exceedingly nice and dutiful in you and likely to please me very much. It is however not in the remotest degree true as you know very well; and a great deal that you say against us, and against me in particular, to very nearly everybody is perfectly untrue. Your stories come back to us from all sides. I do not know what you imagine you gain by blackening and abusing the only people who will ever do anything for you: and I think you actually make enemies, for no-one admires a son for abusing his home, nor will people who know us believe you are greatly ill-used. I have tried to make the best of you for many years and to everyone. If I tried to make the worst of you, I should not have to draw far in my imagination. I am extremely displeased by this last episode and have long been with much that I hear about your complaints of your home. We have always done our very best to make you happy and to give you the advantages other boys of your position have had. The result is no doubt failure but I do not see what we could do more. Picturesque descriptions of your loneliness and ill-treatment will only be laughed at by our friends. Amongst those who do not, you may injure us both more than perhaps, you intend. I thought it better to write this and have it over though it has gone beyond the question of your apparently inadequate diet.

Your affectionate

Mother.

Following this letter, Lionel was interviewed by his father to whom he apologised. Eventually it was decided by his parents that it might be best for him to lead an independent life by going to lodgings while Queen's House remained more or less shut up.

In the autumn, H.R.H. darted over to Belgium to visit two well-known bell foundries and to see Mrs Joy. En route for home, he wrote from his packet boat in mid-channel.

October 1st, 1891

My darling Darling,

I am scribbling a line at sea which I will post on arrival. I spent yesterday most profitably interviewing the great Belgian sculptor Lambeaux in his studio and have material for an article just written for the *Graphic*. In the afternoon I went to Louvain and spent several hours in the Foundry making researches with tuning forks, tone-metres and compasses, analysing sounds and vibrations. I think I have mastered what I wish to know, experimentally. The van Aershodts [a well-known family of bell-makers] have built a splendid new house on the scale of the Hyde Park houses only with a brick and stone facade; half old Amsterdam in style, half Roman-Greek. The boat is tossing and I hear it blows outside. So I have just swallowed a bottle of stout but have small hope of surviving! I foresee from the information I have acquired that there may be in store a good deal of business in connection with Belgian bells by-and-by. You must not be surprised if I do not make large sums. But I must be careful in my position how I go to work! I mean sooner or later to make myself necessary both to the van Aerschodts and to the people who want bells. That can only be done by worming myself into the work naturally and occasional visits like this one create a good impression.

(Later) Rough passage just over. Uncomfortable but not sick. P.B. (Poor Boffin).

On M.E.H.'s return to Cheyne Walk from her long stay in Surrey, she gave two 'carpet dances' for her children at Christmas and several of her lecturette 'At Homes' in the New Year. But she was still suffering from constant headaches and bouts of rheumatism.

On February 13th, 1891, the beautiful long drawing-room at Queen's House was ablaze with shimmering candle-light and packed full with celebrities. Exquisitely gowned ladies escorted by gentlemen in full evening dress with some wearing medals came and went up the tapestry-hung staircase. It was a unique occasion, for the lecture arranged by Mrs Haweis was on 'The Phonograph' given by Colonel Gouraud. To the amazement of everyone present, from a small black instrument placed on a little table the recorded voice of the dead poet Robert Browning came echoing through the room where he himself had stood so often. This evening was reported widely by the press.

A month later, on the 23rd March Mrs Joy died of cancer at her home in Belgium, and her eldest daughter who had long felt estranged from her wept alone in her London drawing-room. H.R.H. hurried over to Malines and took the funeral service. Barely a week later he married Edith Joy to Charles Moureau, an adventurer who afterwards squandered his wife's small inheritance and left her for his mistress, which embittered her still further against her sister, Mary Eliza.

In July of this same year, old Canon Haweis died at Slaugham in Sussex and much family squabbling followed over his

will. M.E.H. thought it a most unfair one, as both her husband's sisters, Mary Paynter and Margaret Haweis, never very
amicable towards her, inherited far more by it than he did.
But H.R.H. refused to make a stand for his rights as eldest
son, to her lasting disappointment.

That summer was passed at Steyning Rectory near Hors-
ham where H.R.H. acted as *locum tenens* and his wife, still
harassed by illness, did little more than lie out on fine days
in a wicker chaise-longue contemplating the lovely shape and
line of the distant Downs. Much to her surprise just after she
had celebrated her eighteenth birthday, Hugolin was asked to
stay a few days with her Aunt Margaret Haweis.

Steyning Rectory
Sept. 14th, 1891

My dear Lionel,

The shirts that I thought of giving you (Jaegers) are at
Queen's House. Hugolin has just returned from a couple
of days at her aunt's who sent for her 'to give her some
little valuables' but did not do so in the end! Hugolin does
not seem to have had the screaming time she expected.
There is a comic side however even to that. I have not
yet discovered what she was really wanted for: it is the
first time she has been asked for several years. Stephen
has begun riding on the black pony and is getting on fine
in spite of several spills. He looks capital on the creature.

With best love,
Your affectionate
Mother

Little did she know that her daughter's visit, to be repeated
so often in the years to come, would have fatal repercussions
resulting in their complete estrangement from one another.

In the meantime the Reverend H. R. Haweis was seldom
at home that autumn. But he kept his wife informed of all
his movements, writing ecstatically from Dundee:

Elmslea, Dundee
Oct. 26th

My darling,

I did a splendid sermon in the evening and the Church presented a wonderful appearance. The pulpit platform on which I stood was crowded and all the avenues and doors blocked with people standing, the whole area one mass and galleries (eighteen rows) deep-crowded to the ceiling. I preached for about an hour and a half, walking about freely. I gave them a whole drama on the 'Unjust Steward.'

After service I was waited on by about thirty Elders who all wanted to shake hands with me. . . . Tonight I do my *Marriage: Is It a Failure?* and tomorrow a stray lecture in Alnwick on my way home. Shall be back at eight p.m. Wednesday for dinner, with pockets full of gold!

Yr. loving,

H.R.H.

But, alas, there never was any gold in those pockets by the time home was reached. As M.E.H. methodically filed his letter did she remember the day when, as one of a group of rapt girls, demurely gloved and bonneted attending a confirmation class in Pimlico, she had asked for the parable of the 'Unjust Steward' to be explained to her? If she did she must have pondered deeply over the strangely mixed bag of good and ill fortune the intervening years had brought her. If only R. could be relied on more often to keep the promises he made, and not always fly off at a tangent, all might still be well. But she could trust him in nothing; least of all in any money affair.

It has been recorded how Hugolin Haweis was heard to say more than once that 'Mother and Father can never rest in our comfortable home for long. They are always wandering.' But early in the New Year of 1892 it was not so much a case of happy wandering on the Continent, visiting museums and art galleries, but dire necessity that drove H.R.H. to take his wife, a very sick woman, to Antibes in search of the sun. He had arranged that they should stay with a friend, Mrs Crawshay. But after ten days spent in dutiful attendance he hurried off to visit the Perdicaris in Tangier. He made the excuse that as his wife would be unable to ride either a mule or a donkey, the sole means of transport in Morocco, on account of her rheumatism, she had better stay quietly with Mrs Crawshay. Actually he wanted to be alone.

From this time most letters received from her husband are marked with comments on their envelopes by M.E.H. Comments that read like 'What does this mean?' or 'In great anxiety for news of me. Of course he could have taken me with him if he had wanted to!'

Something in the nature of a division of interests once so lovingly held in common had opened up between husband and wife. On one side of this division, narrow at first but slowly widening, stood M.E.H. hurt and puzzled by what she has described as R.'s growing 'eccentricity'. This eccentricity took the form of rarely informing her of what he was doing or whom he was seeing; of accusing her of never seeking his advice now, in connection with her new 'philanthropic works'; of flying suddenly into ungovernable rages. Intuitively, she felt that he had fallen under the spell of some alien influence malignant to her. Otherwise, why did he behave in such a peculiar manner to her? What was still more alarming though were the big sums of money that poured like water through his hands and which he could never account for. Was he being blackmailed? If so, for what and by whom? From Antibes she wrote to Lionel in trouble all round, it seemed, in London.

Antibes
February 28*th*

My dear Lionel,
    I am writing to ask you how you like Mr Blackburn and

whether you joined his Art class. You have not answered
and I don't like to throw away my money. It is useless
throwing away chances. When your drawing is marketable
I can market it. Your loving aunts are constantly 'bleur-
ing' on to your Father, implying you are a failure. Now
his letters to me reflect their opinion. Give them the lie
by being a greater success than your Paynter cousins. It
lies in your own hand, but only while you are young. I am
quite willing to push you but not if you sit inert and do
nothing to second me. You must make new friends and
those in your own class of life. People outside your own
world are no use to you in a worldly way though pleasant
for recreation. In whatever class, you must bear in mind
that you will drop out of your place if you do nothing to
keep yourself up. . . . I am afraid this sounds rather a foul
letter. Please don't get out of banking till you are fit for
another post.

The rain has begun to come down in the most English
manner—sky grey, horizon gone, sea drab. It is often of a
positively vulgar blue. But I forget Castellar. It is the
oddest little wild place. A double street of pale pink,
ramshackly houses with windows of inexpressible shapes!
Archways in each of which a murderer lurks but beyond
him shines a distant view of dazzling colour. The smells
would delight Lucifer. The paving is bad for the ankles
but the dark doorways filled with pretty rather Italian
faces tearing olive branches to pieces (not faces, their
fingers!). Perhaps they use the leaves for something and
the wood for fires. In the surrounding woods small children gather the fallen olives for the oil-making. There
seems to be no cruelty to animals. There are some odd
effects in the sea. The colour is deep blue—like blue
paint. Then a pale green or a bright violet streak suddenly
shows, or a white shimmer. Such fountains of snow toss
back from the cliffs. But I do not think their colouring is
as rich as the Scotch hills which are like purple velvet.

I will write as often as you do and I hope you are getting on all right.

Your loving

Mother.

On returning to London from her enforced rest at Antibes M.E.H. did not stay long at home, but went North to Scotland on a round of visits interrupted only by taking Stephen to Madeira Hall at Ventnor, in the Isle of Wight, for the Easter holidays.

Bored with life through her parents being so much away, Hugolin sought consolation by spending a considerable time with her Aunt Margaret who had a small flat in London. It was not long before Margaret Haweis, a confirmed spinster who idolised her eldest brother and had never really liked Mary Eliza Joy, whom she tried to influence Rennie from marrying, realised that her niece was turning more and more to her for adult companionship. Pleased by this unexpected turn of events she began to exert quite an influence over Hugolin to the detriment of the already delicate relationship that existed between mother and daughter. Flattered and made much of, Hugolin found how much easier it was to confide and air her views to Aunt Margaret than to anyone at home except, perhaps, her father.

In the autumn of 1892 Lionel had his wish and left banking to join The Eastern Produce and Estates Company Limited, based at 41 Eastcheap, with the idea of going to Ceylon for them as a tea planter in the near future. He longed to travel, and the Far East particularly attracted him. He was indebted to his mother for his new job and, on removing himself to cheap lodgings in Devonshire Street, Bloomsbury, she helped him 'in'. Deploring the slum atmosphere of the neighbourhood and the insanitary conditions prevailing in his shabby room, she decided to move him to better accommodation when possible.

With Lionel leading his own life in Bloomsbury, Hugolin

made it quite clear that she wished to give up going about socially under her mother's wing and concentrate on carving out her own career. Her career? What was that to be, asked her amused mother?

Ever since Hugolin had been taken to see the Christy Minstrels at St James's Hall by her father who in his capacity of music critic supported negro melodies, writing 'The songs that float down the Ohio River are one in feeling and character with the songs of the Hebrew captives by the waters of Babylon', Hugolin had had aspirations to sing songs such as these. With this view in mind she had taken up the banjo and become quite a proficient performer on it. Now she told her mother that she intended to be a 'variety artiste' specialising in coon songs after the style of the American star May Yohe, shortly to appear in London in a Sims-Caryll opera. Her mother was taken aback by Hugolin's announcement. For her to want to be a music-hall singer was the last thing she had expected to hear. The legitimate stage would have been quite another thing. Ladies could, and did, become actresses, and she would have enlisted Miss Violet Vanburgh's help immediately for she knew her well. So in her usual forthright way she dismissed the whole idea of her daughter becoming a 'variety artiste' as frankly absurd. What musical talent the child possessed was far too slight to make any headway in the gruelling world of professional entertainment. She must stick to appearing as an amateur only in drawing-rooms!

Realising that she would never gain her mother's support in her self-chosen career Hugolin set out to win her father's. Very soon by clever management based largely on flattering him, she achieved this. Furthermore by Christmas she could rely on him to back her up in any kind of personal conflict with her mother. To make matters worse, in an effort to score childishly off his wife whom he felt was drifting further and further away from his sphere of influence, H.R.H. began to confide in his two eldest children. Of course some things which he told them in darkest secrecy drifted back to the ears of his wife. In particular was she incensed by his telling Lionel that she was 'incredibly unjust' to his sister. In fact her behaviour was 'quite abnormal' for a mother. With her innate sense of justice fully aroused she challenged her husband to tell her exactly what he meant by saying she was 'incredibly unjust' to Hugolin or how her behaviour was abnormal?

Immediately H.R.H. crumpled up weakly, evaded answering her questions and departed, as he always did now, to sulk in his club.

The New Year of 1893 opened with freezing weather conditions, and M.E.H. informed her son Lionel that they were in 'miserable conditions at Queen's House with no water, as the main was frozen and nearly every room shut up because of no maids!'

On the eve of departing to lecture in Guernsey, a letter to Lionel from his father contained an odd reference to Miss Souter's growing activities in his life. She was asked to do such personal things for her 'dear Doctor Haweis' that it was not surprising some people began to wonder if she had not become his mistress.

Queen's House

Jan. 23rd, 1893

My dear Lionel,

I suppose I shan't see you before I leave so I send you £5 for the month. My address is the Post Office, Guernsey till further notice. I have asked Miss Souter to arrange about your piano and also a cooking-stove for you. Let me have any news of your work. Be regular and do not ask for leave. Convey the impression that you are really interested. Don't look down on tea! Many engaged in it are quite your equals.

Yr. affect. father,

H.R.H.

P.S.   Avoid mentioning Miss Souter to your mother. She

has an idea that I have a tendency to encourage you to mix) with your social inferiors.

For the rest of the month H.R.H. remained in the Channel Islands gathering material for a commissioned biography of his old friend Sir Morell Mackenzie, the physician. He was hard-pressed for time as 'the good people of Guernsey call on me perpetually and my bell rings on every kind of pretext.' He longed to go to some place where he was not known, but how he would have complained if he had.

In February M.E.H. went to Edinburgh on a long visit to old friends. From their comfortable and warm house she begged Lionel to leave his horrid Devonshire Street lodgings where people spat on the stairs, there were bugs and the drains stank. She would pay for 'his move' and see if his father could increase his allowance by a little.

On her return to Chelsea with her health improved by rest and quiet, but still sleeping badly, a major event took place in the Haweis household. This was the departure—for good this time—of John Brookes Penfold (Pen) as general secretary and when needed, assistant curate, who had been part and parcel of Haweis family life for many years. His departure had been precipitated by an increasing jealousy on H.R.H.'s part who felt that Pen was giving far too much of his time and help to his wife's affairs and not enough to his. So he had jockeyed for and got a living for him in Guernsey from which John Brookes Penfold rose to be Dean of Guernsey and a much-loved figure on the island.

No sooner had Pen departed armed with a full silver tea and coffee service given him as a testimonial from his London friends and colleagues (M.E.H. had contributed the Queen Anne teapot) besides the promise of a £100 cheque which never materialised from his old employer, than H.R.H. left for Rome. He was due to give two lectures on '*The Unification of Italy*' in connection with the Easter Pilgrimage organised by Henry

Lunn. He had asked his sister Mary Paynter to go with him and not his wife. M.E.H. retaliated by answering as few of his letters as possible from Madeira Hall, Ventnor, where she had taken Stephen for his holiday. Upset by his wife's silence, letters began to arrive by every post almost from an 'unutterably lonely Gimmy.' On most envelopes M.E.H. made her usual comment.

Rome
Good Friday, March 28th

My darling,

At last I have got two letters, one from Milan. No one knows the depression I have suffered going to the Post day after day and getting not a line, only a skimpy post card. But I have been rewarded for my work put in. There were great expectations and Doctor Lunn confessed numbers had come abroad simply attracted by my name. I spared them nothing, draping my platform in scarlet with large pictures of the King and Queen of Italy and the great Revolutionaries and the Italian and English flags above in a trophy. I was accompanied on the stage by two Garibaldian heroes in red shirts, armed to the teeth. They presented arms on my ascending the platform and stood right and left behind me; sentinels with fixed bayonets for the whole of my lecture. At times they were overcome with tears; at others shook hands. When I played Garibaldi's 'Hymn' on my violin they sang the chorus and embraced with effusion. The room rose to the highest pitch when I described Garibaldi's capture of Naples and my own adventure as a boy in the Camp. I spoke each night for two hours. The second lecture was even a greater success than the first. When I left the platform the Garibaldians presented arms and great applause rang through the room. Dr Lunn pressed me to return next year. They say 'I was sublime!' Even Mary was overcome with enthusiasm. I have completely demoralised them for

217

other lecturers. I am coming back at once to look after
you and take you away for fresh air.

Yr. loving H.R.H.

On the envelope is M.E.H.'s comment: 'Nice. Says he has
thrown up invitation to return because of my ankle. Is this
true or has his publisher summoned him? Margaret [Haweis]
says the latter'.

On 18th April at Mrs Wynford Phillipps' house M.E.H. gave
her first public talk on Women's Franchise. As she always
felt that she had no aptitude for public speaking (she was
always nervous) she wrote out, in tiny script, every word of
her talk on long strips of thin paper about three inches wide
and from one yard to two long. These rolls were put on to a
little gutta-percha frame of her own invention which she kept
concealed in the palm of her hand. It was worked by turning
a tiny screw which unwound the MSS as she read. An idea
she had adapted from the principle of the Jewish Scripture
parchments mounted on rollers made known to her by
Deutsch, only hers were in miniature. Once launched though
on her talk, she would interpolate in her small clear musical
voice telling remarks, anecdotes and illustrations and so kept
her listeners enthralled. Unlike her husband, she gave no
display of histrionics. Hers was a subtler performance.

That summer the Reverend H. R. Haweis had been booked
to appear as Speaker at the Parliament of Religions being
held in Chicago and his wife was invited to go with him. As
early as July, though, aided and abetted by his sister Margaret
he made secret plans to get Hugolin somehow out to New York
as he wanted to show her America. If he had been open with
his wife and consulted her on the scheme, all might have been
well. But he only let Lionel into the secret, stressing that on
no account must he drop the barest hint to his mother of his
intention in case she put her foot down, forbidding him to take
Hugolin.

I mean Hugolin to have a month with me, going wherever

I go and entertained where I am entertained, he told him.
She will return with me but I shall not take her back to
Queen's House till I see she gets fair play and is treated as
a daughter should be.

For that particular bee still hummed loudly in his bonnet.
He told his son also that he wanted to give up his Chelsea
home and retrench severely. Another continual worry was
how 'to drive the family coach without an upset that will
expose our differences to the outside world.'

No one knew better than he that Victorian convention
required anything of a scandalous or unpleasant nature concerning a family and its members to be kept hidden from the
outside world, irrespective of who was to blame or who might
suffer in consequence. Instead though of exercising the utmost
discretion in regard to his own behaviour H.R.H. came to be
seen increasingly in the company of Miss Souter. To please
her distinguished admirer she gave his eldest children expensive presents and sometimes money. Delighted by this
generosity, Lionel and Hugolin were encouraged by their
father to see her when they could. If M.E.H. went off on a
visit he woefully gave out: 'When I am stranded in London,
alone, I have to live chiefly among the congregation'. This
was said to court pity for such wifely neglect. Actually he
went to stay in Miss Souter's comfortable Marylebone house
where he was treated like a king and lent her his familiar
gold-headed stick while she ran all the parochial errands.
Naturally, people gossiped. On hearing of these visits to Miss
Souter M.E.H. was furious. How much sillier could R. be,
drawing this wrong kind of attention on to himself? But she
knew by now it was useless to remonstrate. He would only
explode into a raging temper.

At the beginning of September the Reverend H.R. and Mrs
Haweis left, not a moment too soon, for New York. In much
better health and welcomed everywhere M.E.H. found herself
being taken for twenty-five and 'your Father's daughter' she
told Lionel joyfully. 'Everyone in America is agog with

Suffrage or No Suffrage for Women, so I am quite in fashion with my fad! I am coming back on the *Majestic* and so will reserve all my news till then.'

With her letter came one from his father informing him of the great ovation he had received from an audience of over 3,000 people attending the Parliament of Religions at the Columbus Hall in Chicago. From Chicago he would go to San Francisco returning by way of Utah, Salt Lake City and Denver. Hugolin would be with him, for he had telegraphed for her, having artfully dissuaded his wife from accompanying him to San Francisco on the pretext of unnecessary expense, though she offered to pay her own way. Little did M.E.H. know that on the very day she sailed for England her daughter would land in New York to take her place beside her husband as his fellow-traveller. By this deceitful act Hugolin made their estrangement complete.

On her arrival home—and a sad and bitter homecoming it must have been to hear how Hugolin had left for America—there came the usual spate of letters from her husband whose disloyalty to her was even harder to bear than her daughter's deceit. From San Francisco they came, from Salt Lake City and New York. But never a word that Hugolin was with him. At last, nearing the end of his lecture tour, he broke the news, adding some very feeble excuses.

October 24*th*

My darling,

I am feeling low at getting no word or wire since you sailed on the 4th. ... Not feeling sure about arrangements for Hugolin on the close of her visits this summer and understanding you did not wish her back on your hands, I wired for Hugolin to join me. Now I have received an offer from Mary [his married sister] to have her for six months or two years as Cam [her son] is going to America and she will be lonely and needs a companion. This will probably be the best arrangement. But it is not the one

I could have suggested. All these complications have much spoiled and embittered my otherwise successful tour. I feel more and more that although I am sometimes driven half crazy with the things you say or do without meaning to worry or embarrass me, I would rather have all that and ten-fold more than be without you. Whatever different views we take of what is right to do in regard to Hugolin I am still miserable without you. The greatest trial is to be so long without a word or sign from you. I still am and never shall be anything but yr. loving if often unhappy H.R.H.

Underscored is this comment on the envelope: 'Not feeling sure? On my hands? The first I have heard of this. If he had wanted me he could have kept me with him. Keep.'

A week before her husband and daughter were due back in England M.E.H. wrote a long letter to her eldest son stating, once and for all, her attitude to her daughter who had behaved so badly to her. Lionel Haweis was shortly leaving for Ceylon and she wanted him to know the true facts about Hugolin's going to America and not hear a garbled version of the whole affair cooked up by his father.

Queen's House,
Cheyne Walk, s.w.
November 7th

My dear Lionel,

I am glad you like the shaving glass. I thought one might be unobtainable in Colombo. Like you I can't say things as well as write. But you know my character sufficiently to be sure that I am immovable in my affections as I am in 'the other thing' and I don't gush (this is both bad and good, but I have seen enough gush in our family to know what it is often worth). Believe me, I shall never alter in my love for my children whatever they do. Even when they go to such lengths as Hugolin has done to annoy me. I don't think there will be a day when I won't think of you and you know I have worked for you more than Father. I really believe you are going to do well in Ceylon and will be happy there. I knew you were low yesterday, as I was, but it is no use giving in. If Father will let me, I will gladly come out and have a month with you in Ceylon. I should enjoy it immensely. Don't think of it as being far. Nothing is far. Not even death. Everything is only for a little while and I want you to go in good spirits and not to think again of a single horrid thing. I shall only say one thing about H. You must not think I am out of sympathy with her or angry with her though I know your sympathies are more with her than me because you and she are both young. Whether she puts her actions on to Father or whether he takes it on himself, her actions show a complete lack of sympathy with me. There is little chance of two people so incompatible in character ever getting on. If either of you understood better what the Aunts have been to me all my married life, you would see the finality of H. going off like that, secretly and not under my care. If she had valued her worldly position more, she would not have done it and if she had previously tried to satisfy my ego or my mind as she could have and pretends to have, but did not, then she would not have set up those conditions which have led to these results. I should never have introduced her at seventeen if I had not wished to make her my companion. I should have enjoyed educating and pushing her. By my knowledge of dress, I could have made her eminent as a beauty if nothing else. But this she stupidly opposed and Father backed her up. Now I have stopped and for good. She must always do as she pleases henceforth. *She is not a child but a woman* and *two women cannot live together unless their tastes and habits coincide.* But my affection is unaltered though I don't respect her character any more. If you can understand that! I shall always do my best for her and you all . . .

When you come back in five years I hope everything will have become harmonious once more. You will find me *exactly* as I am today, inside and out. But I expect to see you before as you are really only a little over a fortnight's journey off—about as far as Oxford in the time of Edward III! I do not wish Hugolin to know what I have written to you. Please remember that. But it was my duty to tell you. What I think right I always do whatever it costs even at the cost of sometimes making a mistake. My best love and envy,

Your loving Mother

So far as she was concerned, she had cut Hugolin out of her life forever.

Some days later M.E.H. made plans to leave London for the country. For it had been mistakenly reported in the Press that Mr and Mrs Haweis were due home on the *Germanic* on 18th November, and this announcement had upset her considerably. She felt in no mood to welcome home either her weak husband or erring daughter. Before leaving, she sent for Lionel to excuse herself from seeing him off to Ceylon and said good-bye to him privately, in the Print Room at Queen's House. In this little room, on a dank November day, they exchanged the briefest of farewells. They were never to meet again.

When H.R.H. and his daughter drove up to Queen's House there was no one at home to greet them. The marked absence of his wife whom he was told by a servant, had left for the country, disturbed him very much. Hurriedly he sent a note off by hand to his son on the eve of sailing from Tilbury, enclosing £10 for his travelling expenses. 'The next few years will be anxious ones' he wrote, 'We must let Queen's House as soon as possible for we are living beyond our income: but if I can live and work long enough I shall put things right'— which proved to be a vain hope so far as he was concerned

Early in the New Year, after Lionel's arrival in Ceylon, his mother wrote him an affectionate letter in answer to two of his.

Queen's House
February 3rd, 1894

Dearest Lionel,

I was very glad to get your letters. You seem to have fallen on your feet. I wish I was in Ceylon. I don't see why we shouldn't visit you some day. I have never felt so well nor had such a nice time. My Sunday lunches are being noticed as rather an institution. I get delightful people together, titles, M.P's and notables. It is a great trouble but such a success that they seldom leave till 5 pm. As Father does not come home regularly, I have to be both host and hostess. I try to make my lunches like the celebrated suppers of Coleridge, Wordsworth, Lamb and de Quincey. I guide the talk to be general on some subject of the day with everyone contributing his part. Sometimes, it is the labour question, commercial morality, Pasteurism, Ibsen, hypnotics or what not. I have never enjoyed anything so much before as at dinners talk is often scrappy and useless. The ladies are generally pretty and always clever and I seat them anyhow. But every lunch is composed of harmonious elements. Last Sunday, Sarah Grand, the authoress (her book is in its 25th thousand!) lunched here, Lady Greville, two M.Ps and Miss Violet Vanburgh, the actress . . .

Father seems very well and in good spirits and form for work; whistles about the house and spends his evenings sorting autographs and uttering cries of surprise at the wealth he possesses. He has not been cranky for nearly a month: not even for one single half hour from which I gather the irritants (your Aunts) are out of town.

One of my poor parrots is dead. It was melancholy to see the forlorn mate sit down by her hour after hour, gently pecking her round the eyes which had never failed to elicit a tender response. He did not touch food for nearly two days but, alas, for male constancy titbits and attention has soothed him into new cheerfulness and now he is better off than before as there is no one to exact half his sugar!

The weather is extraordinarily beautiful for early February. I don't remember such a winter for nearly ten years. No fogs but sunshine daily or warm rain. Father has had hardly any asthma or heart or digestion to trouble him. I think light and climate affect everyone. I hope you will keep alright and don't get fever however tempted. I shall be anxious to hear as often as possible.

With love,

Yr affectionate Mother

Lionel also heard from his father who told him he was extremely gloomy and depressed. Though things were in no acute stage at home, it upset him to have Hugolin's (she had remained with her aunts) name rarely mentioned. Other men's daughters were made much of and 'floated' right and left but his was ignored. Illogically, he refrained from saying that it was his daughter's wish, after all, to lead her own life apart from her mother's.

Again H.R.H. told his son that he was secretly planning a winter campaign on the Pacific Coast with a visit to Australia and Ceylon to follow if possible. Money was still tight and his health poor on account of 'unspeakable worries'. Those same worries that he divulged to no one.

On Shrove Tuesday of that year Stephen Haweis won the 'Pancake' contest at Westminster much to his mother's pride. Her youngest son was doing very well scholastically, and she had great hopes of him. He had become her right hand, too, at her parties, which were now so seldom patronised by his father. But as she came to rely more and more on his bright, affectionate nature in her emotionally barren life, his father came increasingly to turn against him. For he saw that Stephen was succeeding where Hugolin had not and this he could not tolerate.

There came days when unable to contain his feelings, he took himself off in great ire to the New University Club where, seated on a hard chair before an uncomfortable little writing-table, when he would have been far cosier in his study at home, he gave full vent to his feelings to Lionel, living happily so far away. It was his mother's 'public work' with which he had so little to do that came to be the chief target for his sarcasm and anger.

> She does not know how so many people laugh at her and how little fitted she is to do the things she is now bent on doing. Her abilities, if guided, as I guided them in the past and so got her a name, could still make her shine in this new world. She really does need me about to stop her running into this present folly!

Then, biting the end of his pen, he glared about him in the way that was fast growing into a habit. Sooner or later, he thought darkly, his darling would want him back on the old terms, consulting him and asking his every opinion just as she had done as a doting bride in the old Welbeck Street days. Then he would make her drop her present silly charitable works along with those members of the '*fine new circle*' who danced round her but left him alone and neglected.

Easter of that year was spent by the Reverend and Mrs Haweis in Rome where H.R.H. lectured for Henry Lunn as before. Still feeling in splendid physical form, M.E.H. put in a great deal of sight-seeing and was delighted to hear that she was being taken again for her husband's daughter. A case of mistaken identity that never failed to annoy him!

But on returning to London by Venice and Strasbourg and settling down to the old routine at Queen's House, M.E.H. realised that those halcyon days of winter calm and February sunshine were over. They had been but a brief interlude. Her husband was acting strangely once more.

Queen's House
Cheyne Walk, s.w.

My dear Lionel,

I am home and have just received yours. I am glad you seem to have a nice berth and all depends on what you make of it as time goes on. . . . I am sorry to say I don't think Father as well as he was in the winter. I think he must be going through some constitutional change which will leave him for better or worse. Sometimes he is quite his old self, cheerful and whistling about the house. But he has unaccountable fits of nervous excitement that I don't understand—chiefly at night. He gives the most curious reasons sometimes for it all—but I don't think the reasons are the causes. Something is at the back of so many of his actions. All the doctors say he is quite sound. Yet I am very anxious sometimes. I trace it all back six years. However we won't croak. I have been wonderfully well and placed on several very important committees and elected to the Writers' Club. Great 'stars' there. Next Friday I am invited at the celebrated Women Writers' Dinner with all the 'New Women'. It is the first time I have been asked and I suppose it is an important recognition.

At present, all the papers are yelling at me for 'injuring the Evangelical cause' by a paper on the Pope in the *Echo* and *Pulpit*. Poor Cause! Mr Stead has put me on his Civic Church Association to my dismay. Every day some one makes me join a new Crusade against some 'crying evil'. Our evils all cry now. It is a good thing that it is the fashion to be doing something. The Suffrage is thriving. But we are chiefly Anti-Vivisection mad just now.

Best love and try to rise in every way on your own feet.

Your affectionate Mother

His wife was right. H.R.H. *was* going through some 'constitutional change' as many men do in their fifties. But his was a change made even more dangerous because he was suffering from a touch of megalomania. Increasingly, he thought of himself as being almost infallible; as infallible as the God he preached about to thousands of enthralled listeners who became mere puppets through the hypnotic magic of his oratory. For reasons only best known to him, he had taken to writing to Lionel and Hugolin from his Club where he asked to receive their replies. On discovering this furtive new practice of his, M.E.H. was more rightly annoyed than hurt.

In the early summer, Hugolin condescended to return to Queen's House for a few days. She found her mother so 'absolutely amiable' and indifferent to what she did or whom she saw that before long, bored and restless, she was off to Boskenna, much to her father's chagrin. Eventually he departed too to Cornwall where he gave out grumpily that Hugolin was 'vegetating unnecessarily' and should return with him to London. But Hugolin would not be moved and, complaining that her mother's treatment had hardened her, her father went home without her.

I have no idea what is to be done with the rest of the summer, he informed Lionel. I cannot be boxed up with Mother and Stephen by way of a holiday either by the sea or in the country.

His relationship with his youngest son was as bad as it was with his wife. Besides usurping his place as companion to his mother, he declared that Stephen was rude and disobedient to him: insulted his aunts: and was offhand with his sister. Matters came to a violent head, one day, when he flatly refused to sit down at table for luncheon till Stephen had apologised to him for some imaginary rudeness. When this was done he illogically told his son 'to stick to his mother', which the boy did, fully realising by now that she was the only safe and solid element in his life. It was his mother who fought his battles and paid more often than not his schooling fees, besides arranging his holidays and feeding and clothing him. Without her, he was totally without security and he was still only a schoolboy.

In the end, the summer holiday question was solved by H.R.H. taking, as usual, a month's duty in a nice old Sussex rectory where M.E.H. lazed in the garden. Stephen pursued his favourite hobby of photography and H.R.H. brooded on his plan to go to San Francisco, that autumn, either alone or secretly with his daughter. Money matters were never out of his mind. He longed to escape to the New World where he would be free from his numerous creditors and from other claims being made on him. Claims that he never dared admit which stemmed from the mysterious background of his concealed and unsuspected private life.

Once back in London, his plans went ahead but openly now through the channel of a responsible agent for a Pacific Coast-to-Coast Tour of America and Canada by the 'Reverend H. R. Haweis, Author, Artist, Critic and Myriad-Minded Speaker' as he came to be so flamboyantly billed. Moved by a sudden and genuine desire which still overcame him at intervals to heal the unhappy breach between his wife and himself, H.R.H. invited her to accompany him on his tour. It would cost them nothing, he said, as hotel accommodation was being supplied for both lecturer and wife. M.E.H. accepted this offer joyfully as she had longed all her life to visit the romantic Golden West.

On 6th November a major event took place at Queen's House, largely engineered by H.R.H. This was Hugolin's home-coming. A Hugolin who was graciously prepared to take up her winter quarters with her parents in London. Her mother had acquiesced without comment to her return, for had she not made it quite clear, months back, that her daughter could come and go as she liked in her own home? 'It is much better that H. should admit she has a parental roof after the sad mess of past affairs, though she sleeps only under it,' Lionel was informed. 'Her movements are kept the most solemn secret from me in the most amusing way!'

It was only from her intimate friends that M.E.H. ever knew what her daughter was up to. She herself was much occupied in arranging another of her popular 'Lecturette' series, besides helping Mrs Booth by writing up her rescue work in *The Queen* and other papers. Suddenly she was told that her trip to California was off. It would add far too much to his expenses, her husband declared. Besides, he would never be stationary for long and she would be left much alone in hotels. So M.E.H. consented to be left behind. If she had demurred, she knew that she would have been accused of never wanting her husband to go anywhere without her. A week before his departure, H.R.H. was struck down by a violent haemorrhage of the nose. It was arrested only after several days of incessant bleeding by the combined efforts of his wife, doctor and a professional nurse called in to help.

M.E.H. remained at his bedside continually though ordered to rest after fainting once after a long stretch of night duty. She was extremely distressed. As for Hugolin, she was no help, doing little for her father but empty his basin once or twice. In a new winter outfit with a little fur toque set on her curly head, she was out all day, visiting music publishers to find new songs for 'her act' as she described it. Little else mattered to her.

On the other hand, her young brother did his best for his invalid father by running errands for him between Chelsea and his church for which he received little thanks. In consequence of his illness, H.R.H. had to postpone his departure to San Francisco by some weeks. Three days before sailing from Liverpool, he announced to his wife's astonishment that he was taking Hugolin with him as her aunts had offered to finance her. Feeling quite rightly that she had been duped, M.E.H. put her foot down firmly. If Hugolin went, so would she. If a married woman could not be left alone to twiddle her thumbs in a Californian hotel how could a young and pretty girl like Hugolin without a proper chaperone?

A battle royal followed of clashing wills: a battle in which H.R.H. was finally forced to give in. Hugolin stayed in England.

On 4th December after a rather chilly parting with his wife, the Reverend H. R. Haweis departed in a cab to catch the boat-train to Liverpool. Hardly had the front door closed behind him than Hugolin crept out of Queen's House, hailed a hansom and drove to Euston where she said goodbye to her father.

The one-time happy pattern of family life was no more.

9. 'THE MYRIAD-MINDED LECTURER ABROAD'

1894-1895

As the Reverend H. R. Haweis, leaning heavily on Miss Souter's gold-headed stick, paced the deck of the ship cutting her way steadily through deep Atlantic rollers, he must have been not a little thankful to be shot for a while of the warring elements engendered by family life at Queen's House. Not to speak, too, of that Shylock pack of creditors always clamouring for payment and those secret demands being made on him by an ex-mistress turned greedy blackmailer.

By the time though that his ship had reached New York he was feeling lonely again and full of self-pity. In this mood it was extremely gratifying to find an army of reporters rushing forward to interview him when he descended from his train at San Francisco. Here, in this fabulous city, he was needed; here, he was going to be treated as a great man.

Once settled at his hotel, notable people never ceased calling on him while daily he received little notes by hand from distinguished ladies requesting his presence at a dinner party or an At Home they wished to give in his honour. It was not until Christmas Eve that he found time to sit down in his hotel bedroom and write to the one person whom he had so conveniently forgotten that he could have had with him.

Occidental Hotel,
San Francisco
December 24th

My darling,
    I arrived here in better condition than hoped and was

met by two members of the Committee. Every attention is paid me. My first Sunday was a great success, the crowds being quite unable to get into the Church and hundreds standing. I preached for an hour and a half. So you may be thankful you weren't there!

As to H. nothing alters my grief and disappointment at her being done out of the social position I have created and intended her to share with you—nor of my views of her rights and your duties. I could write a great deal in justification of my views but it would be running my head against a stone wall and would make no impression on you and do no good. I prefer to remember that nothing can obliterate the image that I carry about with me in my heart of someone who once loved me and has faint gleams of kindness even now. I shall cling to those gleams as long as they continue. Personal happiness is over and done with. But I shall indulge in no more growls.

It is mid-winter here but mild, clear and sunny. My table is covered with cards. Once I should have enjoyed the homage but it is nothing to me now. I am glad the really influential and important people recognise your labours and do you full justice. But it is not what I married. I certainly thought that your strength lay in Art and a purely literary direction and that you neither had the popular sympathies nor tastes for rubbing elbows with the great unwashed. I did not think you had the strength for Committees and Boards and the boring discussions of Bumbledom. But in all this I have been mistaken. . . . I hope I have grasped the situation now and a good deal of the pain is over. I don't quite see where the husband comes in but I daresay some odd niche will be found which will make him appear more or less suitable. Here I have a sense of being earnestly wanted from the Bishop downwards. What appear to me the veriest platitudes are caught up as inspired words of wisdom. So whilst here, I too in my humble way fill a niche for a time. What there was to laugh at in the post-dated cheques, I don't know. I understood that was what you wanted to know—what money was at your disposal throughout the interval.

I want to say how nicely you did my packing. Thank you for putting in a nice new overcoat and all the other things I was likely to want. No appetite and don't sleep well.

Yr. ever loving and lonely,
H.R.H.

It was early in the New Year of 1895 when M.E.H. received this letter and read it seated at her bureau in the drawing-room of Queen's House. The weather had set in atrociously and it was a bitter, cold afternoon with the Chelsea seagulls silenced for once, as they came and went hungrily over the river, flashing white wings against an iron-grey sky. From where she sat she could see the Embankment lay deserted; as deserted as she felt reading R.'s letter with a sinking heart. How best could she meet these cruel accusations she wondered? Even her poor little joke on the subject of the many horrible post-dated cheques (not one of which she had been able to cash as his account was so overdrawn at the bank) had misfired. Chaos she knew now to her cost reigned in all his financial affairs. So pressed was she for ready money to pay the rent long overdue and the servants' wages that in a panic she had asked for a private interview with their bank manager, and pawned some family silver to tide her over for the time being. At Queen's House she was living on a shoe-string besides using up much of her hard-won savings put aside to pay for Stephen's college education. Despondently she drew a sheet of writing paper towards her and took up her pen.

Queen's House
January 6th

My dear R.,
I am very depressed at your 'blue blazer' and scoldings.

Do you not know how I am always thinking of you and pining for a little help and kindness which I once had so much of? I must occupy myself and if you won't give me any help I must get it myself. I should have thought you would have been glad I had developed and that 'my strength' extended beyond Art and Literature. As for needing a husband's protection or advice, I have had to do without both for five years in many ways. But it was not because I did not need them nor because I did not care about them. No one but the kind hearts that have lived long in this house knows what desperate suffering and struggle my life is! Sometimes, it seems just like the cattle on the cattle-ships only moral instead of physical. Still I expect it is for my eventual good or to detach me from what I used to love and lean upon too much. Even the cattle get to the end of it in time. What you said about the packing made me cry. It is the first word of approbation I can remember really for years. I do all I can for you day after day; there is not an hour when you are not thought of or your wants provided for. I don't appear much myself because I am always told now that 'I upset you'. This same cry has been taught my children. *It is not what I married.* Neither are you twenty-eight any longer, or I eighteen. I shall go on doing well and looking well to the last and I shall die in harness because I am so built. Your letter has made me quite ill. But it does not matter. If you will withdraw yourself from my life as you seem to be doing, do you not see new difficulties with the children? Do look forward and realise how much we might do together with my abilities occupied by you. I am willing at any time to do anything. But if nothing is given the mill to grind, it will grind itself. I think I could help you in many ways but if you don't wish it, endless things will drop in here. How earnestly I wish I was away from this world and on that beautiful hill I dream of. Do write now and then a word of human sympathy, dear R.,

235

but as you know I am a high-spirited woman. I will never be wrenched by the bit, or move an inch by hard belabouring.

Always the same loving TIG at heart.

P.S.　I can't understand this last letter. You said I was not to refrain from telling you all I was doing. I did so but it seems as if I had better not for you begin by saying you are pleased and then there follow four pages of indignation. So I don't know what to be at. You say '*it is not what I married!*' Last year when I told you I had not changed in character or affection for twenty years, you said it was very wrong and unnatural not to change. Well, now I have changed. A bud that never opens is a bud dead. H. went off to one of her aunts today without even a goodbye as usual. Is this your counsel? How do you think it possible for her to be my companion? You have stamped down and pushed away a great love and a good wife even if I say it. I often wonder if I could feel the same if you returned to the old conditions—but they are not present now. I often cry over that dear little man who died.

For sometime in the thickening dusk with the melancholy sound of a distant tug hooting on the river or the creak of carriage wheels passing her house that alone broke the silence outside, M.E.H. sat staring in front of her, her pen laid down. In the near future she knew that she must steel herself somehow into giving up Queen's House, the one secure possession in her life. The house that above all others she had known was so deeply loved and prized. For however cleverly she economised and managed to make both ends meet domestically, her efforts were made null and void by the extraordinary drain from unknown sources beyond her control on an income that should be, *was*, more than adequate to meet all their needs. It was not she but R. who was the extravagant one. Her account books so scrupulously kept, her few bills met immediately, the detailed lists of every item bought for the children and house were proof positive of her genius for economy and for keeping up appearances virtually on nothing. As she herself always maintained, so long as the conversation was brilliant at Queen's House with notable guests thrown in for good measure, no one minded what they ate or drank so long as food was presented on Crown Derby and drink in glittering Waterford glass.

Before rising from her chair, M.E.H. put her usual comment on the envelope just received from California: 'Extraordinary scream from R. Am in great sorrow.'

Then going over to the bell she rang for Edith to come and draw the curtains and add a bucketful of coal to the sinking fire. She would be warm if nothing else and soon Stephen would be home from Westminster for the evening.

Far away in San Francisco, completely indifferent as to how his wife coped or not with the New Year's avalanche of bills coming in, the 'Myriad-Minded' lecturer interviewed his press agent to arrange a whistle-stop tour for him of coastal towns from San Francisco to Vancouver from where he proposed embarking for Australia. An offer to preach and lecture at fifty towns on that vast continent had come which he was determined to accept and, if possible, follow up with other lectures in New Zealand and Ceylon where he planned to visit Lionel.

The success he was enjoying both as preacher and lecturer in San Francisco was phenomenal. People only had to listen once to 'the little lame parson' from London and they fell immediately under his spell. Wherever the Reverend H. R. Haweis was billed to appear, thousands converged, roads were blocked and the police called in. As H.R.H. told his wife: 'Everywhere I am received like a god.' The peak though was not achieved till he gave his much-publicised lecture on 'Marriage and Divorce.' In the hall taken, 'Everywhere a human being could plant two feet was occupied and the applause was thunderous!' wrote one reviewer. This amazing re-action was the very breath of life to Hugh Reginald Haweis; a heady draught that came to be reflected more and more in the over-dramatic tone of his letters to his wife whom he felt completely misunderstood him.

> Occidental Hotel,
> San Francisco
> *February* 11*th*

My darling,

Your longed-for letter arrived as I leave 'Frisco'. It made me feel agitated and unfit for the strain of work now upon me—just like home! Your fainting and your money anxieties cut me up dreadfully. Not a word about the £50 wired but your letter is undated. I enclose a blank signed cheque but hold it till I know in Montreal (7th March) if the balance is restored in my bank at home. If you can let the house or sell, it would be best. I don't see the advantage of your coming out unless you care to join me in Ceylon when my incessant racket of fifty nights in Australia would be over. I am very down-hearted about everything and very hard-worked but well as a wanderer trying to pick up money. I have nothing but grief and disappointment to look forward to at home. . . . I am glad to hear of your success. I don't grudge you any fame or popularity. I have worked all my life to set you off and provide you with means to show to the best advantage till you broke up the family and left nothing for anyone but Stephen and yourself. . . . The adulation I receive here gives me not a spark of pleasure—how can it?—when my heart is emptied and my household gods broken. Your photo is always there with fresh flowers in front but it is incense burned to the dead. I fancy some day if you fail or get ill you may want me and no one could help you so well. Heaven knows what is in store! But you want no more of this, 'The vine still clings to the mouldering wall. But at every blast the dead leaves fall.' That is just what I feel. I think I will write only business letters and keep my thoughts. Sell anything you like but my fiddle and my bells. I don't feel any more interest in 'anything' but am still your P.B. (Poor Boffin).

With this letter came another delivered at Queen's House. It was headed by this cryptic statement:

'One of many written lately but kept back. A forlorn attempt to explain the real situation.'

My darling,
I wish you would not say things to outrage my sense of justice. But these allusions to Hugolin are beyond my powers of endurance. You talk of H. being indulged and favoured the worse she behaves. You do nothing for the child, allow me to do nothing, and she is shoved before all the world from pillar to post, entirely dependent during the best years of her life on the bounty of her Aunts. You deliberately deprived her of the two best chances she had —to visit America and Italy. Neither visit would have cost you anything. Then you talk of her being indulged. You seem utterly blind to the view of the situation and incapable of seeing it. That is why I still hang on to you. I am melted when you drop a word of kindness about 'his old lamb face' and cry over every gentle word you drop. I long never to say another disagreeable word to you in my letters but a worm will turn. But no more of this. There is nothing left now but to live for my Church.

Comment by M.E.H. dated 28th February:

A letter from R. saying I have deprived H. of the two greatest chances of her life. This is simply not true. In 1893 she went to New York, alone, unknown to me and has visited France with us, had many home treats and visited the Antwerp Exhibition with her Aunts. Before R. left I told her that I would be glad for her to go to America again but I must go too, as if her father went on a tour to Australia she could not return alone from California. I reminded him of his constant moving about and that her mother should be with her. I suppose she repudiates this as 'chaperoning.' *She must either be in my place or not there at all.* I fear this is the beginning of the end.

By this time the 'Myriad-Minded' lecturer had whirled off on his spectacular tour from Tacoma to Seattle and from Seattle to Winnipeg where he roused mass hysteria in one church with three hundred people crowded into a cellar below the nave to try and hear the voice of the great Doctor Haweis from London pealing down to them through an iron grating.

What with 'distraints' and 'summonses' and enormous bills constantly coming in, M.E.H. took herself to Brighton for a change, but the cold was so intense that she returned home. No sooner had she got back when a mysterious figure, heavily veiled and accompanied by a child of about six years of age, called at Queen's House and asked to see Mrs Haweis. Giving her name as Mrs Smith she was shown into the long drawing-room where a painful interview followed during the course of which M.E.H. learnt of the association her husband had formed with her visitor who declared that the child holding her hand was his. One glance told her all. He was more like R. than any of her own.

What transpired at this meeting was either destroyed or may never have been recorded. The little that is known comes from Stephen Haweis who saw Mrs Smith before she left. His mother, he said, was calm and dignified and kept her head. She turned the whole case over to Mr Tyndale the family solicitor. If his father had only told his mother about Mrs Smith earlier and how he was being bled white by her she might have treated the situation as 'an intellectual problem' and saved his father many years of financial stress, Stephen Haweis has maintained.

Following this painful interview came a suggestion from the

still 'much-fêted wanderer' that his wife should try to let Queen's House and join him as soon as she could in Sydney. But almost as soon written, this rendezvous was changed to Melbourne and then to Ceylon. At a loss to make head or tail of R's 'kaleidoscopic' changes of plan and very much disturbed by his prolonged absence from St James's where everything was going to sixes and sevens, M.E.H. felt it had become her duty to try and write him 'a perfectly reasonable letter to every word of which I stand'.

Queen's House,
Cheyne Walk
March 20*th*, 1895

My darling,

I did not reply to your last letters, you can guess why. Many of the things ought not to have been written. They do no good. When you were younger and quite as wise, you used to say write 'a blue blazer' and then burn it. Your final letter did have some kind words and those I answer with the usual heartache. I am thankful you are enjoying the excitements that to you are not excitements, and I hope and pray you will be able to go on without a breakdown. If you want to put your poor worn worried head in my lap, the only one that has loved you and is even now keeping house and circle regular and intact for the sake of the past, I am glad and thankful. Things go on just the same. The same hours, same servants, same duties, same friends, same furniture. To replace deaths, new friends drop in and that is the way with everybody, I suppose. I think life and what we can do with one's materials are so much more serious than dissipation that I am putting everything in order that I can put. I am ready to join you wherever you settle, even if it is in India, as you last suggested. I have always said so. And I see it is expected. The congregation, the *better class* are already critical but not of me. The commercial class are more used to conjugal separations for a livelihood so their wives are different. They 'advise' or gossip in proportion to their capacity. Mr Weller [a curate left in charge] is inquisitive though he asks no questions of course, being a gentleman, and offers no remarks. But I can see he does not understand. He is frightened, too, of the Church bills. I hope he won't throw up! He says the waste and muddle are serious. Why not give him authority to lower some of the needless expenses according to his very small congregation and offertories while you are away so long? You must not let anyone know that you have debts. It saps credit. I wish I could see what your plans are for the future. Not knowing, I do not think it would be advantageous to let our well-known house rashly, incurring quite half the expense in storing and damaging the furniture. When I see a definite line, I am quite ready to keep house on a smaller scale, keeping however the carriage which the head of the house requires and has always had. We are both middle-aged and shall not get any stronger. I hope you will consider your Church position and select out of the many aims what to work for in the future so that our old age may be comfortable if we live to be old; and memory-respected if not. Our expenditure (what I know of it) is by no means above your income and without further waste we shall in a few years cover past mistakes. I am living on almost nothing and have even taken to vegetarianism which is most economical. Of course, I would not refuse a good offer for the house. Reasonable, steady, *tortoise-work*, I believe in. It is, perhaps, unwise to allude to the bombshell H. but I will to prove that things are taken out of your hands as well as mine. H. does not intend to settle here and has as good as told me so. She repeatedly complains of the 'distance of Chelsea' and was out all day from ten am till ten pm, once returning alone in a cab at midnight.

I have never prevented H. going to America or anywhere else. I only said she ought to have a chaperone and till she is under her mother's guardianship she won't, so far as I can see, hold her right position again. But she does not intend to settle at home whatever is done for her. I think if you let me—or some good manager—things could be pulled back to a solvent condition. But I am afraid this letter is getting too serious and you will complain of my 'hard commonsense' but somebody in the house must have a little. Much remains to be done to arrive at the impeccable position of five years ago. I am doing all I can to gather up the crumbs and only hope there will be twelve baskets full.

I do not think it matters being away a year for once if you put it on the proper dignified ground that you consider you have earned it and don't go croaking to the public about private worries which they care nothing about and look askance at. I hope after a term in India we may start fair again and take up our old envied position and work on to the end, hand in hand. My interests are still yours and my head pretty level in spite of my 'mad delusions' one of which is that life is *not yet over*. She does not think her old TIG is always himself. He is overwrought by his debts, his women and his contradictory advisers. It would be wise for him to wash his old brown pads of a good many of them. Then we could close the account for things in an acceptable light. Do not keep saying you are shoved aside for Stephen. You know it is not true or ever could be. But if you are always away or absent, a companion for me like Stephen is not unnatural. I do think a more regular and reasonable life together would in the end—even if less exciting—bring you more happiness. You are right. If there had been no children we should never have had a jar but our sedentary habits and 'high level' do not really suit young people, I think, and in middle life one is no longer ductile. It is all very sad. I wish I could have gone to California. I should have

made good use of such a trip but I will not go where I am
not wanted.

Your loving T.I.G.

From the summit of the Rockies as he travelled in jolting
trains; from his small cabin on board the R.M.S. *Miowera,*
Sydney-bound; from the Bishop of Honolulu's bungalow
where he scribbled off an article for *The Queen* on Queen
Liliuokalanie, deposed on account of 'moral turpitude' (he
had wished to interview her but was told she was imprisoned):
from Fiji where the red carpet had been rolled out for him
by the Chief Justice and Administrator, H. E. Mr Berkeley,
a late member of his congregation at St James's, in his peak
years as society's pet preacher, they came, those endless
letters, bombastic and extrovert or groaning in self-pity, till
M.E.H.'s head must have reeled.

On arriving, at last, at Sydney, H.R.H. found to his intense
joy that his surname HAWEIS had been placarded all over
the town in immense two foot letters, white on black. He
was ravished. It almost made up for the bitter disappointment of his Canadian tour, so badly organised by his agent,
who had taken him 2,500 miles out of his way with little to
show for in fees collected.

In Sydney he heard grave news that his brother Willy,
dying in a bush cabin some way out of Sydney, was in dire
need of money. He managed to dash off to see him and parted
with five pounds.

In spite of his wonderful press notices and the huge congregations he attracted in churches where he preached by
request, his lecture dates were poorly attended and his whole
tour seemed at one moment to be on the verge of collapse
from a financial angle.

Deeply grieved at the poor amount of his takings, he despatched another of his 'blue blazers' to M.E.H. in reply to
what she had thought was her 'very reasonable' letter!
Barely a week later, from the Grand Hotel, Melbourne, where

he had met with hysterical applause and adulation once more, he wrote in high fettle, mentioning Mrs Smith for the first time.

> The Grand Hotel
> Melbourne
> *May 6th*

My darling,
This is a hurried line to catch the mail. I have wired you £100 to go on with. I have also signed and returned Power of Attorney to Tyndale. . . . He writes me that Mrs S. is being a nuisance. Quite wrongfully, she considers me her trustee on strength of which hallucination she sends me all her bills at random. She has been living two years with a gentleman who is supposed to be going to marry her. Her hallucinations are endless, usual case of being too mad to be at large but not mad enough to lock up. I hand everything over to Tyndale now and have nothing further to do with her. I have certainly struck oil here. There is a sort of craze about for me evidently. People falling over themselves to be introduced to me. But the more kindness I am shown only makes me feel that there is only one whose kindness I really care for and with whom it seems impossible to come to terms short of renouncing my family and repudiating my daughter. . . .
The next cheque will go to Mr Weller. But how to pay his salary, I know not.

> Your own P.B.

Two weeks later, he was en route for New Zealand in a small ship where the service was bad and his cabin lacked both a bell and reading lamp. All the future seemed dark to him, he wrote. He could only walk with two sticks and sleep evaded him. But 'as long as I can struggle I can earn. I have been worse before so you needn't bother!'
He had heard from the Office of Works that there was a

deficit of £100 for pew rents at St James's and he realised that he had made only enough money by his globe-trotting 'to float them over the coming autumn'.

Towards the end of May, M.E.H. went to stay with her elderly cousins, a Mr and Mrs Josselin, of whom she was very fond. They lived at Stratford St Mary on the Essex-Suffolk border, not far from Colchester in a pretty stone house enclosed by leafy woods, ponds and arable land. 'A place that is delightful to me,' she confessed, 'just like walking into a book of Jane Austen's—great finish and great orthodoxy. What R. calls dull. But I *like* Jane Austen.'

It was from this remote and peaceful country house in whose woods lay great pools of blue bells and pigeons murmured in trees above, that M.E.H. wrote to her husband for the last time on how best it was to deal with Hugolin and the complex situation she had brought about between them.

The Hills,
Stratford St Mary
May 31*st*

My darling,

Painful as so many of your letters have been to me read at this distance, I try to believe that there is still the kernel of something of your old self and to that old self I am devoted as ever. You do know that when you come back it will be for you exactly what you make it for me— utter misery or else confidence. As for the children, remember they are not only yours but mine as well. Do not write another 'blue blazer' about this. It is no earthly good. I want a reasonable working plan with some prospect for our ageing years and decreasing energies which may not be visible yet but must come. Nothing that I ever cared about or looked forward to for the end of life is mine now. But it is quite possible to scriggle along without upsetting the coach and with a little good sense some happiness may be left for us both. But not if there are outsiders in it. Your going away for so long without me has been a decided social mistake, I think.

About H., I had made up my mind not to say another word. But if you return in August, this may be my last chance of answering your repeated attacks on me concerning her. For when we meet, I wish to avoid all subjects of discord. On your voyage home think out the facts and let us arrange something amicably. As I have repeatedly said, *H. does not mean to settle at home* and if you have her back it is only a question of time before she makes the situation impossible with me because that is how she likes it.

When she was here last, I gave her no cause of irritation. She chose her own breakfast-time and never came near me except at ten, to say, daily, she was going out. When this had gone on for a week, I told her quite quietly that I did not wish the fire kept up all day in a room never used at all. She had her answer ready: 'Father had better put me in a flat then.' I said that she had the liberty of a flat now and I did not see what she wanted more as I had agreed to all her stipulations. She did not reply. The next day she told me that she *found Chelsea inconvenient* and preferred to return to her Aunts till you put her in a flat.

I want you to understand that I am not saying all this in some extraordinary and demented spirit of 'hatred'. I have reviewed the situation very seriously. I know, too, what the prevailing feeling is—that whatever a mother has done or failed to do in the home, it is her relation with her husband that counts above all; it is the only one too, the public regards. Children go sooner or later from the home but the parents remain and their mark. The great thing now is to let people *forget*. But every time H. appears with you without me, tongues wag and people

247

are agog again. Women have their own code of propriety and it is in no interest of mine to injure H. But I must protect myself since I have no one else to do so. The safest thing now is for us both to *stand together* and *to let things alone.* Let H. make her home with whoever has her confidence whatever it costs in feeling and money, letting her come here as much as she likes. It is best to put such vagaries of hers down to a wish for 'independence' which people understand, and stop all this secrecy and travelling about with her without my knowledge which they don't. You will ruin her if you go on as you did last year. I do assure you the only way is *to let people forget* and to encourage H. as much as possible to have easy relations with me. I am *quite certain* the position is untenable in any other train. You can try having her back. I oppose nothing. But she feels awkward at home now and does not wish to meet our friends and enjoys nothing. Not coming near me except when invited, or writing except to answer has done neither her nor you as her adviser any good.

Ever your loving T.I.G.

Barely had M.E.H. returned considerably refreshed from her stay at peaceful Stratford St Mary when, on 5th June, a cable from Melbourne, Australia, announced: POWER OF ATTORNEY CANCELLED. The following day came a letter written, it seemed, by a madman. Immediately she tried to contact Mr Tyndale.

Queen's House,
Cheyne Walk
June 6th

Dear Mr Tyndale,

I have just had a letter from my husband which I do not know how to describe. I should like to see you if you can come. After all the strain and privation of this year,

Mrs. Haweis in her early forties

A meeting of the Browning Society at Queen's House (Mr and Mrs Haweis are on centre right), from a drawing which the *Illustrated London News* of 14th February 1841 printed with the caption: *Listening to the Master's Voice* (drawing by J. Finnemore)
Left: Mr. Haweis on the steps outside Queen's House

The Reverend H. R. Haweis

it is a little hard to be accused of all the expenditure of 'my Style of Living' and 'of grudging him his holiday'. I am very nearly at my wits' end. If you came tomorrow either early or to dinner (I am engaged from four to seven) his letter could be answered by this mail.

Yours sincerely,

M. E. Haweis

Far away, blissfully unaware of the distress his cable and letter had caused his wife, H.R.H. planned to visit his son in Ceylon before returning to England. He aimed to prolong his wanderings for he well knew the chaotic conditions which bedevilled his church and home.

'Was it possible,' he asked Lionel, to announce his forthcoming appearance and to try to get him as many paid lectures as he could? Then he wailed what a hard time he was having, tossed about the rough coast of New Zealand in little steamers though there were 'Oases with wonderful recognition and reception from State Governors and Bishops down to humble officials and curates!'

By September, utterly exhausted by financial problems and the worry of having had to make up her mind to send Stephen to Cambridge on her own responsibility as she met only with silence from her husband on this project, M.E.H. retired to Lansdowne Grove House, Bath, to undergo special treatment under a Doctor Wylde. Having been in acute pain for weeks and unable to dress herself, she had taken fright. She could not afford to be ill now that she faced the probability of having to pay for Stephen unaided. But having passed his 'Little Go' so successfully, the boy must be given his chance of a university career.

Lansdowne Grove House,

Bath

September 22nd

My dear Lionel,

I am glad you were pleased with my present and are

getting on well. If you have £150 a year as you say, you have a good income, indeed. You could never make anything like it at journalism in England or at anything else. I have done a great deal of writing this year and been in good writing-form but the strain and privation caused by your father's curious forgetfulness of home responsibilities is telling on my health though I shall not tell him so! I am here for treatment. For what I thought was pure rheumatism is not the case. Doctor Wylde here says I am in such a dangerous way that any little shock or chill would turn my present complaint to rheumatic fever. A medical confrère of Doctor Wylde got it in this way and was dead in two days. I regret that I have missed so good a chance for the sake of those family members who wish me away. Doctor Wylde says I have been too much strained. I only know that when Hugolin was home last autumn making the house as she alone can make it, my brain felt as if it was tied up in a knot inside me. All last winter I felt dreadfully ill and weak and fainted repeatedly. I shall not tell the family though, as it delights them but not you. I am now being boiled every afternoon and my arm stretched—very painful—but I have got back some use. I hope Father was all right when with you. He is stronger than he thinks to bear the mere physical fatigue of this year's scampering. His affairs, however, are in a strange condition. I had to carry off the carriage and horse in a hurry to prevent them from being seized and distraints have been twice threatened at the house and only saved by Mr Tyndale's prompt kindness.

I don't think Father realises how much harm this kind of neglect does him for tiny Jacks in office gossip and so do their wives! I think I could pull him round if he would be pulled. . . .

Well, now for more pleasant topics. Stephen takes up residence at Peterhouse almost immediately. There is sure to be some row directly the aunts and H. hear of it and turn it all into something sinister. I would much rather Father had been home before he went up but this can't be helped now. I think Father 'fusses about taking no interest in Stephen' are largely that he does not want the trouble of responsibility. He really cannot mean all he says about him. It would be too unnatural. Anyhow, I have done my best which was my duty as I always do whether others do theirs or not. One gets more happiness that way. How happy was my life till H. came back with her Aunt M's 'little ways' (as they are called in Slaugham) and set the whole of Queen's House ajar. However, I daresay, one day, she'll have her own turn of trial as her horoscope shows.

Did I tell you I was sent for by Lady Henry Somerset whom I hardly know but who has been following the Turner controversy in the *Times* which I set going. I think I am the first member of the family to have a Leader in the *Times*. I stayed a couple of days at the Priory—an old monastery—delightfully fitted up and full of old pictures, Romneys, etc. The principal drawing-room (one of half a dozen) was furnished with old French furniture upholstered in white moiré. My bedroom was vast. Enamelled white walls, a carved bed in the Gibbons school, furniture, curtains (edged with old point lace) in richest yellow satin antique damask and wardrobes hand-painted with delicate arabesques in colour on a white background. Something like a bedroom that! I was reminded of many a great nobleman's house which Father and I used to visit years ago but now never do. I am afraid he is regarded as 'too eccentric'!

I am glad and thankful to hear that you have never done anything to be ashamed of. Keep your standard *high* and be useful to others too. It is what you do for others that tells in the long run and makes one feel contented and jolly. When you say you have made 'life-friends', I hope you are premature. Circumstances change and so does character and one's associates belong to each phase. 'Upwards and onward'!!

Now with love,

Your affectionate Mother

P.S. Re your 'Chevalier', is it published and *in the market*? I must warn you that sensuality has a *very* small public and close thought and a crisp, rapid style necessary. Read Rudyard Kipling and Anthony Hope for *style*. But for matter, Thomas Hardy.

After sealing and addressing her letter to Lionel, M.E.H. took her chair over to the window of her bedroom at Lansdowne House from where she could see the distant old tiled roofs and buildings of elegant Bath. It was a view she loved. Here she sat in the late afternoon sun, pondering over the events of the past few months spent at Queen's House without R. in London. Though she had stood for 'the Vestry' in Chelsea as a member of the Progressive Party opposed to the Moderates, she had failed to get in. Not that she minded, for the Moderates were the better party, she knew. Anyway she had little use for politics. Politicians never put 'measures' before party interests and it was only 'measures' in which she was interested! What was going to happen on R.'s return, she wondered? Would he ever settle down again after all these wanderings? She prayed that his roving tastes had been satisfied at last, especially as several people had been asking her awkward questions recently about St James's—had the church been taken away from him? She had done her best to reassure them. It was hopeless to mention anything of this nature in her letters, she had learnt from experience. It only inflamed him. She sighed. Much as she tried not to be anxious and worry as Doctor Wylde begged her to, worry she did, continually, about the future.

There came a low knock at her door followed by dear Nurse Blanche's welcome appearance with the tea tray. Smiling, M.E.H. rose to greet her.

10. FAREWELL TO CHELSEA

1895-1896

AT THE BEGINNING of November, the long-absent Incumbent of St James's, Marylebone, arrived home having been
away almost a year. His wife received him at Queen's House
and no reference was made on either side to Mrs Smith's visit.
Much to his satisfaction, he found Hugolin settled in her
room and apparently quite happy going her own way and
seeing her own friends. In fact, domestic conditions appeared
normal on the surface, the only drawback so far as H.R.H.
was concerned being that he faced an almost empty church on
taking his first Sunday service.

Hardly though was he back when he attacked his wife on
the old score of her extravagant housekeeping. She retaliated
by showing him her account books. Going over them, he
could not fault her on a single item. Calmly she pointed out
how she had reduced their living costs to a fine art. Was he
aware that food cost them now only between seven and eight
shillings per head a week? Their entire lighting by oil barely
amount to £6 a year. By letting off part of their stabling she
kept the horse in free food and litter. If she died tomorrow,
she announced, he would find her affairs in perfect order with
every shilling accounted for! Completely floored by facts and
figures, H.R.H. retired to the library to write to Lionel.

> Queen's House
> London
> *December 4th*

My dear Lionel,
    We are somewhat in a hole. Mother proves she is as

economical as possible and every attempt to get out of this house and retrench is defeated. Hugolin is back, free and happy and very little in the house. But not taken anywhere. Still she appears at our parties, has hosts of friends and Mother tolerates her presence at dinner but never sees her else. I go my own way a great deal more, finding that being tied to chariot wheels does no good. The house is simply exploited for Mother's friends—not mine. Many important congregation people like Miss Souter dropped. She is no longer invited here in spite of my remonstrances. Stephen is at Cambridge. Who's to pay for him I don't know.

Yr affectionate father,
H.R.H.

It was M.E.H. who was paying for her son's college fees and to do so she 'bespatted the Press' as she described her journalistic activities on every topic under the sun and every thing she wrote, told. A fragmentary newspaper column dealing from a housewife's point of view with the value offered by shopping at a certain public stores was reprinted in tens of thousand by them though she had no idea when writing her 'column' that she was producing a fine trade advertisement. In the same way, the White Star Line used another article called 'Goblin Market' which described 'the Souks' of Tangier and offered her a free trip to Cairo and Constantinople in one of their ships by way of payment.

By now, the week-end habit had established itself among the rich and it was fashionable to boast of owning some bijou house or villa in the Home Counties. From time to time, M.E.H. had taken rustic cottages and done them up for her children's holidays. Now she cashed in on this experience doing a series on 'Woman's home in Miniature' for *The Lady's Realm*. She high-lighted one cottage [Franklyn's Green] declaring that she had entirely re-decorated it for £50 by using rush-matting and colourful Japanese cotton rugs instead of expensive carpets; curtains of fishing-net bought from Craigg's in Lowestoft because 'when washed and hung outside, this net dries by itself' (an early form of drip-dry material); and, finally, by hunting about for second-hand furniture in country 'junk' shops she found and converted, an old spinet into a dressing-table for her bedroom. For chairs, she commandeered a dozen rush-bottomed ones from a derelict church hall at one shilling each. This series brought her instant notoriety through Punch. For this celebrated weekly made her the subject of a lampoon.

> Home cheap home,
> Thine be a cot beside a hill,
> Hums Mrs Haweis in our ear.
> Such cots are in the market still
> At thirty pounds a year.

With his wife winning such kudos from the Press and her name making 'news' wherever she appeared as a public Speaker on the Women's Suffrage Movement or merely as a social celebrity, R.H. concentrated, glumly, on trying Sunday by Sunday, to win back his old congregation, lost to him by his long absence. It was hard going, made the harder by rumours circulating—as M.E.H. said they were—of his insolvency. In fact, most of his private affairs were now public.

So after all it had been a bleak and depressing homecoming-for the 'Myriad-Minded Lecturer'. But worse was to follow. In spite of his having won international fame as a preacher and lecturer, this achievement had by no means impressed his Ecclesiastical superiors. Very soon he received a hint from high quarters that he could look for no more preferment.

His only reaction to such news was to say grandly to his wife: 'I have preferred a wide sphere and I think a nobler calling. To stand on my feet and beg for cheese is absurd at my time of life.' M.E.H. listened to these words in tactful silence. Alas, if poor R. had known, as she did, that had he been in any way less of a powerful personality in the pulpit, he might have been asked to resign from St James's. But those in high office thought it might be better to keep the Reverend H. R. Haweis acknowledged as the best Anglican preacher since Canon Liddon inside, rather than outside, the Church. So after one uncomfortable interview with the Bishop of London which necessitated his replying to several awkward questions put to him in regard to parochial gossip, the Incumbent of St James's was left to put both his religious and domestic house in order.

By the New Year he had made considerable headway and almost filled his church again. But it was not so easy to reconstitute home life on any satisfactory basis. His old jealousy of his son, Stephen, now reasserted itself to a really alarming degree.

Queen's House,
Chelsea
March 16*th*, 1896

My dear Lionel,

I am working harder than ever I did in my life though not so young as I was and almost without hope of seeing any of my dreams realised, my wishes accomplished or my affections satisfied. Hugolin and Stephen are under the same roof but do not speak. Neither does Mother to Hugolin. I have nothing to do with Stephen. He is quite *tête monté* with his College and his mother's flattery. He makes a bid now and then for my approbation but I consider his attitude to his aunts and myself not to speak of his gross impertinence to his sister, equivalent to open defiance of me and I let him know it. But as long as he can hide behind his mother, I can only strike at him through her and this I will not do. Hugolin I only see at snatches. She is as good as gold and universally popular though out of our circle with hosts of friends of her own and dead set against marriage. But a more blameless and blithe little creature does not breathe. Thank God, my health holds out though the wear and tear is great.

Mother knows I must keep up appearances and have no open breach with her. In my profession this would be bad for us all. I am working on the first two volumes of my Travels. If they succeed another two are in tow from 1856 to 1885. Remember me to all kind friends and keep my memory green.

Yr affectionate father,
H.R.H.

In June the situation at Queen's House had deteriorated still further. Lionel is told by his father how he is 'only just keeping his head above water financially. Mother is more extravagant than ever and Hugolin, poor child, creeping in and out of the house (a habit she always had) like a convict. Mother never notices her. *Her* conduct is my misfortune but Stephen's an affront which I should be wanting in self-respect not to resent and mark with my great displeasure.'

A reverse side to this sorry portrait of family life by H.R.H. is given at exactly the same time by his wife again to Lionel.

Queen's House,
Chelsea, s.w.
June 19th

My dear Lionel,

I shall send you some clothes for your birthday as you prefer but I feel rather afraid of buying boots! I hope you are well and keeping clear of fever. We have tried your curries and they are much liked. A great novelty. I have been wonderfully well, having a good time and writing a good deal. Bespattering the Press all spring with my articles and 'constant' interviews.

Father says you detest me, and so does Hugolin, and that you don't want my letters. Mind, I do not believe this and a great deal of nonsense he sometimes talks now. I do not know why. I shall always write to you as I have always done and do all I can for you as long as I see a glimmer of return. But Father is often very odd, these days. I think he can't help it. Then he is all right again and merry. I only tell you this to show you I have sometimes much to bear and to warn you not to believe things that may be said if they sound very unlikely. All my children, like everybody else, are at liberty to go or stay and be hateful to me or nice, and learn by their own experience, for no man learns by any other. I am very thankful to hear from you, dear Lionel, that Father's crankiness is all on the surface and that you have natural feelings for your mother.

Stephen is very good and popular, and apart from the trouble which your aunts have made, and are still making, I am enjoying life as I never thought I should again two years ago, which I should not, if I was the creature they represent. It is a very gay season and we have been going out a great deal. The grand garden parties are now beginning. Father is in excellent preaching and writing form. He has invented a new way to increase the 'collections' but still says he is strained for money more than ever.

Your loving,
Muz

P.S. Did I tell you I opened the May Session of Debates at the Pioneer Club. Father proffered himself for the chair —he does not like to be out of things.

In August, spent at Davos Platz, Switzerland, there came a brief respite from the strained atmosphere and conflicting cross-currents that prevailed at Queen's House. In the High Alps, in the stinging mountain air surrounded by a crowd of admiring young people with whom he raced and joked all day and to whom at night he gave the inaugural Conference lecture, H.R.H. was in splendid spirits and enjoyed himself hugely. According to his wife, he was his old and perfectly good-tempered self. But on their return to London the unhappy conditions of home life soon revived. It seemed impossible for Hugolin and her mother to be under the same roof without altercations ensuing between husband and wife. This was nearly always due to H.R.H. who could not leave well alone and let his wife and daughter each go their own way without interfering. He would keep nagging his wife to notice Hugolin more, and take her about, which was the last thing she wanted of her mother.

Christmas saw Queen's House partially shut up and the Haweis family divided. Hugolin went off to stay with friends and M.E.H. and Stephen left for Suffolk to stay with the Josselyns. It was arranged for H.R.H. to join them but at the last moment, disgruntled and with a painful knee, he decided to stay where he was with only a manservant, Richard, to look after him.

His letter to his wife, without affectionate beginning or end follows the pattern of several others written at this time. It was posted to Suffolk.

Queen's House, s.w.
December 28th

I do not wish to appear exacting or to speak unkindly but I have had a week now of great pain and helplessness —hardly able to dress myself or even to get into a cab and hobble off to the Club. It may seem strange, but after struggling through Saturday and Sunday in great pain, I need rest and some sort of care if I am to attempt the midnight Service and next Sunday. This is out of the question with no cook and only Richard who has done his best. So I shall struggle down to Brook Cottage (his sister Margaret's Sussex home) and there do the best I can for myself. I feel no obligation to stay in a house where S. is supported in open defiance although I still claim the right of having the roof of my own house over my head. I am always sorry when you are ill and no one nurses you more tenderly. Just now I can neither nurse myself or you so I am doubly useless. No one seems to know when you return and I have received no information. This has been not the least wretched of several recent Xmases.

Comment. Blue blazer. Poor man! If he would only keep away from those wretched sisters.

But early in January 1897 H.R.H. found himself almost on the brink of ruin with no money whatsoever in hand and bills amounting to £250 for which he might be summonsed at any moment. What few investments of his remained had so depreciated in value that he could not sell out except at great disadvantage. Besides, the little interest his shares brought in had to be used for repaying the large sums of money that Mr Tyndale had loaned him to meet the claims of Mrs Smith.

Dropping his role of the unhappy and much neglected husband, he went in despair to his wife. They must leave Queen's House, selling the remainder of their lease for a good price, he told her. By this means they could get a smaller and cheaper house near to his church in Marylebone which would be bought in her name. His wife acquiesced to everything he suggested. 'For the fortieth time I agree,' she said colourlessly. 'Furthermore I shall be glad to go. You may then become a little more reasonable to live with.'

They parted coldly. M.E.H. to cheap lodgings in Brighton and her husband to Brook Cottage, Slaugham, where he received all the flattery and cherishing essential to him.

A week later though, H.R.H. and wife were together again at Queen's House and on much better terms than they had been for some time past. In fact, while lecturing on Tennyson in Newcastle, there came a letter dated 7th February in which M.E.H. was her husband's 'darling' once more. Enclosed was a most welcome £5 note.

Hugolin Haweis now took herself off to lodge with a doctor's wife in preference to living at Queen's House. Her father paid for her rooms and her travelling and dress expenses. Much to her mother's annoyance she refused to take up any form of paid work. M.E.H. had been taken on to the staff of *The Lady's Realm* and with a steady salary coming in quite apart from her numerous press payments she relieved her husband of all her travelling fares besides maintaining the carriage and paying for Stephen. From Brighton she wrote to Lionel:

33 Oriental Place

Brighton

March 31*st,* 1897

My dear Lionel,

I was glad to get your bi-annual letter though not over-joyed by its contents. I have not written for some time as you write so seldom and say you do not want to hear of 'bones of contention' [i.e. family matters]. What remains to write about when public interests which occupy me do not interest you? I never said you were 'destitute of filial feeling' and if anyone else has it is the usual gossiping that goes on in the family which I have entirely withdrawn from. Why you are 'to establish a ground of sympathy with me so terribly shaken in the past' I don't know. I am quite unaware of the shaking! I must say the things you write about to your father and H. and your aunts about me rather help the bothers than not. I have done more for you than H. and the aunts and I do not intend to go shares with those interfering and rude women either in my children's affection or anything else. With Hugolin's help they have broken up the whole family and whoever is friends with them is not likely to 'have any use for me' as the Americans say. I cannot tell whether you really want any news of your 'affectionate brother' as you call him! Remember that Stephen has the Haweis temper and is obstinate as ten and is not more enthusiastic about you than you are of him. He considers his aunts and Hugolin have behaved scandalously to me. In this he may be wrong. But it is no use talking. His father every now and then under influence writes the most extraordinary letters to him appealing to his one-time happy associations with his aunts (of which he has had none) and to 'all he owes his sister' which is exactly nothing. He says she used to frighten him at night when he was a baby. Stephen is a boy of shrewd and fixed opinions and I cannot influence him in the least though the family pretend he is my hyponotised slave and echo. But all these things are in your horoscopes and we must make the best of your mixed blood [*his great-grandmother came from Baluchistan.*] Why I am accused now of keeping you from College and kicking you out of England and driving Hugolin naked into the streets, I don't know. Why didn't the police intervene? It all sounds like Gilbert and Sullivan and I often shake with laughter at the nonsense the family talks.

Have you seen what successes the Suffragists have had? No one expected the bill to carry on for the Second Reading this season. But it did by a queer chance long before the proposed day. Most singular. It happened on the same day of Mrs Massingbred's (popular founder of many women's societies) Memorial Service when the Suffrage Bill got slipped in through an Irish Bill failing. We all met in the House of Commons where the excitement was great. Women laughing and kissing and crying and some M.P.s running about like school boys saying they were so glad of our triumph. Lord Templetown who has a Suffrage Bill in the Lords was wild with joy. We are not without hope that the Bill may actually pass this Session. Still that is too much good luck. But it has since gone into Committee which no one hoped for. Lord Salisbury has made himself unpopular enough about Armenia and Greece he might restore the balance easily by giving women the suffrage in the Queen's sixtieth year. That would be monumental!

With love,

Your affectionate,

Mother

But alas for M.E.H. and other supporters of the movement, the Suffrage Bill was not passed until 1918.

With a friendlier atmosphere at Queen's House largely due to Hugolin's departure, and her husband behaving more logically than he had for months, M.E.H. tossed off article after article and tackled the 'sensational novel' of her youth which had been put aside so many years ago. She was determined to finish it. In between times, she worked hard at her astrology. She worked in the peace and quiet of her beloved drawing-room with its seven tall windows looking out on to the distant flowing Thames. A picture so dear and familiar by now that with all the delicate clarity of an aquatint, it was imprinted on her mind for ever. Always she knew that she would remember those changing cloudscapes and rapid swoop of gull; the passage of tug and coal barge or paddle steamer churning its way up-river amid diamond sparkle of water.

So far no offer for Queen's House good enough to warrant acceptance had been received. But come that offer would, and soon. Far too soon, sighed the inner voice of M.E.H.'s secret intuition. For on that day so dreaded, her beloved house would be lost to her for ever.

Easter that year was spent by the Haweises, as so often before, in Rome. M.E.H. had been commissioned to write a series of articles on some royal ladies, describing their personalities and homes for *The Lady's Realm*. In this august assembly was Queen Marguerite of Italy whom she had long admired and met on more than one occasion. A private interview with the Queen was arranged for her at the Quirinal Palace, an interview much enjoyed both by Her Majesty and Mrs Haweis. Other interviewes followed that necessitated travelling on to Germany. Assisted by her husband who supplied the historical details and background, M.E.H. interviewed the Empress Frederick at her country residence Friedrichshof, near Frankfurt, the Duchess of Saxe-Coburg, only daughter of the Czar Alexander II and wife of Prince Alfred, second son of Queen Victoria at Schloss Edinburg;

and later, in London, the Duchess of Albany and Princess Christian.

Queen's House,
Cheyne Walk, s.w.
May 13*th*

My dear Lionel,

We are just back from Rome where I succeeded at last in being presented privately to Her Majesty Queen Marguerite and got Father in too. A great privilege, the receptions which equal our 'Drawing-rooms' being all over. I have always adored the Queen of Italy and presented her with my book *Chaucer* with the daisies of her royal name on the cover richly bound. I had a copy of Father's *Music and Morals* bound, too. It was very funny how Father pretended not to take any interest in the interview till he was 'presented'. Then you should have heard him talking to the Queen! Lord, how he talked! Exceeding well, but no one else had a look in, not even the Queen. I told him afterwards that his arms went round like a windmill and his voice thundered. But that is a slight exaggeration. I send you the first copy of my 'firebrand' [*Flame of Fire*], I hope it will cause a few apoplectic fits. Your Aunt Margaret used to get into such tempers as a girl that leeches had to be applied behind the ears, the coachman driving ten miles to get them. I am sure my small writing successes deprive her of reason! I dance and Topsy Sindon (a popular pantomime dancer of the nineties) isn't in it.

With love
Your affectionate,
Mother

P.S. I forgot to say that Stephen has designed my book cover. I think it's hideous but he said 'it would take' and it has. I made a better one but they preferred his.

Her novel did not make money and was soon forgotten.

On 27th July came the long-dreaded news that a tenant had been found for Queen's House who was willing to pay £200 a year for the remainder of their lease. 'Where we shall go, goodness knows!' wrote his mother to Lionel. She was in low spirits for R. had come begging another loan from her. He was being threatened once more and the bankruptcy court loomed near. She gave him what she could spare, and then, to try and console them both, lobbied for and achieved an invitation to the State Garden Party being held in honour of the Queen's Diamond Jubilee.

As M.E.H., parasol in hand and on very high heels, stood beside her husband on the crowded lawn of Buckingham Palace watching the diminutive figure of her beloved Queen being driven in a small, open carriage through aisles of bowing figures, she was deeply moved. For she remembered the day ten years ago when she had seen Her Majesty take another drive; that memorable Golden Jubilee drive to St Paul's (rather reluctantly) against her will. This drive taken in the grounds of her own home before many who were known to her, was quite different, thought Mary Eliza Haweis, stirred to the depths with loyalty.

As people came up and spoke to her, little did she know that she was making her own last public appearance and would die before her Queen.

The rest of that summer was spent in looking for a new home. At one time M.E.H. despaired of ever finding one, and was on the point of storing all her belongings and going into lodgings, when she saw Number 31, Devonshire Street, Marylebone, and decided that it might do.

Queen's House,
Cheyne Walk, s.w.
August 19th

My dear Lionel,

I meant to have written sooner, but partly the Jubilee

celebrations, and partly troubles, have prevented. The troubles are too melancholy to enter into. But a certain amount of brain mischief in your father suspected lately by me has induced him to put himself under medical advice for a while and a regimen, *which he is doing*. I hope after a time things will improve. He has had a slight stroke or two this summer with absolute and sudden loss of memory without the faintest cause or any irritation at all. Every excitement for him is dangerous. All this may sound gloomy but I am only telling you the facts. I shall stand by your poor father however he behaves. I cannot leave him at the end of his life. I can only do my best for everybody and, as I say, I think things will mend.

I am sending you an account of the State Garden Party. I was so glad to go. We met heaps of people we knew. It was a record attendance. I am also sending you a 'judgement' of your horoscope but I am afraid it will be too late for your birthday. I find astrology of ever increasing interest. Much truth lies therein: the more so as the destiny is only indicated and not inevitable which shows the value of the free will and persistent effort in the right direction.

Your father's affairs are in a frightful condition and we are leaving this house in a month. Only my help keeps him out of the bankruptcy court. He has not a penny to leave; not even the insurance of his life. If Hugolin does not put her hand to earn now she will be a disgrace to us. Stephen will get a post as soon as I hear of one. Meantime, I am paying for him and I am glad to, for he is a thoroughly good boy so far. One more year will give him his degree and then not a penny more! I am sorry I can't send you a nice birthday present owing to things being as they are.

Your loving,

Muz

Before leaving Queen's House she drew a plan of it with such careful measurements that if it was put into the hands of a competent builder a miniature Queen's House could have been built from it. For this was her dream now, even as it had once been her dream to live in Rossetti's house.

Dry-eyed she had made her plan and dry-eyed on the 24th September she walked slowly down the front staircase for the last time and out through the front door into the familiar courtyard. It was a warm still afternoon. The virginia creeper had not yet turned crimson but the white blossom of the two flourishing jessamines had long since faded. Never again would she smell that sweet scent which penetrated up to the drawing-room window where she sat at her bureau, writing. She paused. There was such a sparkle on the river that she had to raise one hand to shade her eyes while she took a long last look at her beloved Thames flowing past at full tide. Never again, she knew, would she live beside its banks. Never again if she could help it would she put foot in Chelsea. To pass by Queen's House knowing that it was no longer hers to enter would be beyond all bearing.

Resolutely, without a single glance back at that house, so beloved, she reached her carriage and drove away, alone, to Marylebone.

11. NUMBER 31 DEVONSHIRE STREET

1897-1898

In a few weeks the Reverend H. R. Haweis and Mrs Haweis were more or less installed at Number 31, Devonshire Street, Marylebone. It was a tall, narrow house rising at the end of Devonshire Street which is nearest to Marylebone High Street and almost opposite a brick-red edifice which still survives called the *Devonshire Arms*. M.E.H. had never lived so close to a public-house; she hated it on sight, besides the neighbourhood, a near-slum in some parts. As for the mean proportions of the rooms she had to decorate and furnish now as best she could, they offended her artistic pride. 'I don't think I can bear to live here after Queen's House' she told her husband.

He could not help but agree and suggested that as soon as they obtained the freehold they could put the house up for sale. Freshly cleaned and painted, they might even make a slight profit on it with which sum of money another house could be bought more suited to their taste.

Early in the New Year, feeling extremely ill but saying nothing of it, M.E.H. dragged herself off to 'frugal lodgings' in Brighton. She simply could not bear to stay in 'The Devil's Den', as she called 31 Devonshire Street, a moment longer.

On the eve of her fiftieth birthday, the 21st February, as she sat alone in her sitting-room, M.E.H. came to the conclusion that never before had she felt so wretchedly ill and depressed. She was losing weight rapidly and the effort of writing anything but a brief note to her editors was beyond her. She longed to lay down her pen and rest. The whole of her small fragile body seemed to have become the battle-ground for a hundred-and-one nameless aches and pains. It was possible, of course, that she had arrived at a woman's change of life. If this was so, she must face up to and conquer the extraordinary malaise affecting her mind and body.

Her thoughts kept turning to her three children: to Lionel, Hugolin and Stephen. Stephen was busy trying to get his degree at Cambridge, she knew. A good boy, revealing some-times a touch of the unpredictable Haweis temper, but affectionate always. He had to be led, not driven. She longed to see Lionel, her first-born, once more, and, perhaps, help him find a more congenial job. For he was still a square peg in a round hole. But there was no money available now for her to visit him. As for Hugolin who managed like no one else to create needless differences of opinion between R. and her-self, she was still in her own flat: and still, she refused to do any form of paid, regular work, even to help her father whom she professed to love. Now and then M.E.H. heard that her daughter had made a fleeting appearance on some stage or other in striped trousers, singing—what? And for whom? No one knew till a friend of Stephen's reported that he had seen her perform and registered his disapproval of her plantation costume in the style of Mary Yohe. Like her she sang 'Oh, honey, ma honey' from Ivan Caryll's *Christopher Columbus*.

M.E.H. was still absorbed in her astrology and when sleep evaded her at night she tried to forget the melancholy sound of the distant, tossing sea by studying her Ephemeris or one of the queer little black-lettered 'magic books' which she collected now. They were better reading than her old 'sleep' books once ordered from Mudie's. One evening after supper she sat down to write to Lionel from whom a letter had just come.

St Marine Square,
Brighton
February 25th

My dear Lionel,

I was very pleased to get your nice long letter though it did not contain very reassuring news. It is rather a mercy though that you did not sell up all your sticks, as you say, for passage money and come home. For I do not see how we could help you here unless it was to go into a bank again. Do not be like your Uncle Willy who gave up the Navy because he was bored and restless and was always just going to get something wonderful but never did and after fearful vicissitudes died, as you know, of drink. Would it not be better to eat a little humble-pie and ask for your old job back at E.P.E.C. now this present one with Mr Barker has turned out so badly? I do assure you it is better to be bored with a small salary than to starve on none. I will help you in any way I can. Your father still never seems to have any money unless that which is borrowed. I fear Hugolin is a regular drain. She is just as rude and undutiful to me as ever. She has a very bad horoscope, but one lives and hopes.

I am still dreadfully grieved at losing Queen's House, but it had to be. Your father could not meet such a rent. These lodgings are somewhat frugal but Brighton is never cheap. Has your Polka been accepted? What is it called? I wonder whether an article or two on Ceylon with a smart style and local colour might not suit the *Echo* here? They give a guinea a column. Stephen gets his pocket-money by doing illuminations and initial letters. . . .

I have come to the conclusion that this life is not intended for happiness, but for discipline, and as we model our characters, if we get some happiness *en route* we may be glad, but cannot *claim* it. I have got very philosophic and I believe the greatest happiness comes from hard work and mental and physical activity. Not that the last is much in my line! Did I tell you that I have charge of the Chaucer course in the 'National Home Reading Union'? Now with the best love and hoping to hear again soon.

Your loving

Mother

P.S. Tell me if there is something I can do.

Struggling on then in her dreary lodgings, M.E.H. managed to stage a half-recovery and returned to London where on 4th April she suffered a grievous loss. For on that day Pompey, her beloved old pug whom she rated as almost human, died as he lay as usual at her feet while she scribbled away at her bureau. One moment he was there, snoring away, the next with a little groan and stir of his aged body, which immediately brought her hand down to caress him, he was gone and she was left alone in the drawing-room, bereft of her companion.

But R. could not have been kinder. Together they took Pompey in a box to the Woking Crematorium where he was cremated just like (and just after) a Christian, M.E.H. told Stephen. His ashes were handed over to her in a little Greek pot that she had brought for that purpose.

M.E.H. was so impressed by the whole procedure of cremation that she gave her husband instructions as to how she was to be cremated like Pompey when the time came.

In May she resuscitated her Saturday 'At Homes' on a reduced scale but without her old enthusiasm. Everything had become too much of a physical effort. Then, from Ceylon, came a short book of stories by Lionel which he wished her to read and criticise.

31 Devonshire Street, w.

May 8th

Dearest Lionel,

Father has just disgorged your book in which I find my

271

name and I write to tell you how much I like it! I consider the stories capital. I am going to try and see if any copies can be taken up over here and stir up Father to do likewise. I really think you might make a speciality of Ceylon stories as just now Indian ones by Kipling have a great vogue.

I am giving a series of Saturday 'At Homes' but nothing much can be done in this pokey house although when people come they profess delight. Father is running *beautifully straight* now and I think we shall revive the congregations gradually which have certainly suffered from family 'eccentricities'. I am sending you a small birthday present. I wish it could be more. But hard as I may work, a good deal is put on me to pay till Stephen's education is finished. I only hope we shall tide through the deep water. The worries are great. Do make a solemn pact with yourself, my dear boy, never to back a bill. It is old-fashioned advice but it works. Do recommend Hugolin if you have any influence to stop this semi-music hall business she pursues and join some accredited dramatic company. If she has any real ability she could.

My dear old Pompey is dead. I miss him every day. He was cremated and I have his ashes in a Greek pot that once contained those human—so there! He can't say on the astral plane that he was not cared for. All the same I remain depressed.

I often wish I could see you but I shall not likely go to Ceylon now. However tell me at any time if you think I can help.

With best love,
Your loving Mother

She did not know how great the worries were to be till she received a letter while in Scotland in which R. wrote some very complicated and odd details concerning the negotiations

over buying the freehold of Number 31 Devonshire Street
that still dragged on.

31 Devonshire Street, w.

June 2nd

My darling,

Farmer [a cousin and a solicitor] strongly advises us to
save further litigation which at present only amounts to
£10, to let Tyndale hold the lease and papers etc. and on
that security advance the whole purchase-money, i.e.
with £600 I shall pay from 'Ayres Villa' (a small property).
He will advance £500 which with £300 will make the house
ours. Only we have to pay 5% on Tyndale's £500 till we
pay it off which we can do as soon as ever we sell. If we
sell for £2000 we shall sail off and be clean out of Tyndale's
hands which is what you want and with a clear £1400 to
£1500 in our pockets. Of course, I shall have to pay off
Tyndale's loans out of my Canadian-Pacific and B.A.
shares. But this plan stops Chancery at once and all
further litigation, and with that £1500 or less we can buy
a freehold elsewhere. This plan requires your assent as
both the house and furniture are settled on you and will
be held as security for purchase money till we pay the
£500. If we now delay or pause the lawyers for Devonshire Street will have no mercy and will plunge us into
Chancery complications. So I have yielded to Farmer's
advice and he is writing to you for your assent which I
hope you will not delay. . . .

Today has been a day of horror. A scaffolding gave way
in sight of this house—one man carried by dead, three
others buried, one not expected to live. Crowds and fire-
engines all the morning. Just now as I write a young
woman plunged through the window next door. Smashed
glass and flower-pots. For several minutes she struggled,
only a nightgown on and with both legs and half her body
over the balcony. Two policemen rushed into our house

and helped three nurses to save her. I shall enquire about it all. I hope you are better. This house is evidently in the neighbourhood of horrors and we had better get out. Disease, madness, sudden death and disaster.

Yr loving H.R.H.

On receiving this letter M.E.H. played a game of delaying tactics. Somehow she did not trust either her husband or Tyndale, whom she had come to dislike, feeling that he had her weak and unbusinesslike husband in his clutches. But she knew that she could trust Herbert Farmer and so she wrote to him to explain everything. In the meanwhile agonised letters came from Devonshire Street that accused her of '"blocking the way." Very hard when I was just floating into calmer waters.' If matters were being arranged so satisfactorily at last, why, argued M.E.H., did she have to sign yet another cheque for £135 after selling at a loss more of her good securities, to free them from being in Mr Tyndale's debt?

In between hysterical scrawls from her husband came others joyfully telling her how St James's had been crammed to hear him preach on the death of Gladstone. Black-coated, top-hatted men had mopped their eyes or uanashmedly wept, while in the evening he had thrown open the vestry with illustrations from the great statesman's life including his portrait swathed in black. His open service in Hyde Park had been attended by no less than 10,000 people. How was it possible for her to take in any seriousness his emotional accusations that she was driving him to the verge of a breakdown by withholding her signature when he was here, there and everywhere giving star performances in pulpit and on platform?

By the end of July she had lost so much weight that it was too physically tiring for her to fulfil any social engagement, while her once pretty skin was like parchment. She ate little and drank nothing. When meals became the bane of her life she bypassed them.

Suddenly H.R.H.'s eyes were opened. He realised that it was his wife not he who was on the verge of a complete breakdown. To get her out of London he arranged to officiate as *locum tenens* for two months at Epsom.

On August 3rd he went ahead to make the necessary arrangements for moving into their Surrey vicarage, a commonplace house he warned his wife, but with a nice garden.

Through August M.E.H. continued to fade away before his anxious eyes. She rarely left the garden and when they entertained Lord Rosebery and other local magnates she talked and laughed as brightly as ever to cover up that she ate nothing.

Soon a long-standing lecture date in the North, forced H.R.H. to leave Epsom for Newcastle. From here, staying at a big country house, he sent a magnificent trophy of fruit, black grapes, peaches and pears to his wife with a note—'Don't let anyone gobble these up. They are for you. We must loose ourselves of Devonshire Street at all costs and remain out of London till you are stronger.'

But his present anxiety for her, and care, had come too late. A telegram received from Epsom sent him scurrying home. 'Mrs Haweis' kidneys badly affected' wired Doctor Wright, 'Advise consultation with a specialist.'

Suddenly M.E.H. took matters into her own hands. She would go to Bath and put herself once more in the charge of Doctor Wylde.

On 3rd October, by a supreme effort of will, she travelled to London, calling at Devonshire Street to recover some private letters and her keys. Before the 'Devil's Den' stood a board with the words 'For Sale' printed large on it, which pleased her. After an hour's rest she went on by cab to Paddington. But when she arrived at the platform where the Bath train was puffing uneasily and filling the air with steam, she sank down on a porter's discarded barrow and cried. Cried as if her heart would break. Her husband gazed at her, appalled. Never in his life before had he seen her break down and cry in public. Always her self-control had been iron. With her face drained of all colour and her limbs shaking she looked a dying woman. Desperately he called to a porter to help him and together they lifted her into an empty compartment and laid her down.

Tenderly, H.R.H. coaxed her to sip a little brandy and eat a tiny piece of cake. A few minutes later their train left. When the ugly back streets and grime-blackened houses of London gave way to the flat green market gardens of Middlesex and they approached Staines, M.E.H's spirits began to revive. She sat up and began to speak quite cheerfully.

On reaching Bath, an unnatual strength seized her and she was her old self driving to Lansdowne Grove House in a carriage. Standing at the front door, waiting to receive her, was Matron and dear Nurse Blanche of whom she was so fond.

Together they led her to her old room on the second floor where one window faced east, the other west. So she could see the sun both rise and set.

But as she sat down on a chair and Nurse Blanche hurried away to make her a cup of tea, she turned to the figure, silenced for once, beside her. 'Rennie' she said in a moment of flashing illumination, 'Rennie, I shall not come out of this place alive.'

She began her treatment that same evening by taking a vapour bath.

'You look like a varnished guinea-pig, my dear Mrs Haweis,' declared Doctor Wylde on seeing her. He had diagnosed at once that the pores of her skin were clogged and, having ceased functioning, the accumulated poison was being driven into her kidneys.

Her bath brought instant relief and the following morning when her husband came to say goodbye she assured him that she felt better already.

Two days later, a subcutaneous eruption broke out all over

her body, causing great pain and skin irritability but, in spite of this condition, she insisted on leaving her bed to sit by the window. Every now and then her tired eyes kept turning to a large poster that hung from the end of her bed. This poster announced her appearance at the Browning Hall, Walworth, where she had promised Mr W. T. Stead to give a talk on Chaucer to a Society of Working Men in which he was interested. That she might not be able to fulfil this promise was preying on her mind.

On her husband's next visit she asked him what she could do in regard to her Chaucer lecture. When he proposed that he might do it for her she accepted his offer gratefully. There and then, they got out the box of coloured glass slides which she had had made as illustrations from the chromo-lithographs for her book *Chaucer for Children*. Amicably, they made notes together and then she asked for pencil and paper.

In half an hour she handed the following prophetic lines to her husband. Would he recite them as an apology for her absence?

> I am not nigh yet fain I would be here:
> Pray you, good people, hold old Chaucer dear.
> No man e'er sang more truly from the heart,
> Nor wedded speech to thought with subtler art!
> Pray you be patient with my poorer speech,
> My pictures limned to place within your reach
> The sights he saw, the people he portrayed,
> The lessons that he taught, the songs he made.
> Great Chaucer's dumb, and broken is my spell:
> So now to all good-night—and fare ye well!

So in Bath M.E.H. wrote her swan song. For the next day she suffered a severe relapse. An alarming tendency to dropsy became apparent. She swelled all over and spoke in a thick, slurred tone with difficulty. This last symptom terrified her.

Some days later when on a flying visit, H.R.H. entered his wife's room and heard her speak, not in her clear, musical voice, but like one with an impediment, such a feeling of fear swept through him that, after a light kiss, he hurriedly left on the pretext of going to buy her some special food in the town. For the first time in his life, Hugh Reginald Haweis faced the shattering possibility that his wife might die and nothing in the world mattered so much to him now as to try and keep her alive.

On his return with a basket of delicacies such as she had once enjoyed, he began his vigil at her bedside, fulfilling at least one promise that he would tend her if she was ever ill and in need of him.

At last, husband and wife were together with no fear of interruption from the outside world. Vanished for ever the troublesome ghosts of those whom H.R.H. had once jealously called 'her ill-advised attendants'. Adoring Deutsch, John Richard Greene. Poor Jack Penfold and that virile lion-hunter Colonel Godwin Austen whom he had disliked so much. But the knowledge that he had got his wife, at last, to himself brought little consolation. For he was desperately aware that in her utter physical exhaustion, her complete indifference to anything outside the compass of her room's four walls, she had floated far beyond his reach for him to stage any form of emotional come-back by way of tears, pleading her forgiveness. An invisible Presence was in her room. That Presence which terminates all human relationships.

So, as H.R.H. put a glass of lemonade to his wife's lips or smoothed her pillow, he was haunted by past acts regretted or left undone; words spoken that might have been left unsaid; explanations never given; and letters he should not have sent.

One afternoon in that heavy stillness which fills the interior of a nursing-home when patients try to rest or sleep the tedious hours away, H.R.H. heard these words come, halting and slow, from the motionless face on the pillow: 'Oh, I wish some kind angel would come and take me across!'

So the monotonous hours passed till he had to leave for

Edinburgh where he was due to preach. Back in London the following day, he found no news from Bath.

31 Devonshire Street, w.

November 10*th*

My own precious,

My whole heart yearns towards you now and nothing you can say or do will shake my love. Till you are better do be guided by me. Postpone immediate expense and worry which you can't bear and try to see that the moment we are subpoena'd against my wish and there is a woman, a money question and you in opposition, even if you get hundreds,—you will get nothing. We are both done for. Don't deal me this other knockdown blow before I have got you well. You have taken a turn. I can see it. I watch so closely I haven't had my clothes off for three days. But a night's rest may help me through Sunday. Back soon and no more discordant words.

Yours in love,

H.R.H.

P.S.   I have Chaucer proofs with me.

The following afternoon he gave his wife's talk on Chaucer at Walworth which was extremely successful. Rushing back to Landsdowne Grove House, he found a far livelier M.E.H. waiting in her room to hear how he had got on with Chaucer. She even smiled, faintly, on hearing of his wonderful reception and how many in the audience had sent kind messages and good wishes for her speedy recovery.

Her talk on Chaucer dealt with, she began to worry over another commitment: an article on *Servants and Served* commissioned by *The Contemporary Review*.

At length, it was decided that she should dictate what she could say by way of short sentences which her husband would then write-up in essay form. As she assembled her ideas as best she could in drowsy weakness, did she remember the day when she and a certain young Mr Haweis had travelled by train to Sevenoaks and argued so long and to no purpose on this very same subject of 'servants and served'? If she did, she kept this memory to herself. For she had finished with the past and the present concerned her only so far as it saw the end of her literary commitments.

That Sunday prayers were asked at St James's for Mrs Haweis lying dangerously ill in Bath. It was the first intimation received by the outside world of her breakdown. For M.E.H. had been adamant that no one should know she was ill. Above all, none of her editors in case it should prejudice her work with them.

After the service people gathered in groups to discuss the sad news. Poor Doctor Haweis! No wonder he appeared distraught, waving away anyone who approached him except, of course, Miss Souter.

On his return to Bath he lunched by appointment with Doctor Wylde and Sir William Crookes, an expert on stomach diseases. Both men assured him that though his wife was in a precarious condition they had her various complaints successfully under their control.

Her recovery depended now on getting her to take nourishment for she was literally starving to death.

After lunch, on going to her room H.R.H. was amazed to find her sitting up dressed, in her chair, waiting for him.

'I don't want to stop here. Take me somewhere else. They have done all they can,' she said to him fretfully.

'Yes I know, darling, but all your symptoms are better. In fact Doctor Wylde is quite optimistic. Why, even your voice is more like your own today. So much stronger,' he replied, soothing her.

'Yes, that may be. But you don't know how hard I try to speak clearly and to pronounce each word well. Please, take me out, Rennie. Please.'

There was nothing for him to do but to call for Nurse Blanche. Carefully she was carried downstairs and propped up on cushions in Doctor Wylde's open victoria. Hot water bottles were placed to her feet; another on her lap. Then getting into the carriage her husband put his arm round her stiff, doll-like body and almost holding her up, they made a slow tour of Bath for three-quarters of an hour.

As if she had received a shot of superhuman strength, M.E.H. gazed intently at everything round her. She seemed like one clinging desperately to life, thought her husband. He did not know that in her stoical way she was saying farewell to the world she loved: to the trees in their mournful loveliness of dull crimson and yellowing leaf: to the faint blue sky overhead delicately marbled by a pattern of small clouds: to the dwindling rays of the sun barely warm on her face and hands. A nostalgic, last breath of summer enclosed Bath and its environs like a charm. Slowly they drove round till H.R.H. told the coachman it was time to go home.

Early on 13th November H.R.H. left for London in high spirits. He felt sure that he was not going to lose his wife after all. God had stayed His Hand. She would recover and they would begin a new life together by going abroad for the winter. But as the countryside slid past the window of his railway compartment he began to think of the many differences of opinion still existing between his wife and himself and of conversations recently held. In one she had told him of her Will made in favour of Stephen whom she wanted to finish his university career and obtain a degree. The more he thought about this will the more he began to worry and fret. For he envisaged great difficulties. As soon as he was home he dashed off a note to Bath.

> 31 Devonshire Street, w.
> *November 15th*

My darling
I am waiting anxiously for every post to hear from you. If you are going to do anything to your Will remember I don't want your money. But I should like my own books,

papers and the Haweis family pictures and relics, such as they are, secured to me, which might all be willed away with the house as, by the deed, all go together. I shall be grieved if you leave your personal jewellery away from me as it is intimately associated with you and shall be worn by no one else but kept together in a case. I do not know who are your trustees and executors. Of course, I should be. But if you prefer a solicitor have Johnson or Farmer. I do think that all papers supposed to be incriminating or of a private nature should not be opened by executors but either destroyed or handed to me. Certainly your books and papers should be left to my care. No one could deal with them more lovingly and wisely than I could. But I pray and believe that there is no chance of such questions arising. You may outlive me. My Will has become very simple. You have got all I can give except my labour and love while life lasts. I am working at your article. Post just in but no word from you. Hope you are well.

Yrs

H.R.H.

In the meantime, with her husband away, M.E.H. sent for her son, Stephen, to whom she gave her last instructions.

'Whatever they say or do, Stephen, I won't leave this room except in a box, I know. My Will provides for you to finish your university career. After that, it is up to you to make good in whatever work you choose to do. I have left you all my papers, private journals, and MSS. Don't trust any member of the family, Stephen. Not even your Father. He is not reliable,' she murmured weakly, 'though I do believe in his own way he loves me.'

Stephen was far too stunned listening to his mother's calm acceptance of death to say anything. Bewildered and unhappy he sat, motionless, beside her bed. On his departure, M.E.H. wrote a short letter to her husband and then asked

Nurse Blanche's help for another to Lionel. In the end, Nurse Blanche wrote it for her.

Lansdowne Grove House,
Bath
November 15*th*

My dear Lionel,

I have just got your second letter—your first would have been answered but I have been so dangerously ill that I could write no letters. Even now I am not out of the wood. I have had a very complete and sudden breakdown after feeling ill and miserable for all the summer. Nearly every organ has given way at once and all the diseases contradicting the rest so that remedies have been very difficult. But they are very kind and capable here, the nurses young and merry, and Doctor Wylde really a genius. He has got rid of all the worst symptoms but the rallying power seems weak. I think he will cure everything in turn and then I shall die. The strain of the past five or six years has been too much even for my pluck. I cannot advise you to come home for there is no home. My furniture is stored in Devonshire Street which may be let at any moment. I don't see what you are to do except peg along. I do wish you had remained in Tea where I put you and done your writing etc. in between whiles. Every penny that I saved up—and what his father left him—is gone, no one knows where, squandered by your Father. Of what he earns from week to week Hugolin has to have a good allowance. Your Father is doing nothing to help S. and how we are to live I cannot see. I hope you will find some good girl with some money who will make you a home some day. You are a clever personable young fellow and if you are steady many girls would like you. I shall do everything I can to help you. I hope the Editor of the *Lady's Realm* will take your stories. They came safely but I was too ill to read them. On October 6th no one thought I would live through the night but I did. I shall never forget the feeling of slowly dying but Doctor Wylde sat up with me all night and certainly saved my life. Your Father comes down constantly to see me and writes me letters of the utmost devotion and affection. S. is very miserable about me. I have been here six weeks and cannot stand yet. But if I live through the winter I shall soon begin to work again. You must keep up heart. I should like to see you but I know to come back would be a worse disappointment than your worries where you are. Life does not get easier as one gets older. I think all life is a lesson of patience. . . . I am not able to write or dictate any more.

Your loving Mother,

M.E.H.

As soon as M.E.H's note from Bath concerning further details of her will dropped through the letter box in Devonshire Street and her husband had it in his hand, scanning its contents, he was writing off again to her feverishly.

31 Devonshire Street, w.

November 17th

My darling and most precious one,

The account of your weakness this morning is most dreadful to me. I was rooted in the hope that you had taken a real turn for the better and felt buoyant till just now your dreadful details about your *Will* has prostrated me. I will start off for Bath tomorrow morning though your note contains no words of wanting to see me. Let us leave all discussion. I shall at least know that if you never alter your will which reflects such indignity on me and despoils me of all I have given you together with the house and private possessions in favour of Stephen, you at least *meant* to alter it and probably never quite realised the inconceivably strange use and disposition you were making of the power and property I so confidingly placed unreservedly in your hands. But no more of this. Again nothing matters to me really but your health.

Yr loving,

H.R.H.

The 'power' he had confided to his wife was the Deed of Gift drawn up in the summer to prevent his few remaining assets and possessions being claimed by his creditors.

On entering his wife's bedroom a day later, H.R.H. received his last and most terrible shock. For she had changed beyond all recognition. So small and shrunken she appeared in bed with her arms like two little withered sticks lying outside the sheet drawn up to her chin and her once lovely hands shrivelled paper-thin, that there was nothing literally left of her. Her face was quite expressionless.

When, dazed and trembling, H.R.H. bent over to kiss her he saw that her eyes, once so alive and challenging, were empty and dull—the light fading from them. Why had he not been told of what was happening? Why had he left her when Time was so short?

As he put his lips to her cold forehead, she murmured: 'I have been here quite long enough.'

To Nurse Blanche's grief, her appetite had not returned. She could not swallow a crumb. Doctor Wylde had ordered that she must be fed artificially. Not that dear Mrs Haweis minded. 'I think it saves her all effort,' the nurse told her stricken husband.

The following morning M.E.H. became very restless, complaining of ceaseless pains in all her joints. By evening this condition had passed, like others before it. Doctor Wylde declared that all signs of dropsy had vanished.

Throughout the day of 22nd November, the last he was to spend with her, H.R.H. tried to tempt his wife with delicacies. With much coaxing and many endearments, he got her to take a few grapes, some raisins and a teaspoonful of jelly.

285

Then he asked her if she would not see her daughter. But her answer was only a blank stare.

Early the following morning, due that day to lecture at Leeds, he went into her room about eight o'clock and found her asleep. She had had a poor night, said Nurse Blanche. So he did not wake her. For a few minutes he lingered beside her bed across which a long thin bar of sunlight quivered from a crack in the drawn blinds. Then, with one last look, he left to pick up his bag where he was staying with Stephen.

Richmond Lodge,
Bath
November 23rd

My own darling,

My one desire is that your real wishes should be carried out as expressed by you to me. If all you have is *now* as you say left to Stephen, *the house and all that is in it will go from me* (if at any time I am wretched enough to survive you) as it is now all yours. Let Johnson know you mean me to have for my life *all I had power to make over and did settle on you in that Deed*, drawn up by Farmer. If you can see J., I will send him down to you. If you can't, send him the enclosed slip and say you wish a clause inserted embodying it—*if I have rightly understood your intention.*

Your ever devoted and loving,
H.R.H.

P.S. Wire or notes at any time to 31 Devonshire St.

But even if M.E.H. did read this note from her husband, she had no wish to alter her will. Since 1891 she knew R. had squandered nearly £10,000 and even his own solicitor, Tyndale, had admitted to her that he was not fit to have even £100 at his disposal! Stephen must be protected till his education was completed.

On his arrival in London, H.R.H. posted a second hastily scribbled note prompted by some strange premonition.

Euston
Wednesday, 10.15 *a.m.*

My own most precious darling,

I came to your room at eight am this morning and found you asleep. So had not the heart to wake you. But I longed for the dear eyes to open upon me. I am trying to fix lecture matters in my head for Leeds tonight but my whole heart is by your side. I would not go did I not need the fees so as to be able to pay and you lack for nothing. Say a word to anyone who is about that you *love* me and *want* me as I do you. Nothing else in all the World do I want or ever have or ever shall in comparison.

Your loving husband ever

'God be with us and we with Him.'

Reaching Leeds about eight p.m. that evening he found at the hall where he was to lecture a telegram from Doctor Wylde recalling him instantly: 'Mrs Haweis sinking and asking for you,' he read.

But there was no train back till midnight, so he made his distraught way on to the platform with his wife's death warrant in his pocket. For once, that night, he spoke like a man in a dream, indifferent to the applause of the huge audience gathered to hear him. His lecture finished, he stumbled down off the rostrum and made his way to the exit door like an unconscious sleep-walker, unaware of anyone pressing forward to speak to him.

He got into the waiting cab and left for the station. Of that hideous night journey he remembered nothing as he sat huddled and cold in the corner of his empty compartment. All was a blank before him. He could only pray silently that he would not be too late to see his beloved again, as he had left her, breathing gently like a child.

But in the cold, grey, unsubstantial light of early morning

when the front door of Lansdowne Grove House opened at his knock, it revealed the figure of Nurse Blanche. One look at her pale tired face told him he was too late.

Silently she escorted him to the room whose blinds were drawn down. There she left him standing, alone, beside a figure lying composed and still. She looked like one asleep. With every little line smoothed away from her serene face, it was the face of the pretty young girl he had married years ago. He broke down and wept.

Later he was told that Mrs Haweis had died about three am that morning the 24th of November while seated in her chair by the window. In the afternoon, when she had insisted on leaving her bed for her chair, Doctor Wylde had known she was sinking and sent his telegram. They had asked if she wanted to see her son, Stephen, but she had shaken her head. At intervals, though, said Nurse Blanche, 'She kept asking for you, Mr Haweis.'

By the evening post his note written at Euston Station arrived and was held up before her eyes to read. She seemed content, murmuring: 'God be with us both,' her husband's final message.

Matron and Nurse Blanche had stayed with her till the end. 'She smiled often during the last hours and asked when you would arrive. Then, just before she stopped breathing, she leant her head on Matron's shoulder and fell asleep. We hardly knew she was gone.'

Had that kind angel come and 'taken her across' as she had once wished he would, wondered her grief-stricken husband?

When he saw her again, she had been dressed in white with white flowers put into her hands and more at her feet. She seemed diaphanous to him. No longer of this earth but a wraith all spirit. He kissed her ice-cold forehead and then covered her face with a small handkerchief that Nurse Blanche had given him. After another last long look, he turned away, sobbing. His whole life, he felt, had come to an end in this room.

'I will go on and will continue to go on,' he told his son, Stephen, when he arrived some hours later at Lansdowne Grove House, 'but it is not the same person doing it. It will never be the same person.'

Then he broke down again and wept. Looking at the poor little broken man whom he hardly knew but called father, Stephen Haweis felt that they had changed places. He was no longer a child but his father seemed one crying there before him, bereft and helpless.

Three days later, father and son stood alone outside the door of a brick building at the Crematorium, Woking. All had been done as Mary Eliza Haweis had directed. Her body had been wrapped in asbestos and a vein in her arm opened just before the lid of her coffin was screwed down. Now that frail shell containing her remains had been consigned to the white heat of a blazing furnace which would consume it in an instant of time.

But Mary Eliza had stipulated that the furnace which was her funeral pyre should not be inspected under an hour. As the slow minutes dragged by, H.R. turned to his son and said fretfully: 'It is nearly an hour. Let us go in and order the inspection.'

But Stephen Haweis replied, obstinately: 'No, it is not yet an hour. I shall stay here until it is.'

In the uncertain light of that dismal November day father and son waited for the Crematorium clock to strike. When it did, they moved forward and entered the door before them to claim the ashes of Mary Eliza Haweis.

Two days later, there came the ring of a bell at the front door of the vicarage of Boughton Monchelsea which was immediately answered by the Vicar who had been waiting in his study to hear it. Before him in the dusk stood the small slight figure of a boy in heavy mourning. He carried a small parcel. 'Come in, please. Come in. You are Stephen Haweis, I take it.' The boy nodded. He looked pale and drawn. 'No, I won't, if you don't mind. There isn't time. I have to get

back to London tonight. My father said so. Here, here is . . . '
He came to a full stop and silently, with trembling lips handed
his small parcel, the little urn containing his mother's ashes, to
the tall, kindly faced man standing before him. Then he vanished into the night.

12. DEATH STRIKES AGAIN

1898-1901

IT WAS a dark and foggy December afternoon and the street lamps identified only by an eerie glimmer had already been lit in Devonshire Street. Behind the folds of a half-drawn curtain in the ground floor window of one house stood a figure, peering out. It was the Reverend H. R. Haweis anxiously awaiting the arrival of Herbert Farmer acting, legally, for his late wife, and Tyndale coping, as usual, with the chaotic state of his own affairs.

H.R.H. was a worried man, for the Deed of Gift which had been the cause of so much tragic wrangling between his 'darling' and himself as she lay dying had not been revoked by her as he had prayed it might be till the last moment. Under the terms of her will, Stephen was sole legatee and he, her loving husband, received nothing. As M.E.H. had had to raise the sum of £600 to secure the leasehold of 31 Devonshire Street in her name, her hard won savings amounted to little more now than £1,500. Still the house, her property, went to Stephen and her husband no longer possessed the right to keep or sell it. Quite rightly, he was incensed. The more so when he learnt that Stephen also inherited all the Joy family pictures, furniture, china and plate besides his mother's MSS., papers and letters.

Fortunately, there was a loophole. His son was still a minor and as his father he was his lawful guardian. In this capacity, by nefarious planning, he was determined to put right, quietly and secretly, what he considered to be unjust and wrong. Lionel and Hugolin were as much M.E.H.'s children as Stephen. He must provide for them as no one else would.

Staring out into the fog which had obliterated *The Devonshire Arms*, usually visible from where he stood, he thought how his darling would have expostulated against the depressing gloom of this scene if she had been with him. But she was gone and he was utterly alone. Never more would her light musical voice ring in his ear; never more, her step be heard on the stairs. Like some empty shell cast up on an alien shore, a shell whose vanished occupant had once given it entrancing colour, life, form, the house lay behind him empty; dead.

Finishing his task of drawing the curtains together, he returned to his writing-table strewn all over with bundles of letters and papers. He must continue his labour of scrutinising everything that had once belonged to his wife while he still had the chance. Farmer and Tyndale must have been held up by the fog. They would appear in time, he thought.

Querulously, he put two of four stout leather volumes marked with the well-known gilt monogram of M.E.H. in a drawer which he, then double locked. After reading his wife's *Thought Books,* he had decided that two must be destroyed before Stephen left for Paris. For the boy had obstinately refused to continue his university career on the plea that it was a waste of money as he wished to be an artist. Maybe he was right, thought his father. Painter's blood coursed through him and money was tight. Far too tight to ensure him an easy, cushioned passage through college as his mother had wished. He anticipated no trouble in getting Stephen's consent to destroy any one of his mother's private journals after stressing their sacred and personal nature to him. The boy understood well enough that he should have been named her literary executor.

How thankful was he to have gone ahead with his reading of everything that recorded the last muddled years of their marriage. Years in which, according to his darling, he had played too often the role of an absentee cleric and erring husband.

But he must be generous and forgive those strange aberrations of her mind. So much of what she had put down in writing simply was not true in his opinion but figments of her sick, distorted imagination. Better than anyone, he knew how her once so clear and logical mind had deteriorated under the stress of illness; or so he liked to tell himself.

His hand went hovering over a bulky packet of letters which he had separated from those to be kept. These letters from Emmanuel Deutsch and John Richard Green told their own tale of the admiration—in the case of Deutsch of love—that both men had felt for his wife. There were other letters, too. Those from slavishly adoring Pen whom he had discovered had often come to May's rescue with small sums of money to meet a pressing bill (usually his) during his absences from home, and others from that absurd lion-hunting explorer, Colonel Godwin Austen. His letters tied up with ribbon actually accused him, Hugh Reginald Haweis, of neglecting his beloved. They pointed out that her husband was incapable of appreciating her courage in adversity besides her beauty, wit and intelligence. How dare he? This man who, in spite of his notorious expeditions out East, was a fool and a charlatan in his view? But he would take his revenge of him now and destroy his letters with the rest.

Picking up several bundles, he hobbled painfully over to the fire (his knee had begun to pain him, again, and there was no one to rub it as M.E.H. had done) and flung the first packet, defiantly, on to the red-hot coals. Brittle, thin and dry, the envelopes caught alight and flames shot up. As he watched the scrawled-over sheets penned by hands not his being reduced to nothing but ashes, he could not help thinking of another fire which had so recently consumed the body of his beloved wife. All that was left now of her beauty, wit and intelligence, so long admired, was a pinch of grey-white ash reposing in a small urn in a lonely Kentish graveyard. Tears came into his eyes. Tears which were always his to command whenever he thought or spoke of his wife.

Suddenly, from far off, echoing down through the well of the silent house, came the faint, twanging sound of a banjo. Hugolin must have crept in (that mouse-like habit of hers familiar for years) and be practising, upstairs, in her room. She should have come and seen him. He needed to tell her of the lawyers' visit and that tea must be provided for them. It was a pity but she was no housekeeper like her mother. She had to be constantly reminded of her duties. Pushing down the last packet of offending letters into the glowing bed of the fire with a poker, he went to the door, opened it and called petulantly:

'Hugolin! Hugolin! Come down. I want you.'

That very moment, there came a peal at the front door. Farmer and Tyndal had arrived.

A few days later, a letter was delivered at Devonshire Street from kind Mrs Josselin. It contained a cheque for £1,000. This sum, wrote Mrs Josselin, she had intended leaving 'dear May' but now at her death, knowing her wishes, she wanted it to be paid into her estate for Stephen. *Her* wishes? What did Mrs Josselin, that old country bore who had never liked him, know of *his* darling's wishes, thought H.R.H., furious. Stephen was well provided for. Hugolin was not and neither was Lionel! In a violent fit of temper, he rang his bell and informed a flustered maidservant that he would not be home for lunch. He hurried off to his Club. Here he remained brooding over his persistent bad luck; in particular his misfortune of never being able to put his hand on ready money when it did turn up! Eventually, he unburdened himself to Lionel.

New University Club
December 5th

My Dear Lionel

I have delayed writing, hoping to give you some definite news but Mother's Will business drags on. Nothing anywhere finished yet. Meanwhile creditors won't wait and I have to pay debt after debt which has to come out of the estate besides advancing Stephen money to go to Paris, an expense which will also be refunded. Hugolin has settled in and keeps house quite well. I miss Mother more and more. She was absolutely a part of my life and the world is wondrously empty without her. Often I am under an influence bordering on despair. Every detail, event, object reminds me of her—with all those inconceivable worries and misunderstandings. I would have lived anywhere, done anything, suffered anything could I have kept her. I know now how unutterably deep was my life in her and how for thirty years of toil and labour of love and planning for her, I had really lived only for her. She never really had a rival in my inmost heart whatever were my failings and blunders and fiascos in money relations with others and inconceivably complicated and difficult circumstances of life.

Yr. affect. father

H.R.H.

Christmas came and went; a dreary melancholy Christmas. Nothing seemed to be going right for H.R.H. so often closeted with his lawyers. There were endless arguments but in spite of using his most persuasive powers of speech he could not get that unlucky Deed of Gift rescinded. Besides this, he heard that a codicil added to his wife's will on the day of her death, leaving him £50, had been declared invalid. This was the last straw. Fuming and fretting with Hugolin as his only listener, he felt that in every way he had been most cruelly defrauded by fate.

Before Stephen left for Paris, his father called him into the library and announced that he planned a memorial to his mother which would take the form of a fund raised in her name to aid Working Girls. A meeting to discuss the preliminary arrangements would take place at which he wished him, Stephen, to take the Chair. Friends of his mother who had promised to attend included Lady Henry Somerset, Lady

Arnold, Mrs Wynford Phillipps, Mr W. T. Stead and Mr Wilkins, Editor of *The Lady's Realm*.

On the day arranged, a small slight boy feeling rather bewildered and not knowing exactly why he had to occupy such an important place, took the Chair. It was not long, though, before he heard his father announce to the assembled company that his youngest son would start the monetary ball rolling by donating the sum of £1,000 to his mother's Memorial Fund. The money, in fact, that Mrs Josselin had presented to him.

The following day Stephen Haweis left for Paris.

March came, gusty and cold, and another letter was sent off to Lionel in Ceylon.

31 Devonshire Street
Portland Place
March 12th, 1899

My dear Lionel

Your letter just received. Stephen is in Paris roughing it, I fancy, after the lap of luxury for years. We are all on good terms but his head is a little turned by inheriting his mother's money, though it won't turn out as much as he fancies. I feel deeply her leaving him all her lace and jewels but I know it was done to prevent Hugolin or any woman in whom I might be interested getting them. Intense jealousy born of love of me but ending in injustice to all. When all is done I shall make a division of all my property between you and Hugolin. Money I now have little or none to leave. Plate and property somewhat but before I depart I may be able to lay by some more. [This he did, by hiding Stephen's furniture left by his mother in a cellar of his church. The furniture was appropriated at his death by Hugolin.] As long as I live, there is always a home for you. I am very hard worked just now, lecturing and preaching. Asthma and bronchitis my two great enemies. I go to Tangier with

Hugolin for about a month in April. We all think of you and there may be brighter days in store. Hugolin is adverse to marriage which is a pity, but I leave things alone. I preach at Manchester Cathedral before I leave for Tangier.

Yr. loving father,

H. R. Haweis

That spring in spite of a good holiday spent with his old friends the Perdicardis which cost him nothing, he was in low spirits. The London season was in full swing but, of course, not for him, a bereaved widower. He was missing M.E.H. more and more. He missed, too, as he repeatedly told Lionel, what she had contributed to household expenses through her press earnings. Those many little extra luxuries were no more. Although the 'collections' at St James's were good and the congregation large, the fashion for pew-holding by the monied set was fast dying out. So the summer weeks dragged by with little entertaining done in Devonshire Street. July came and on the first Sunday of that month, 1899, the Reverend H. R. Haweis, M.A., preached one of his longest and most publicised sermons in connection with the International Congress of Women which had been convened by the Countess of Aberdeen at Queen's Hall in order to give support to the cause of Peace and Arbitration. He took as his subject *Woman As A Peace-maker*, opening his sermon with the words 'And many women were there' from chapter XXVII of the Gospel of St Matthew.

As he clambered up the familiar pulpit steps to take his usual stance, half-standing, half-leaning, against the low brass rail in front of him, did he see in that sea of up-turned faces a small rapt one with blue eyes fixed on him, adoring; the face of his girl-bride, Mary Eliza Haweis? For his whole sermon, that morning might be taken as a belated tribute paid by him to her life-long interest in the cause of women and the role that they could, if allowed to, play in the world political as well as the world domestic.

Wherever the interests of humanity are concerned you will find as a rule many women are [there he thundered out]. My friends, this last week has witnessed a spectacle quite unique in the history of the world. There never has been such a thing before as a large International Congress of Women met together in this way for such a purpose. It marks an epoch in the evolution of women's influence. They are met together for no party purpose or to consult merely the wide interests of their own sex but for the general welfare of humanity. There never was such a movement. Women have moved and acted in the old days as though they were moved by the Holy Ghost. But there was at no time such co-operation, such unanimity, such organisation for great and eternal purpose, for interests which, touching earth, aspire and reach up to Heaven. When I looked through the programme of the Congress of Women, I was amazed at the large variety of subjects which found a place in it. There was sociology, there was literature, there was hygiene, there was drama and there was politics. The days are past when the shallow sneer about women attempting to engage in politics is heard with any kind of patience.

In conclusion, thumping on the edge of his pulpit, he told his congregation of how he gave his full support to those great aspirations expressed by good and noble women from all countries who have borne on their hearts the burden of humanity and who have tried to do something for Christ and followed in His footsteps in the paths of Peace.

An exhausted but, perhaps, happier man for having struck his own blow in the defence of a cause so intimately associated with his vanished wife, he went home to Devonshire Street accompanied by a completely disinterested Hugolin.

At the end of July the Reverend H. R. Haweis put cleaners into his church, a caretaker into his house and departed with his daughter to Norwood where he was relieving the Vicar of his parochial duties for five weeks.

On his return home in September, he began to go through his wife's MSS. with a view to publishing a book composed of her last writings. For money was needed as usual.

Barely had he begun work when London heard that Kruger had presented an ultimatum to Britain. On 18th October, the Boer War was declared.

In Devonshire Street, life went on in much the same way with H.R.H. immersed in church and literary affairs. But he found time to write to Lionel, airing his grievances as always.

> 31 Devonshire Street
> Portland Place
> *November* 21*st*, 1899

My dear Lionel,

Stephen is not earning a farthing as yet though he is doing his best to prepare for it and I think working honestly. Of course, I have to support him. Mother's money, after paying endless bills and expenses, will only bring him in £25 a year. Hugolin is admirable in every way, almost perfect in character to me. Very bright and clever though we naturally haven't much in common. I am at the top of my powers just now but it doesn't seem to lead to anything. I need a new sphere sadly. I have just finished putting together some essays and addresses of poor Mother's with biographical links in between the chapters to give glimpses of her. The very best and most favourable that I could choose. This is the fatal week (last year!) and I am filled with immense depression. I realize intensely that, in spite of all the worry and anxiety I had, life to me is nothing without her. She was so entirely a part of my scheme for better or worse. Now the central figure is gone.

> Yr. affec.
>
> Wuz

But the trouble with H.R.H. was that he could never play a consistent role for long. After a recent, fairly amicable though detached relationship with his youngest son, giving no trouble in Paris, Lionel is told that 'We [presumably Hugolin and himself] cannot put up with him [Stephen] any longer and would sooner pay to keep him as a non-resident.' Even his beloved daughter is no longer the 'almost perfect being' she had been. 'She has no tact with men,' her father told Lionel, 'and tires of them, one after the other, in so short a time. They see they are not wanted and get choked off. She is, in fact, without much of the woman's instinct for the male, *qua* male, and that is the one thing the male will not pardon. Just as a woman resents the apathy of a man indifferent to her charm.'

The trouble was that Hugolin Haweis, unmoved by her father's loneliness, was pursuing her own life in Devonshire Street in exactly the same egotistical way that she had in Queen's House during her mother's lifetime. She spent little or no time housekeeping or in entertaining her father's few remaining friends; flowers were rarely arranged by her or attractive meals planned ahead on an economical basis. However loudly H.R.H. had railed once at his wife's supposed domestic extravagances, he still missed the many little extra luxuries she had once provided and her individual touch about the house.

31 Devonshire Street
Portland Place
April 1st, 1900

My dear Lionel

I do feel I have been very backward in writing but have thought of you a great deal. The settling of Mother's affairs is undergoing new developments. It now turns out that the disastrous Deed of Gift was irregular so she could not dispose of a good deal which under it would have gone to Stephen. Most of it remains mine, i.e. yours and Hugolin's. The lease of 31 Devonshire Street is now in my hands—not Stephen's—to dispose of as well as most of the plate and jewels. We are going to sell up and go to live in the country not far from town so that I can come up for Sunday and, perhaps, in summer take a flat for a few months. Any living in style, such as I am now thankful to have been able to keep up during poor Mother's lifetime, is at an end and my humble ambition is limited to live in a small way in sufficient comfort and to do what I can by preaching, lecturing and writing. I am as fit as ever I was in the pulpit and much in request. All through Lent I have preached in my own church to large congregations and every Wednesday at Ealing.

Hugolin seems to live a contented life with no liking for Society. The remains of the old, distinguished circle hang about but there is no one to hold them together. I have dropped out of all the big influential houses. In fact, dropped out of the London world having no longer a social right-hand. I see now what a force dear Mother was and what a centre she made by her genius in spite of her later developed peculiarities. Of course, she also earned and spent on common objects. I miss that, too. . . .

Miss Souter flourishes and is very fat from vegetarianism. She is gone largely into the Indian religions and has always got some Swami *guru*. But she still pays up for the Church, though not quite so warmly as once . . . Money is short and the Church not so remunerative as once.

Yrs.

H. R. Haweis

Miss Emmeline Souter had largely cooled off because H.R.H.'s promise of marriage if and when he became a free man had never materialised. No longer did he drop in at her house or sleep there as he had in the past. She had her pride and though she retained her pew in St James's and invited Hugolin occasionally for tea, she avoided meeting her old admirer as it was right and lady-like for her to do.

On receiving the galley-proofs of his wife's posthumous book which was to be called *Words to Women,* he planned to arrange a meeting of her friends and well-wishers in the hope of reviving interest in her work. But he failed to bring it off. Instead, he gave a small dinner party to a few of 'the old distinguished circle'.

31 Devonshire Street
Portland Place
July 10*th*

My dear Lionel

I feel I owe you a long letter. Things are now comparatively simple. The only injustice is that I am obliged to pay Stephen £600 which came out of Mother's *so-called money* [her savings] as part of the purchase money of 31 Devonshire Street lease. Of course, this money, though nominally Mother's, was really *accumulated by me* [quite untrue] . . . We do not like this house and if we could sell the lease and get some place in the country we could pay off Stephen at once. I have put my five volumes of *Christ and Christianity* into a cheap edition for the people, a great success.

I still do not feel that anything or anyone can take Mother's place though there was such a fatality about her mind and life. Stephen will remain under the glamour of her delusions to the end.

Hugolin is now getting on towards thirty though she looks younger, but so far as I can see there are no prospects of marriage nor any liking for the idea on her part. She is singularly like her mother in some things; that want of quick emotional perception, I should say, allied to great dullness or dread of sexual sensibilities which men quickly feel and so sheer off. This is a comfort in one way as I am quite easy about her never being betrayed into any indiscretion by her feelings which in this matter are light as air or totally non-existent. She is excellent according to her lights; dependable, active, ingenious and tolerably equable. These traits are not intensified as yet though I note the maternal ones are deepening. Still I am fortunate to have her though she never gives me the least feeling of having 'a woman in the house' which, in one form or another, is what a man wants. However I don't care, as my life is pretty well done with. In Mother, I had my ruling occupation and an absorbing centre for which I pretty well lived and was drawn to with terrible force just as she was slipping away. I have cast my die and not been successful. But Mother was all I cared for and I feel her loss now as much as ever . . . Nothing central remains to me nor will be found, again. We have had a fairly gay season though Hugolin does not care for dancing now. We give few parties but tonight we have had the Earl and Countess of Mar, Lord Garioch, the Perdicaris of Tangier, Miss Rudd (daughter of the millionaire), Sir Laurence Jones, Sir Thomas and Lady Sutherland, etc., with some fine artists to amuse them. This will be our only splash before we leave town. The Church keeps up and I am shutting it up in August for repairs. I think of trying the experiment of taking a big hall at Margate for several Sundays from where I can tap Broadstairs, Ramsgate, Westgate and Birchington. Stephen is on quite good terms but so warped, fundamentally, that I do not look forward to seeing him with any pleasure or having him at home. You know we would always find a place for you though I don't earn enough really to support Stephen, Hugolin and self in the style to which we have been used. I don't see far ahead and neither Hugolin or I feel settled though we have got through the season somehow and have not lost ground except that a few big houses have dropped out. I have not seen a green field nor smelt the sea for months. I am at work on an illustrated *Child's Life of Christ* to order. My last real success is a sixpenny edition of the *Story of Four* and the *Picture of Jesus.* 1,000th edition sold out in a week. But the price is low —£2 on a 1,000. If I could get a church and a house and endowment, I should be easier. The Bishop of London is polite, nice, lunches with me but gives me nothing! So I continue to depend after thirty-two years on the breath of my mouth. Since Mother's death, I am sensible of having aged and am forced to rest more to get through the business of life. I have to economise force but when I am screwed up, I am as good as ever I was in public. Outside London I seem very widely known and invariably draw. Notwithstanding money-making is hard.

Yr. affect:

Wuz

It was rumoured that the Bishop of London with other high Church dignitaries were still chary in giving the Reverend Haweis even a country living, although if his old friend and patron, the late Archbishop of Canterbury (Archibald Campbell Tait) had been living things might have been different. In the eyes of the Church, the character of Hugh Reginald Haweis had been weighed and found wanting; a judgment of his peers which he failed to recognise or, what was more likely, had not the courage to accept.

On his return from Margate at the beginning of October, he re-opened St James's and saw the appearance of *Words to Women: Addresses and Essays by the late Mrs Haweis. Edited by the Reverend H. R. Haweis with Memoir.*

For a brief interlude, Mrs Haweis's name was brought forward once more to members of the reading public and some admirers recalled her witty and pungently-phrased support of worthwhile causes. Then, as other writers took her place, she was forgotten and her books with her.

Gradually, the war news from South Africa improved with British troops beind led to victory by Lord Roberts and Lord Kitchener. But the Queen was in poor health at Balmoral. The tragic loss of her soldier grandson, Prince Christian Victor of Schleswig-Holstein at Pretoria, of enteric fever, had severely taxed her failing strength.

By November, a wretchedly dark and gloomy winter had set in. Much alone and depressed that so few contributions had come in for the M. E. Haweis Memorial Fund For Working Girls, H.R.H. decided to close it at the instigation of his sister, Margaret, and Hugolin. In time, unknown to Stephen, the sum of £1,000 (Mrs Josselin's gift) which had been donated in his name was given to the only 'poor working girl' known to his father: his daughter Hugolin. That the money was his son's and not his to give either did not enter his head or, if it did, was conveniently forgotten.

At the beginning of December, H.R.H. wrote his last letter to Lionel.

> 31 Devonshire Street
> Portland Place
> *December 1st*, 1900

My dear Lionel

I hope Hugolin keeps you posted up in our affairs. As you know, I am a bad correspondent although my correspondence reaches now all over the world. I spend a little fortune in stamps. This winter, I am better but leave in January for the Alps for a month. The Church is still crowded and collections are about £400 but pew-rents down to £250 instead of £600 and I don't get even all of them.

We have put down the carriage at last which I could not keep up without her (M.E.H's) money. I have been dropped by most of the big London houses once open to her because she was a personage. There is no personage now but me, such as I am, and I have had enough of the

"Igh Life' except individuals. It is quite clear that no "Igh Life' means to do anything about me professionally. Still, amidst this quiet neglect, the popular sentiment asserts itself now and then and places me close to the Bishop of London when public classification has got to be made. I write. I preach. *Voilá tout!* When I cease I have next to nothing to fall back on. Hugolin will have my Insurance £1,000. Furniture, jewels and house will be divided between you. Meanwhile I send you a paper to sign, as should Stephen die before he is twenty-five you are the next to inherit whatever he holds from his Mother. Please let me have the paper back. I am sending you a real parcel and Hugolin too. She is admirable in many ways and I never bother her about anything. So she has her own way. As to her men, I've given them up. A new one every few weeks and none retained or cared for as far as I can see. As happy an Xmas as you can have at all events.

> With loving thoughts from home,
> Yr. Affect. Father
>
> H. R. Haweis

With his carriage put down, H.R.H. took to riding a tricycle like old Lord Salisbury. Crouched up like some gnome against the handlebars, the Reverend H. R. Haweis in sombre black with cloak-ends flying became a familiar sight pedalling furiously up and down Devonshire Street.

On 18th December, after attending the Irish Industries Exhibition held at Windsor (her last public function), the Queen left the Castle for Osborne. At St James's, H.R.H. preached his last Christmas sermon while the Old Year wailed itself out in high winds and violent storms.

New Year celebrations meant little to the inmates of Devonshire Street. Hugolin Haweis was away and her father immured in his library writing. But, one afternoon, there came a caller. A young woman, recently widowed, who sought advice and comfort from the Incumbent of St James's where she attended services. A friendship struck up between this lonely pair and they went to a few concerts together, for the young widow had musical tastes.

On the 18th of January, the Royal Family was summoned to Osborne and, on the following day, the first bulletin regarding the Queen's illness was issued to a shocked and distressed nation. From that moment, nothing was spoken or thought of but Her Majesty's health, and special prayers were said in every church throughout the kingdom for her recovery.

On Thursday, 24th January, as dusk was falling, London heard that the Queen was sinking. The end came at six-thirty p.m. that evening.

Queen Victoria's death not only plunged Great Britain and the Empire but a whole world into deep mourning. For an epoch had ended and none felt this more than Hugh Reginald Haweis. On Sunday, 27th January, in a deeply emotional state, he climbed into the pulpit of St James's, Westmoreland Street, to face an enormous congregation. Never had the building been so full. Wherever he looked, people sat, knelt, or stood in heavy black. To these people, rich and humble, known and unknown, Stephen Haweis, who was present, has recorded that his father preached his finest sermon on the passing of his beloved Queen and Empress. Then, immediately following this service, without food or respite, he went to Hyde Park Corner, that meeting-ground open to the common people who had always upheld him, and preached to them. He returned home as dusk fell, worn out and exhausted.

Early the following morning, when there came no reply to her timid knock on the door, a maidservant entered the library at Devonshire Street to find her master slumped, unconscious, across the top of his paper-strewn writing table. His doctor was sent for but there was nothing to be done. Without regaining consciousness, Hugh Reginald Haweis died early on the morning of Tuesday, 29th January.

Some hours later, a placard was placed on the door of

Number 31, announcing the sudden death of The Reverend
H. R. Haweis, Incumbent of St James's Church, a few hours
earlier. It remains for the newest member of his congregation,
that young woman, so recently widowed, to whom he had
generously given his last advice and sympathetic help, to
write the following testimonial as a comparative stranger:

He was by far the most remarkable man I have known.

At first, he did not strike one as at all impressive except
that he was unusual. But when he was talking to you or
speaking in public, you forgot his small stature. Everything but his personality. He had the most wonderful
eyes—they seemed to glow—and a very expressive
mouth. He was the most kindly man, too, always trying
to help someone.

I heard him play his violin many times. He seemed,
somehow, to swell into far greater proportions then than
his real stature and he would stop to interpolate some
brilliant comment on what he was playing. No one who
heard him play can forget it.

He was always hard up, having no idea of the value of
money. It seemed to me, he was always being sued for his
taxes and rather enjoyed it.

I shall never forget him on his tricycle—he looked so
funny. But he had the pluck of the devil and if he tackled
a thing, he tackled it. He did not mind the traffic.

I heard him preach a great sermon on Queen Victoria
just before he died. I shall never forget my impression of
his death. I was in Kent at the time and when I got back
to London, I took a cab to his home in Devonshire Street
and there I found staring me in the face a notice on the
door telling of his death the day before. I was completely
dazed. I cannot remember where I went but I found myself sitting on a seat in Victoria Station. I could not realize
I should never see him again and I was too upset to go to
his funeral.

This ceremony took place by special permission of the

Bishop of London in the Crown Chapel of St James's, whose Incumbent he had been for close on thirty-six years. Cremation then followed, as he had left instructions it should. For all his working life, had he not crusaded for the ultimate 'Pure and simple disinfectant of Fire, the reign of Cremation and the Field of Rest'? In this matter, his wishes were respected.

Thus, in a small urn, the ashes of Hugh Reginald Haweis were deposited in the great table tomb of Thomas Joy, Gent., at St Peter's, Broughton Monchelsea, beside those of his wife. Today, no record of their resting-place remains either on the moss-stained surface of this tomb or in the Parish Register. But still the apple orchards of Boughton Monchelsea come into fragile bloom each spring, while the deer continue to browse in the park overlooked by that quiet little Kentish churchyard along whose paths the child, Mary Eliza, and her father Thomas Musgrove Joy before her, loved to wander.

ACKNOWLEDGEMENTS

BIBLIOGRAPHY

INDEX

ACKNOWLEDGEMENTS

I am much indebted to the late Mr Lionel Haweis for the careful typescript copies which he made of his mother's correspondence and journals that rendered my own work easier.

I am grateful also to Mr Robert Mackworth-Young, Librarian at Windsor Castle and to Mr Oliver Millar, m.v.o., Deputy Surveyor of The Queen's Paintings for confirming the presence of Thomas Musgrove Joy at Windsor Castle and giving me details of his activities there; to Lady Mander (Rosalie Glynn Grylls) and Mr Gale Pedrick for permission to use certain information connected with Queen's House that appeared in their recent books on Rossetti; to Mr Reginald Colby for drawing my attention to Thomas Joy's portrait of Mrs Fitzgeorge (Louisa Fairbrother) in the collection of Princess Iris Galitzine; to Mr James D. Boyd, Curator of The City of Dundee Art Gallery for information concerning Thomas Joy's three pictures on loan there; to the Vicar of Boughton Monchelsea, Kent, for kindly supplying notes from the Parish Register on the Tomkin and Joy families; to Miss Coombes who lives at Tilts House, Boughton Monchelsea (one time home of the Tomkins) for data in regard to their residence there besides local lore; and to Miss Branstone for her care, till now, her retirement, in typing my books over the many years we have known each other.

Lastly, I wish to thank Sylvia Townsend Warner for reading my final draft and my husband, Mark Lubbock, for invariably finding the necessary second-hand book to assist my research.

BIBLIOGRAPHY

Mrs Haweis, 1848-1898

Chaucer for Children: A Golden Key. Chatto & Windus, 1877.
The Art of Beauty. Chatto & Windus, 1878.
The Art of Dress. Chatto & Windus, 1879.
The Art of Decoration. Chatto & Windus, 1881.
Chaucer for Schools. 1881.
Beautiful Houses. Sampson & Low, 1882.
Chaucer's Beads: a Birthday Book. 1884.
Rus in Urbe; or, Flowers that Thrive in London Gardens. Field & Tuer. 1886.
Tales from Chaucer. Adapted by Mrs Haweis. 1887.
The Art of Housekeeping: A Bridal Garland. Sampson & Low, 1889.
A Flame of Fire: A Novel. Hurst & Blackett, 1897.
Words to Women: Addresses and Essays. Edited by the Reverend H. R. Haweis (with Memoir). Burnet & Isbister, 1900.
Unpublished mss. Memoranda, 1864-1867.
Thought Book, 1865-1876.
Letters. Poems. Sketches. 1858-1898.
Four to Fourteen. By a Victorian Child (Hugolin Haweis). Robert Hale. 1939.

Reverend H. R. Haweis, M.A.

Music and Morals. Longmans, Green & Co., 1871.
Thoughts for the Times. Henry S. King & Co., 1872.
Speech in Season. Henry S. King & Co., 1874.
Ashes to Ashes: A Cremation Prelude. W. H. Allen & Co., 1884.
My Musical Life. Daldy, Isbister & Co., 1875.

Books Consulted

Hints on Household Taste, Charles Eastlake, 1864.
Memories of Victorian London, L. B. Walford. Edwin Arnold, 1912.
Elizabeth Rigby, Lady Eastlake, Marion Lockhead. Murray, 1961.
The Victorian Household, Marion Lockhead. Murray, 1964.
London by Gaslight, Michael Harrison. Peter Davies, 1963.
Victorian Book Design, Ruari Maclean. Faber & Faber, 1963.
Art and The Formation of Taste, Lucy Crane. Macmillan, 1882.
An Artist's Reminiscences, Walter Crane. Methuen, 1907.
L. Alma Tadema, R.A. His Life & Work, H. Zimmern. The Art Journal, 1886.
Life of William Morris, J. W. Mackail. Longmans & Green, 1897.
Memorial of Edward Burne-Jones, G.B-J. Macmillan, 1904.
The Wonderful Village, R. Blunt. Peter D. & Boon, 1918.
Illustrated Historical Handbook to the Parish of Chelsea, R. Blunt. Lamley, 1900.
Book of the Seven Seals, Anon. Cayme Press, 1928.
Dante Gabriel Rossetti, R. L. Megroz.
Recollections by Treffry Dunn, Faber & Gwyer, 1928.
Life with Rossetti, Edited by Gale Pedrick. Macdonald, 1964.
Portrait of Rossetti, Rosalie Glynn Grylls. Macdonald, 1965.
Christina Rossetti, Lona Mosk Packer. Cambridge University Press, 1963.
The Perfect Lady, C. Willet Cunnington. Max Parrish, 1948.
The 'Art at Home' Series: The Drawing-room, Mrs. Orrinsmith.
The Boudoir, Lady Barker. Macmillan, 1878.
Shops and Shopping, Alison Adburgham. George & Allen, 1964.
The Victorian Church, Owen Chadwick, 1966.

INDEX

In this index MEH = *Mary Eliza Haweis*